Ghosts Of My Life

Writings on Depression, Hauntology and Lost Futures

Ghosts Of My Life

Writings on Depression, Hauntology
and Lost Futures

Mark Fisher

Winchester, UK
Washington, USA

First published by Zero Books, 2014
Zero Books is an imprint of John Hunt Publishing Ltd., Laurel House, Station Approach,
Alresford, Hants, SO24 9JH, UK
office1@jhpbooks.net
www.johnhuntpublishing.com
www.zero-books.net

For distributor details and how to order please visit the 'Ordering' section on our website.

Text copyright: Mark Fisher 2013

ISBN: 978 1 78099 226 6

A CIP catalogue record for this book is available from the British Library.

Design: Stuart Davies
Cover photograph by Chris Heppell
Illustrations by Laura Oldfield Ford

Printed and bound by CPI Group (UK) Ltd, Croydon, CR0 4YY

We operate a distinctive and ethical publishing philosophy in all
areas of our business, from our global network of authors to
production and worldwide distribution.

CONTENTS

For my wife, Zöe and my son, George

Mark Fisher is the author of *Capitalist Realism: Is There No Alternative?* (Zer0, 2009). His writing has appeared in many publications, including Sight & Sound, The Wire, The Guardian, Film Quarterly and frieze. He is Programme Leader of the MA in Aural and Visual Cultures at Goldsmiths, University of London, and a lecturer at the University of East London. He lives in Suffolk.

Acknowledgements

Many of the ideas in *Ghosts Of My Life* were first auditioned on my blog, k-punk. I'm grateful to the k-punk readers who responded to the ideas there and helped them to propagate. I'm also grateful to the publishers who kindly allowed me to reprint material in *Ghosts*, in particular Rob Winter at *Sight & Sound* and Tony Herrington at *The Wire*. Some of the pieces that originally appeared elsewhere have been altered for inclusion here. Needless to say, all responsibility for the edits in *Ghosts* lies with me.

If I were to list everyone who inspired or supported the writing of *Ghosts Of My Life*, the book would never get started, so I will concentrate only on those who worked closely on the manuscript. Thanks, therefore, to Tariq Goddard for his patience, Liam Sprod and Alex Niven for their attentive copy-editing and proofreading, Laura Oldfield Ford for allowing me to use her drawings to illustrate the text, Chris Heppell for the cover photograph, and Rob White for his customarily insightful and incisive comments.

Lately I've been feeling like Guy Pearce in
Memento
- Drake

00: LOST FUTURES

'The Slow Cancellation of the Future'

'There's no time here, not any more'

The final image of the British television series *Sapphire and Steel* seemed designed to haunt the adolescent mind. The two lead characters, played by Joanna Lumley and David McCallum, find themselves in what seems to be a 1940s roadside café. The radio is playing a simulation of Glenn Miller-style smooth Big Band jazz. Another couple, a man and a woman dressed in 1940s clothes, are sitting at an adjacent table. The woman rises, saying: 'This is the trap. This is nowhere, and it's forever.' She and her companion then disappear, leaving spectral outlines, then nothingness. Sapphire and Steel panic. They rifle through the few objects in the café, looking for something they can use to escape. There is nothing, and when they pull back the curtains, there is only a black starry void beyond the window. The café, it seems, is some kind of capsule floating in deep space.

Watching this extraordinary final sequence now, the juxtaposition of the café with the cosmos is likely to put in mind some combination of Edward Hopper and René Magritte. Neither of those references were available to me at the time; in fact, when I later encountered Hopper and Magritte, I no doubt thought of Sapphire and Steel. It was August 1982 and I had just turned 15 years old. It would be more than 20 years later before I would see these images again. By then, thanks to VHS, DVD and YouTube, it seemed that practically everything was available for re-watching. In conditions of digital recall, loss is itself lost.

The passage of 30 years has only made the series appear even stranger than it did at the time. This was science fiction with none of the traditional trappings of the genre, no spaceships, no ray guns, no anthropomorphic foes: only the unraveling fabric of the corridor of time, along which malevolent entities would crawl, exploiting and expanding gaps and fissures in temporal continuity. All we knew about Sapphire and Steel was that they were 'detectives' of a peculiar kind, probably not human, sent from a mysterious 'agency' to repair these breaks in time. 'The basis of *Sapphire and Steel*,' the series's creator P. J. Hammond explained, 'came from my desire to write a detective story, into which I wanted to incorporate Time. I've always been interested in Time, particularly the ideas of J. B. Priestley and H. G. Wells, but I wanted to take a different approach to the subject. So instead of having them go backwards and forwards in Time, it was about Time breaking in, and having set the precedent I realised the potential that it offered with two people whose job it was to stop the break-ins.' (Steve O'Brien, 'The Story Behind Sapphire & Steel', The Fan Can, http://www.thefancan.com/fancandy/features/tvfeatures/steel.html)

Hammond had previously worked as a writer on police dramas such as *The Gentle Touch* and *Hunter's Walk* and on children's fantasy shows like *Ace of Wands* and *Dramarama*. With *Sapphire and Steel*, he attained a kind of auteurship that he would never manage to repeat. The conditions for this kind of visionary public broadcasting would disappear during the 1980s, as the British media became taken over by what another television auteur, Dennis Potter, would call the 'occupying powers' of neoliberalism. The result of that occupation is that it is now hard to believe that such a programme could ever have been transmitted on prime-time television, still less on what was then Britain's sole commercial network, ITV. There were only three television channels in Britain then: BBC1, BBC2 and ITV; Channel 4 would make its first broadcast only a few months later.

By comparison with the expectations created by *Star Wars*, *Sapphire and Steel* came off as very cheap and cheerful. Even in 1982, the chroma-key special effects looked unconvincing. The fact that the stage sets were minimal, and the cast small (most of the 'assignments' only featured Lumley and McCallum and a couple of others), gave the impression of a theatre production. Yet there was none of the *homeliness* of kitchen sink naturalism; *Sapphire and Steel* had more in common with the enigmatic oppressiveness of Harold Pinter, whose plays were frequently broadcast on BBC television during the 1970s.

A number of things about the series are particularly striking from the perspective of the 21st century. The first is its absolute refusal to 'meet the audience halfway' in the way that we've come to expect. This is partly a conceptual matter: *Sapphire and Steel* was cryptic, its stories and its world never fully disclosed, still less explained. The series was much closer to something like the BBC's adaptation of John Le Carré's Smiley novels – *Tinker Tailor Soldier Spy* had been broadcast in 1979; its sequel *Smiley's People* would begin transmission a month after *Sapphire and Steel* ended – than it was to *Star Wars*. It was also a question of emotional tenor: the series and its two lead characters are lacking in the warmth and wisecracking humour that is now so much a taken-for-granted feature of entertainment media. McCallum's Steel had a technician's indifference towards the lives in which he became reluctantly enmeshed; although he never loses his sense of duty, he is testy and impatient, frequently exasperated by the way humans 'clutter their lives'. If Lumley's Sapphire appeared more sympathetic, there was always the suspicion that her apparent affection towards humans was something like an owner's benign fascination for her pets. The emotional austerity that had characterised the series from the start assumes a more explicitly pessimistic quality in this final assignment. The Le Carré parallels are reinforced by the strong suspicion that, just as in *Tinker Tailor Soldier Spy*, the lead characters have been betrayed by their own side.

Then there was Cyril Ornadel's incidental music. As Nick Edwards explained in a 2009 blog post, this was '[a]rranged for a small ensemble of musicians (predominantly woodwind) with liberal use of electronic treatments (ring modulation, echo/delay) to intensify the drama and *suggestion* of horror, Ornadel's cues are far more powerfully chilling and evocative than anything you're likely hear in the mainstream media today.' ('Sapphire and Steel', gutterbreakz.blogspot.co.uk/2009/05/sapphire-steel .html)

One aim of *Sapphire and Steel* was to transpose ghost stories out of the Victorian context and into contemporary places, the still inhabited or the recently abandoned. In the final assignment, Sapphire and Steel arrive at a small service station. Corporate logos – Access, 7 Up, Castrol GTX, LV – are pasted on the windows and the walls of the garage and the adjoining café. This 'halfway place' is a prototype version of what the anthropologist Marc Augé will call in a 1995 book of the same title, 'non-places' – the generic zones of transit (retail parks, airports) which will come to increasingly dominate the spaces of late capitalism. In truth, the modest service station in Sapphire and Steel is quaintly idiosyncratic compared to the cloned generic monoliths which will proliferate besides motorways over the coming 30 years.

The problem that Sapphire and Steel have come to solve is, as ever, to do with time. At the service station, there is temporal bleed-through from earlier periods: images and figures from 1925 and 1948 keep appearing, so that, as Sapphire and Steel's colleague Silver puts it 'time just got mixed, jumbled up, together, making no sort of sense'. Anachronism, the slippage of discrete time periods into one another, was throughout the series the major symptom of time breaking down. In one of the earlier assignments, Steel complains that these temporal anomalies are triggered by human beings' predilection for the mixing of artefacts from different eras. In this final assignment, the anachronism has led to stasis: time has stopped. The service station is in 'a pocket, a vacuum'. There's 'still traffic, but it's not going anywhere': the sound of cars is locked into a looped drone. Silver says, 'there is no time here, not any more'. It's as if the whole scenario is a literalisation of the lines in Pinter's *No Man's*

Land: 'No man's land, which never moves, which never changes, which never grows older, which remains forever icy and silent.' Hammond said that he had not necessarily intended the series to end there. He had thought that it would be rested, to return at some point in the future. There would be no return – at least, not on network television. In 2004, Sapphire and Steel would come back for a series of audio adventures; though Hammond, McCallum and Lumley were not involved, and by then the audience was not the television-viewing public, but the kind of special interest niche easily catered for in digital culture. Eternally suspended, never to be freed, their plight – and indeed their provenance – never to be fully explained, Sapphire and Steel's internment in this café from nowhere is prophetic for a general condition: in which life continues, but time has somehow stopped.

The slow cancellation of the future

It is the contention of this book that 21st-century culture is marked by the same anachronism and inertia which afflicted Sapphire and Steel in their final adventure. But this stasis has been buried, interred behind a superficial frenzy of 'newness', of perpetual movement. The 'jumbling up of time', the montaging of earlier eras, has ceased to be worthy of comment; it is now so prevalent that is no longer even noticed.

In his book *After The Future*, Franco 'Bifo' Berardi refers to the 'the slow cancellation of the future [that] got underway in the 1970s and 1980s.' 'But when I say "future"', he elaborates,

> I am not referring to the direction of time. I am thinking, rather, of the psychological perception, which emerged in the cultural situation of progressive modernity, the cultural expectations that were fabricated during the long period of modern civilization, reaching a peak after the Second World War. These expectations were shaped in the conceptual frame-

works of an ever progressing development, albeit through different methodologies: the Hegel-Marxist mythology of *Aufhebung* and founding of the new totality of Communism; the bourgeois mythology of a linear development of welfare and democracy; the technocratic mythology of the all-encompassing power of scientific knowledge; and so on.

My generation grew up at the peak of this mythological temporalization, and it is very difficult, maybe impossible, to get rid of it, and look at reality without this kind of temporal lens. I'll never be able to live in accordance with the new reality, no matter how evident, unmistakable, or even dazzling its social planetary trends. (*After The* Future, AK Books, 2011, pp18-19)

Bifo is a generation older than me, but he and I are on the same side of a temporal split here. I, too, will never be able to adjust to the paradoxes of this new situation. The immediate temptation here is to fit what I'm saying into a wearily familiar narrative: it is a matter of the old failing to come to terms with the new, saying it was better in their day. Yet it is just this picture – with its assumption that the young are automatically at the leading edge of cultural change – that is now out of date.

Rather than the old recoiling from the 'new' in fear and incomprehension, those whose expectations were formed in an earlier era are more likely to be startled by the sheer persistence of recognisable forms. Nowhere is this clearer than in popular music culture. It was through the mutations of popular music that many of those of us who grew up in the 1960s, 70s and 80s learned to measure the passage of cultural time. But faced with 21st-century music, it is the very sense of future shock which has disappeared. This is quickly established by performing a simple thought experiment. Imagine any record released in the past couple of years being beamed back in time to, say, 1995 and played on the radio. It's hard to think that it will produce any jolt in the listeners. On the contrary, what would be likely to shock our 1995 audience would be the very recognisability of the sounds: would music really have changed so little in the next 17 years? Contrast this with the rapid turnover of styles between the 1960s and the 90s: play a jungle record from 1993 to someone in 1989 and it would have sounded like something so new that it would have challenged them to rethink what music was, or could be. While 20th-century experimental culture was seized by a recombinatorial delirium, which made it feel as if newness was infinitely available, the 21st century is oppressed by a crushing sense of finitude and exhaustion. It doesn't feel like the future. Or, alternatively, it doesn't feel as if the 21st century has started yet. We remain trapped in the 20th century, just as Sapphire and Steel were incarcerated in their roadside café.

The slow cancellation of the future has been accompanied by a deflation of expectations. There can be few who believe that in the coming year a record as great as, say, the Stooges' *Funhouse* or Sly Stone's *There's a Riot Goin' On* will be released. Still less do we expect the kind of ruptures brought about by The Beatles or disco. The feeling of belatedness, of living after the gold rush, is as omnipresent as it is disavowed. Compare the fallow terrain of the current moment with the fecundity of previous periods and you will quickly be accused of 'nostalgia'. But the reliance of current artists on styles that were established long ago suggests that the current moment is in the grip of a *formal* nostalgia, of which more shortly.

It is not that nothing happened in the period when the slow cancellation of the future set in. On the contrary, those 30 years have been a time of massive, traumatic change. In the UK, the election of Margaret Thatcher had brought to an end the uneasy compromises of the so-called postwar social consensus. Thatcher's neoliberal programme in politics was reinforced by a transnational restructuring of the capitalist economy. The shift into so-called Post-Fordism – with globalisation, ubiquitous computerisation and the casualisation of labour – resulted in a complete transformation in the way that work and leisure were organised. In the last 10 to 15 years, meanwhile, the internet and mobile telecommunications technology have altered the texture of everyday experience beyond all recognition. Yet, perhaps *because* of all this, there's an increasing sense that culture has lost the ability to grasp and articulate the present. Or it could be that, in one very important sense, there is no present to grasp and articulate any more.

Consider the fate of the concept of 'futuristic' music. The 'futuristic' in music has long since ceased to refer to any future that we expect to be different; it has become an established style, much like a particular typographical font. Invited to think of the futuristic, we will still come up with something like the music of Kraftwerk, even though this is now as antique as Glenn Miller's big band jazz was when the German group began experimenting with synthesizers in the early 1970s.

Where is the 21st-century equivalent of Kraftwerk? If Kraftwerk's music came out of a casual intolerance of the already-established, then the present moment is marked by its extraordinary accommodation towards the past. More than that, the very distinction between past and present is breaking down. In 1981, the 1960s seemed much further away than they do today. Since then, cultural time has folded back on itself, and the impression of linear development has given way to a strange simultaneity.

Two examples will suffice to introduce this peculiar temporality. When I first saw the video for the Arctic Monkeys' 2005 single 'I Bet You Look Good on the Dancefloor', I genuinely believed that it was some lost artifact from circa 1980. Everything in the video – the lighting, the haircuts, the clothes – had been assembled to give the impression that this was a performance on BBC2's 'serious rock show' *The Old Grey Whistle Test*. Furthermore, there was no discordance between the look and the sound. At least to a casual listen, this could quite easily have been a postpunk group from the early 1980s. Certainly, if one performs a version of the thought experiment I described above, it's easy to imagine 'I Bet You Look Good On The Dancefloor' being broadcast on *The Old Grey Whistle Test* in 1980, and producing no sense of disorientation in the audience. Like me, they might have imagined that the references to '1984' in the lyrics referred to the future.

There ought to be something astonishing about this. Count back 25 years from 1980, and you are at the beginning of rock and roll. A record that sounded like Buddy Holly or Elvis in 1980 would have sounded out of time. Of course, such records were released in 1980, but they were marketed as retro. If the Arctic Monkeys weren't positioned as a 'retro' group, it is partly because, by 2005, there was no 'now' with which to contrast their retrospection. In the 1990s, it was possible to hold something like Britpop revivalism to account by comparing it to the experimentalism happening on the UK dance underground or in US R&B. By 2005, the rates of innovation in both these areas had enormously slackened. UK dance music remains much more vibrant than rock, but the changes that happen there are tiny, incremental, and detectable largely only by initiates – there is none of the dislocation of sensation that you heard in the shift from Rave to Jungle and from Jungle to Garage in the 1990s. As I write this, one of the dominant sounds in pop (the globalised club music that has supplanted R&B) resembles nothing more than Eurotrance, a particularly bland European 1990s cocktail made from some of the most flavourless components of House and Techno.

Second example. I first heard Amy Winehouse's version of 'Valerie' while walking through a shopping mall, perhaps the perfect venue for consuming it. Up until then, I had believed that 'Valerie' was first recorded by indie plodders the Zutons. But, for a moment, the record's antiqued 1960s soul sound and the vocal (which on a casual listen I didn't at first recognise as Winehouse) made me temporarily revise this belief: surely the Zutons' version of the track was a cover of *this* apparently 'older' track, which I had not heard until now? Naturally, it didn't take me long to realise that the '60s soul sound' was actually a simulation; this was indeed a cover of the Zutons' track, done in the souped-up retro style in which the record's producer, Mark Ronson, has specialised.

Ronson's productions might have been designed to illustrate what Fredric Jameson called the 'nostalgia mode'. Jameson identifies this tendency in his remarkably prescient writings on postmodernism, beginning in the 1980s. What makes 'Valerie' and the Arctic Monkeys typical of postmodern retro is the way in which they perform anachronism. While they are sufficiently 'historical'–sounding to pass on first listen as belonging to the period which they ape – there is something not quite right about them. Discrepancies in texture – the results of modern studio and recording techniques – mean that they belong neither to the present nor to the past but to some implied 'timeless' era, an eternal 1960s or an eternal 80s. The 'classic' sound, its elements now serenely liberated from the pressures of historical becoming, can now be periodically buffed up by new technology.

It is important to be clear about what Jameson means by the 'nostalgia mode'. He is not referring to psychological nostalgia – indeed, the nostalgia mode as Jameson theorises it might be said to preclude psychological nostalgia, since it arises only when a coherent sense of historical time breaks down. The kind of figure capable of exhibiting and expressing a yearning for the past belongs, actually, to a paradigmatically modernist moment – think, for instance, of Proust's and Joyce's ingenious exercises in recovering lost time. Jameson's nostalgia mode is better under-stood in terms of a *formal* attachment to the techniques and formulas of the past, a consequence of a retreat from the modernist challenge of innovating cultural forms adequate to

contemporary experience. Jameson's example is Lawrence
Kasdan's now half-forgotten film *Body Heat* (1981), which,
although it was *officially* set in the 1980s, feels as if it belongs to
the 30s. '*Body Heat* is technically not a nostalgia film,' Jameson
writes,

> since it takes place in a contemporary setting, in a little Florida
> village near Miami. On the other hand, this technical contem-
> poraneity is most ambiguous indeed . . . Technically, . . . its
> objects (its cars, for instance) are 1980s products, but every-
> thing in the film conspires to blur that immediate contem-
> porary reference and to make it possible to receive this too as
> nostalgia work – as a narrative set in some indefinable
> nostalgic past, an eternal 1930s, say, beyond history. It seems
> to me exceedingly symptomatic to find the very style of
> nostalgia films invading and colonizing even those movies
> today which have contemporary settings, as though, for some
> reason, we were unable today to focus our own present, as
> though we had become incapable of achieving aesthetic repre-
> sentations of our own current experience. But if that is so, then
> it is a terrible indictment of consumer capitalism itself – or, at
> the very least, an alarming and pathological symptom of a
> society that has become incapable of dealing with time and
> history. ('Postmodernism and Consumer Society' in *The
> Cultural Turn: Selected Writings on the Postmodern, 1983-1998*,
> Verso, 1998, pp9-10.)

What blocks *Body Heat* from being a period piece or a nostalgia
picture in any straightforward way is its disavowal of any explicit
reference to the past. The result is anachronism, and the paradox
is that this 'blurring of official contemporaneity', this 'waning of
historicity' is increasingly typical of our experience of cultural
products. Another of Jameson's examples of the nostalgia mode is
Star Wars:

one of the most important cultural experiences of the genera-
tions that grew up from the 1930s to the 1950s was the
Saturday afternoon series of the Buck Rogers type – alien
villains, true American heroes, heroines in distress, the death
ray or the doomsday box, and the cliff-hanger at the end
whose miraculous solution was to be witnessed next Saturday
afternoon. *Star Wars* reinvents this experience in the form of a
pastiche; there is no point to a parody of such series, since
they are long extinct. Far from being a pointless satire of such
dead forms, *Star Wars* satisfies a deep (might I even say
repressed?) longing to experience them again: it is a complex
object in which on some first level children and adolescents
can take the adventures straight, while the adult public is able
to gratify a deeper and more properly nostalgic desire to
return to that older period and to live its strange old aesthetic
artefacts through once again. ('Postmodernism and
Consumer Society', p8)

There is no nostalgia for a historical period here (or if there is, it
is only indirect): the longing of which Jameson writes is a
yearning for a form. *Star Wars* is a particularly resonant example
of postmodern anachronism, because of the way it used
technology to obfuscate its archaic form. Belying its origins in
these fusty adventure series forms, *Star Wars* could appear new
because its then unprecedented special effects relied upon the
latest technology. If, in a paradigmatically modernist way,
Kraftwerk used technology to allow new forms to emerge, the
nostalgia mode subordinated technology to the task of refur-
bishing the old. The effect was to disguise the disappearance of
the future as its opposite.

The future didn't disappear overnight. Berardi's phrase 'the
slow cancellation of the future' is so apt because it captures the
gradual yet relentless way in which the future has been eroded
over the last 30 years. If the late 1970s and early 80s were the

moment when the current crisis of cultural temporality could first be felt, it was only during the first decade of the 21st century that what Simon Reynolds calls 'dyschronia' has become endemic. This dyschronia, this temporal disjuncture, ought to feel uncanny, yet the predominance of what Reynolds calls 'retromania' means that it has lost any *unheimlich* charge: anachronism is now taken for granted. Jameson's postmodernism – with its tendencies towards retrospection and pastiche – has been naturalised. Take someone like the stupendously successful Adele: although her music is not marketed as retro, there is nothing that marks out her records as belonging to the 21st century either. Like so much contemporary cultural production, Adele's recordings are saturated with a vague but persistent feeling of the past without recalling any specific historical moment.

Jameson equates the postmodern 'waning of historicity' with the 'cultural logic of late capitalism', but he says little about why the two are synonymous. Why did the arrival of neoliberal, post-Fordist capitalism lead to a culture of retrospection and pastiche? Perhaps we can venture a couple of provisional conjectures here. The first concerns consumption. Could it be that neoliberal capitalism's destruction of solidarity and security brought about a compensatory hungering for the well-established and the familiar? Paul Virilio has written of a 'polar inertia' that is a kind of effect of and counterweight to the massive speeding up of communication. Virilio's example is Howard Hughes, living in one hotel room for 15 years, endlessly rewatching *Ice Station Zebra*. Hughes, once a pioneer in aeronautics, became an early explorer of the existential terrain that cyberspace will open up, where it is no longer necessary to physically move in order to access the whole history of culture. Or, as Berardi has argued, the intensity and precariousness of late capitalist work culture leaves people in a state where they are simultaneously exhausted and overstimulated. The combination of precarious work and digital communications leads to a besieging of attention. In this insomniac, inundated state, Berardi claims, culture becomes de-eroticised. The art of seduction takes too much time, and, according to Berardi, something like Viagra answers not to a biological but to a cultural deficit: desperately short of time, energy and attention, we demand quick fixes. Like another of Berardi's examples, pornography, retro offers the quick and easy promise of a minimal variation on an already familiar satisfaction.

The other explanation for the link between late capitalism and retrospection centres on production. Despite all its rhetoric of novelty and innovation, neoliberal capitalism has gradually but systematically deprived artists of the resources necessary to produce the new. In the UK, the postwar welfare state and higher education maintenance grants constituted an indirect source of funding for most of the experiments in popular culture between the 1960s and the 80s. The subsequent ideological and practical attack on public services meant that one of the spaces where artists could be sheltered from the pressure to produce something that was immediately successful was severely circumscribed. As public service broadcasting became 'marketised', there was an increased tendency to turn out cultural productions that resembled what was already successful. The result of all of this is that the social time available for withdrawing from work and immersing oneself in cultural production drastically declined. If there's one factor above all else which contributes to cultural conservatism, it is the vast inflation in the cost of rent and mortgages. It's no accident that the efflorescence of cultural invention in London and New York in the late 1970s and early 80s (in the punk and postpunk scenes) coincided with the availability of squatted and cheap property in those cities. Since then, the decline of social housing, the attacks on squatting, and the delirious rise in property prices have meant that the amount of time and energy available for cultural production has massively diminished. But perhaps it was only with the arrival of digital communicative capitalism that this reached terminal crisis point. Naturally, the besieging of attention described by Berardi applies to producers as much as consumers. Producing the new depends upon certain kinds of withdrawal – from, for instance, sociality as much as from pre-existing cultural forms – but the currently dominant form of socially networked cyberspace, with its endless opportunities for micro-contact and its deluge of YouTube links, has made withdrawal more difficult than ever before. Or, as Simon Reynolds so pithily put it, in recent years, everyday life has sped up, but culture has slowed down.

No matter what the causes for this temporal pathology are, it is clear that no area of Western culture is immune from them. The former redoubts of futurism, such as electronic music, no longer offer escape from formal nostalgia. Music culture is in many ways paradigmatic of the fate of culture under post-Fordist capitalism. At the level of form, music is locked into pastiche and repetition. But its infrastructure has been subject to massive, unpredictable change: the old paradigms of consumption, retail and distribution are disintegrating, with downloading eclipsing the physical object, record shops closing and cover art disappearing.

Why hauntology?

What has the concept of hauntology to do with all this? It was in fact with some reluctance that hauntology started to be applied to the electronic music of the middle of the last decade. I'd generally found Jacques Derrida, the inventor of the term, a frustrating thinker. As soon as it was established in certain areas of the academy, deconstruction, the philosophical project which Derrida founded, installed itself as a pious cult of indeterminacy, which at its worst made a lawyerly virtue of avoiding any definitive claim. Deconstruction was a kind of pathology of scepticism, which induced hedging, infirmity of purpose and compulsory doubt in its followers. It elevated particular modes of academic practice – Heidegger's priestly opacity, literary theory's emphasis on the ultimate instability of any interpretation – into quasi-theological imperatives. Derrida's circumlocutions seemed like a disintensifying influence.

It's by no means irrelevant to point out here that my first encounter with Derrida took place in what is now a vanished milieu. It came in the pages of the *New Musical Express* in the 1980s, where Derrida's name would be mentioned by the most exciting writers. (And, actually, part of my frustration with Derrida's work came out of disappointment. The enthusiasm of NME writers like Ian Penman and Mark Sinker for Derrida, and the formal and conceptual inventiveness it seemed to provoke in their writing, created expectations which Derrida's own work couldn't meet when I eventually came to read it.) It's hard to believe this now but, along with public service broadcasting, the NME constituted a kind of supplementary-informal education system, in which theory acquired a strange, lustrous glamour. I had also seen Derrida in Ken McMullen's film *Ghost Dance*, shown late at night on Channel 4 in the early days of the network, at a time before we had a VCR, when I had to resort to washing my face with cold water to try to keep myself awake.

Derrida coined the term 'hauntology' in his *Specters of Marx: The State of the Debt, the Work of Mourning and the New International*. 'To haunt does not mean to be present, and it is necessary to introduce haunting into the very construction of a concept,' he wrote. (Jacques Derrida, *Specters of Marx: The State of the Debt, the Work of Mourning and the New International*, Routledge, 1994, p202) Hauntology was this concept, or puncept. The pun was on the philosophical concept of ontology, the philosophical study of what can be said to exist. Hauntology was the successor to previous concepts of Derrida's such as the trace and *différance*; like those earlier terms, it referred to the way in which nothing enjoys a purely positive existence. Everything that exists is possible only on the basis of a whole series of absences, which precede and surround it, allowing it to possess such consistency and intelligibility that it does. In the famous example, any particular linguistic term gains its meaning not from its own positive qualities but from its difference from other terms. Hence Derrida's ingenious deconstructions of the 'metaphysics of presence' and 'phonocentrism', which expose the way in which particular dominant forms of thought had (incoherently) privileged the voice over writing.

But hauntology explicitly brings into play the question of time in a way that had not quite been the case with the trace or *différance*. One of the repeated phrases in *Specters of Marx* is from *Hamlet*, 'the time is out of joint' and in his recent *Radical Atheism: Derrida and the Time of Life*, Martin Hägglund argues that it is possible to see all of Derrida's work in relation to this concept of broken time. 'Derrida's aim,' Hägglund argues, 'is to formulate a general 'hauntology' (*hantologie*), in contrast to the traditional 'ontology' that thinks being in terms of self-identical presence. What is important about the figure of the specter, then, is that it cannot be fully present: it has no being in itself but marks a relation to what is *no longer* or *not yet*' (*Radical Atheism: Derrida and the Time of* Life, Stanford University Press, 2008, p82)

Is hauntology, then, some attempt to revive the supernatural, or is it just a figure of speech? The way out of this unhelpful opposition is to think of hauntology as *the agency of the virtual*, with the spectre understood not as anything supernatural, but as that which acts without (physically) existing. The great thinkers of modernity, Freud as well as Marx, had discovered different modes of this spectral causality. The late capitalist world, governed by the abstractions of finance, is very clearly a world in which virtualities are effective, and perhaps the most ominous 'spectre of Marx' is capital itself. But as Derrida underlines in his interviews in the *Ghost Dance* film, psychoanalysis is also a 'science of ghosts', a study of how reverberant events in the psyche become revenants.

Referring back to Hägglund's distinction between the *no longer* and the *not yet*, we can provisionally distinguish two directions in hauntology. The first refers to that which is (in actuality is) *no longer*, but which *remains* effective as a virtuality (the traumatic 'compulsion to repeat', a fatal pattern). The second sense of hauntology refers to that which (in actuality) has *not yet* happened, but which is *already* effective in the virtual (an attractor, an anticipation shaping current behaviour). The 'spectre of communism' that Marx and Engels had warned of in the first lines of the *Communist Manifesto* was just this kind of ghost: a virtuality whose threatened coming was already playing a part in undermining the present state of things.

In addition to being another moment in Derrida's own philosophical project of deconstruction, *Specters of Marx* was also a specific engagement with the immediate historical context provided by the disintegration of the Soviet empire. Or rather, it was an engagement with the alleged disappearance of history trumpeted by Francis Fukuyama in his *The End of History and the Last Man*. What would happen now that actually existing socialism had collapsed, and capitalism could assume full spectrum dominance, its claims to global dominion were thwarted not any longer by the existence of a whole other bloc, but by small islands of resistance such as Cuba and North Korea? The era of what I have called 'capitalist realism' – the widespread belief that there is no alternative to capitalism – has been haunted not by the apparition of the spectre of communism, but by its disappearance. As Derrida wrote:

> There is today in the world a dominant discourse . . . This dominating discourse often has the manic, jubilatory, and incantatory form that Freud assigned to the so-called triumphant phase of mourning work. The incantation repeats and ritualizes itself, it holds forth and holds to formulas, like

any animistic magic. To the rhythm of a cadenced march, it proclaims: Marx is dead, communism is dead, very dead, and along with it its hopes, its discourse, its theories, and its practices. It says: long live capitalism, long live the market, here's to the survival of economic and political liberalism! (*Specters of Marx*, p64)

Specters of Marx was also a series of speculations about the media (or post-media) technologies that capital had installed on its now global territory. In this sense, hauntology was by no means something rarefied; it was endemic in the time of 'techno-tele-discursivity, techno-tele-iconicity' 'simulacra' and 'synthetic images'. This discussion of the 'tele-' shows that hauntology concerns a crisis of space as well as time. As theorists such as Virilio and Jean Baudrillard had long acknowledged – and *Specters of Marx* can also be read as Derrida settling his account with these thinkers – 'tele-technologies' collapse both space and time. Events that are spatially distant become available to an audience instantaneously. Neither Baudrillard nor Derrida would live to see the full effects – no doubt I should say the full effects so far – of the 'tele-technology' that has most radically contracted space and time, cyberspace. But here we have a first reason why the concept of hauntology should have become attached to popular culture in the first decade of the 21st century. For it was at this moment when cyberspace enjoyed unprecedented dominion over the reception, distribution and consumption of culture – especially music culture.

When it was applied to music culture – in my own writing, and in that of other critics such as Simon Reynolds and Joseph Stannard – hauntology first of all named a confluence of artists. The word confluence is crucial here. For these artists – William Basinski, the Ghost Box label, The Caretaker, Burial, Mordant Music, Philip Jeck, amongst others – had converged on a certain terrain without actually influencing one another. What they shared was not a sound so much as a sensibility, an existential orientation. The artists that came to be labelled hauntological were suffused with an overwhelming melancholy; and they were preoccupied with the way in which technology materialised memory – hence a fascination with television, vinyl records, audiotape, and with the sounds of these technologies breaking down. This fixation on materialised memory led to what is perhaps the principal sonic signature of hauntology: the use of crackle, the surface noise made by vinyl. Crackle makes us aware that we are listening to a time that is out of joint; it won't allow us to fall into the illusion of presence. It reverses the normal order of listening according to which, as Ian Penman put it, we are habituated to the 're' of recording being repressed. We aren't only made aware that the sounds we are hearing are recorded, we are also made conscious of the playback systems we use to access the recordings. And hovering behind much sonic hauntology is the difference between analogue and digital: so many hauntological tracks have been about revisiting the physicality of analogue media in the era of digital ether. MP3 files remain material, of course, but their materiality is occulted from us, by contrast with the tactile materiality of vinyl records and even compact discs.

No doubt a yearning for this older regime of materiality plays a part in the melancholia that saturates hauntological music. As to the deeper causes of this melancholia, we need look no further than the title of Leyland Kirby's album: *Sadly, The Future Is No Longer What It Was*. In hauntological music there is an implicit acknowledgement that the hopes created by postwar electronica or by the euphoric dance music of the 1990s have evaporated – not only has the future not arrived, it no longer seems possible. Yet at the same time, the music constitutes a refusal to give up on the desire for the future. This refusal gives the melancholia a political dimension, because it amounts to a failure to accommodate to the closed horizons of capitalist realism.

Not giving up the ghost

In Freud's terms, both mourning and melancholia are about loss. But whereas mourning is the slow, painful withdrawal of libido from the lost object, in melancholia, libido remains attached to what has disappeared. For mourning to properly begin, Derrida says in *Specters of Marx*, the dead must be conjured away: 'the conjuration has to make sure that the dead will not come back: quick, do whatever is needed to keep the cadaver localised, in a safe place, decomposing right where it was inhumed, or even embalmed as they liked to do in Moscow' (*Specters of Marx*, p120) But there are those who refuse to allow the body to be interred, just as there is a danger of (over)killing something to such an extent that it becomes a spectre, a pure virtuality. 'Capitalist societies,' Derrida writes, 'can always heave a sigh of relief and say to themselves: communism is finished, but it did not take place, it was only a ghost. They do no more than disavow the undeniable itself: a ghost never dies, it remains always to come and to come-back.' (*Specters of Marx*, p123)

Haunting, then, can be construed as a failed mourning. It is about refusing to give up the ghost or – and this can sometimes amount to the same thing – the refusal of the ghost to give up on us. The spectre will not allow us to settle into/ for the mediocre satisfactions one can glean in a world governed by capitalist realism.

What's at stake in 21st century hauntology is not the disappearance of a particular object. What has vanished is a tendency, a virtual trajectory. One name for this tendency is popular modernism. The cultural ecology that I referred to above – the music press and the more challenging parts of public service broadcasting – were part of a UK popular modernism, as were postpunk, brutalist architecture, Penguin paperbacks and the BBC Radiophonic Workshop. In popular modernism, the elitist project of modernism was retrospectively vindicated. At the same time, popular culture definitively established that it did not have to be populist. Particular modernist techniques were not only disseminated but collectively reworked and extended, just as the modernist task of producing forms which were adequate to the present moment was taken up and renewed. Which is to say that, although of course I didn't realise it at the time, the culture which shaped most of my early expectations was essentially popular modernist, and the writing that has been collected in *Ghosts Of My Life* is about coming to terms with the disappearance of the conditions which allowed it to exist.

It's worth pausing a moment here to distinguish the haunto-logical melancholia I'm talking about from two other kinds of melancholia. The first is what Wendy Brown calls 'left melancholy'. On the face of it, what I've said risks being heard as a kind of leftist melancholic resignation: *although they weren't perfect, the institutions of social democracy were much better than anything we can hope for now, perhaps the best we can ever hope for* . . . In her essay 'Resisting Left Melancholy', Brown attacks 'a Left that operates without either a deep and radical critique of the status quo or a compelling alternative to the existing order of things. But perhaps even more troubling, it is a Left that has become more attached to its impossibility than to its potential fruitfulness, a Left that is most at home dwelling not in hopefulness but in its own marginality and failure, a Left that is thus caught in a structure of melancholic attachment to a certain strain of its own dead past, whose spirit is ghostly, whose structure of desire is backward looking and punishing.' (Wendy Brown, 'Resisting Left Melancholy', *boundary* 2 26:3, 1999, p26). Yet much of what makes the melancholy Brown analyses so pernicious is its disavowed quality. Brown's left melancholic is a depressive who believes he is realistic; someone who no longer has any expectation that his desire for radical transformation could be achieved, but who doesn't recognise that he has given up. In her discussion of Brown's essay in *The Communist Horizon*, Jodi Dean refers to Lacan's formula: 'the only thing one can be

23

guilty of is giving ground relative to one's desire' and the shift that Brown describes – from a left that confidently assumed the future belonged to it, to a left that makes a virtue of its own incapacity to act – seems to exemplify the transition from desire (which in Lacanian terms is the desire to desire) to drive (an enjoyment through failure). The kind of melancholia I'm talking about, by contrast, consists not in giving up on desire but in refusing to yield. It consists, that is to say, in a refusal to adjust to what current conditions call 'reality' – even if the cost of that refusal is that you feel like an outcast in your own time . . .

The second kind of melancholia that hauntological melancholia must be distinguished from is what Paul Gilroy calls 'postcolonial melancholia'. Gilroy defines this melancholia in terms of an avoidance; it is about evading 'the painful obligations to work through the grim details of imperial and colonial history and to transform paralyzing guilt into a more productive shame that would be conducive to the building of a multicultural nationality that is no longer phobic about the prospect of exposure to either strangers or otherness.' (Paul Gilroy, *Postcolonial Melancholia*, Columbia University Press, 2005, p99) It comes out of a 'loss of a fantasy of omnipotence'. Like Brown's left melancholy, then, postcolonial melancholia is a disavowed form of melancholia: its 'signature combination', Gilroy writes, is that of 'manic elation with misery, self-loathing, and ambivalence.' (*Postcolonial Melancholia*, p104) The postcolonial melancholic doesn't (just) refuse to accept change; at some level, he refuses to accept that change has happened at all. He incoherently holds on to the fantasy of omnipotence by experiencing change only as decline and failure, for which, naturally, the immigrant other must be blamed (the incoherence here is obvious: if the postcolonial melancholic were really omnipotent, how could he be harmed by the immigrant?). At first sight, it might be possible to see hauntological melancholia as a variant of postcolonial melancholia: another example of white boy whingeing over lost privileges . . . Yet this would be to grasp what has been lost only in the terms of the worst kind of resentment *ressentiment*, or in terms of what Alex Williams has called negative solidarity, in which we are invited to celebrate, not an increase in liberation, but the fact that another group has now been immiserated; and this is especially sad when the group in question was predominantly working class.

Nostalgia compared to what?

This raises the question of nostalgia again: is hauntology, as many of its critics have maintained, simply a name for nostalgia? Is it about pining for social democracy and its institutions? Given the ubiquity of the formal nostalgia I described above, the question has to be, *nostalgia compared to what*? It seems strange to have to *argue* that comparing the present unfavourably with the past is not automatically nostalgic in any culpable way, but such is the power of the dehistoricising pressures of populism and PR that the claim has to be explicitly made. PR and populism propagate the relativistic illusion that intensity and innovation are equally distributed throughout all cultural periods. It is the tendency to falsely overestimate the past that makes nostalgia egregious: but, one of the lessons of Andy Beckett's history of Britain in the 1970s, *When The Lights Went Out* is that, in many ways, we falsely underestimate a period like the 70s – Beckett in effect shows that capitalist realism was built on a myth-monstering of the decade. Conversely, we are induced by ubiquitous PR into falsely overestimating the present, and those who can't remember the past are condemned to have it resold to them forever.

If the 1970s were in many respects better than neoliberalism wants us to remember them, we must also recognise the extent to which the capitalist dystopia of 21st-century culture is not something that was simply imposed on us – it was built out of our captured desires. 'Almost everything I was afraid of happening over the past 30 years has happened,' Jeremy Gilbert has observed. 'Everything my political mentors warned might happen, since I was a boy growing up on a poor council estate (that's a housing project, if you're American) in the North of England in the early 80s, or a high–school student reading denunciations of Thatcherism in the left press a few years later, has turned out just as badly as they said it would. And yet I don't wish I was living 40 years ago. The point seems to be: this is the world we were all afraid of; but it's also sort of the world we wanted.' (Jeremy Gilbert, 'Moving on from the Market Society: Culture (and Cultural Studies) in a Post-Democratic Age', http://www.opendemocracy.net/ourkingdom/jeremy-gilbert/moving-on-from-market-society-culture-and-cultural-studies-in-post-democra) But we shouldn't have to choose between, say, the internet and social security. One way of thinking about hauntology is that its lost futures do not force such false choices; instead, what haunts is the spectre of a world in which all the marvels of communicative technology could be combined with a sense of solidarity much stronger than anything social democracy could muster.

Popular modernism was by no means a completed project, some pristine zenith that needed no further improvement. In the 1970s, certainly, culture was opened up to working-class inventiveness in a way that is now scarcely imaginable to us; but this was also a time when casual racism, sexism and homophobia were routine features of the mainstream. Needless to say, the struggles against racism and (hetero)sexism have not in the meantime been won, but they have made significant hegemonic advances, even as neoliberalism has corroded the social democratic infrastructure which allowed increased working class participation in cultural production. The disarticulation of class from race, gender and sexuality has in fact been central to the success of the neoliberal project – making it seem, grotesquely, as if neoliberalism were in some way a precondition of the gains

26

made in anti-racist, anti-sexist and anti-heterosexist struggles.

What is being longed for in hauntology is not a particular period, but the resumption of the *processes* of democratisation and pluralism for which Gilroy calls. Perhaps it's useful to remind ourselves here that social democracy has only become a resolved totality in retrospect; at the time, it was a compromise formation, which those on the left saw as a temporary bridgehead from which further gains could be won. What should haunt us is not the *no longer* of actually existing social democracy, but the *not yet* of the futures that popular modernism trained us to expect, but which never materialised. These spectres – the spectres of lost futures – reproach the formal nostalgia of the capitalist realist world.

Music culture was central to the projection of the futures which have been lost. The term music *culture* is crucial here, because it is the culture constellated around music (fashion, discourse, cover art) that has been as important as the music itself in conjuring seductively unfamiliar worlds. The *destranging* of music culture in the 21st century – the ghastly return of industry moguls and boys next door to mainstream pop; the premium put on 'reality' in popular entertainment; the increased tendency of those in music culture to dress and look like digitally and surgically enhanced versions of regular folk; the emphasis placed on gymnastic emoting in singing – has played a major role in conditioning us to accept consumer capitalism's model of ordinariness. Michael Hardt and Antonio Negri are right when they say that the revolutionary take on race, gender and sexuality struggles goes far beyond the demand that different identities be recognised. Ultimately, it is about the dismantling of identity. The 'revolutionary process of the abolition of identity, we should keep in mind, is monstrous, violent, and traumatic. Don't try to save yourself—in fact, your *self has*, to be sacrificed! This does not mean that liberation casts us into an indifferent sea with no objects of identification, but rather the existing identities will no longer serve as anchors.' (Michael Hardt and Antonio Negri, *Commonwealth*, Harvard University Press, 2011, p339) While Hardt and Negri are correct to warn of the traumatic dimensions of this transformation, as they are also aware, it also has its joyful aspects. Throughout the 20th century, music culture was a probe that played a major role in preparing the population to *enjoy* a future that was no longer white, male or heterosexual, a future in which the relinquishing of identities that were in any case poor fictions would be a blessed relief. In the 21st century, by contrast – and the fusion of pop with reality TV is absolutely indicative of this – popular music culture has been reduced to being a mirror held up to late capitalist subjectivity.

By now, it should already be very clear that there are different senses of the word hauntology at play in *Ghosts Of My Life*. There is the specific sense in which it has been applied to music culture, and a more general sense, where it refers to persistences, repetitions, prefigurations. There are also more or less benign versions of hauntology. *Ghosts Of My Life* will move amongst these different uses of the term.

The book is about the ghosts of *my* life, so there is necessarily a personal dimension to what follows. Yet my take on the old phrase 'the personal is political' has been to look for the (cultural, structural, political) conditions of subjectivity. The most productive way of reading the 'personal is political' is to interpret it as saying: the personal is impersonal. It's miserable for anyone at all to *be themselves* (still more, to be forced to sell themselves). Culture, and the analysis of culture, is valuable insofar as it allows an escape from ourselves.

Such insights have been hard won. Depression is the most malign spectre that has dogged my life – and I use the term depression to distinguish the dreary solipsism of the condition from the more lyrical (and collective) desolations of hauntological melancholia. I started blogging in 2003 whilst still in such a state of depression that I found everyday life scarcely bearable.

Some of these writings were part of the working through of the condition, and it's no accident that my (so far successful) escape from depression coincided with a certain externalisation of negativity: the problem wasn't (just) me but the culture around me. It's clear to me that now the period from roughly 2003 to the present will be recognised – not in the far distant future, but very soon – as the worst period for (popular) culture since the 1950s. To say that the culture was desolate is not to say that there weren't traces of other possibilities. *Ghosts Of My Life* is an attempt to engage with some of these traces.

Ghosts Of My Life: Goldie, Japan, Tricky

It must have been 1994 when I first saw Rufige Kru's 'Ghosts Of My Life' on the shelves of a high street record store. The four-track EP had been released in 1993, but this was a time – before internet hype and online discographies – when the traces of the underground took longer to surface. The EP was a prime example of darkside Jungle. Jungle was a moment in what Simon Reynolds would come to call the 'hardcore continuum': the series of mutations on the British dance music underground triggered by the introduction of the breakbeat into Rave, passing from hardcore Rave into Jungle, Speed Garage, 2-step.

I'll always prefer the name Jungle to the more pallid and misleading term drum and bass, because much of the allure of the genre came from the fact that no drums or bass guitar were played. Instead of simulating the already-existing qualities of 'real' instruments, digital technology was exploited to produce sounds that had no pre-existing correlates. The function of timestretching – which allowed the time signature of a sound to be changed, without its pitch being altered – transformed sampled breakbeats into rhythms that no human could play. Producers would also use the strange metallic excrescence that was produced when samples were slowed down and the software had to fill in the gaps. The result was an abstract rush that made chemicals all but redundant: accelerating our metabolisms, heightening our expectations, reconstructing our nervous systems.

It is also worth holding onto the name Jungle because it evokes a terrain: the urban Jungle, or rather the underside of a metropolis that was just in the process of being digitalised. It has sometimes seemed as if the use of the word 'urban' is a polite synonym for 'black' music. Yet it's possible to hear 'urban', not as some disavowal of race, but as an invocation of the powers of cosmopolitan conviviality. At the same time, however, Jungle was by no means an unequivocal *celebration* of the urban. If Jungle celebrated anything, it was the lure of *the dark*. Jungle liberated the suppressed libido in the dystopian impulse, releasing and amplifying the jouissance that comes from anticipating the annihilation of all current certainties. As Kodwo Eshun argued, in Jungle there was a libidinisation of anxiety itself, a transformation of fight and flight impulses into enjoyment.

This was deeply ambivalent: at one level, what we were hearing here was a kind of sonic fictional intensification and extrapolation of the neoliberal world's destruction of solidarity and security. Nostalgia for the familiarity of smalltown life was rejected in Jungle, but its digital city was devoid of the comfort of strangers: no-one could be trusted here. Jungle took many of its cues from the Hobbesian scenarios of 1980s films such as *Blade Runner*, *Terminator* and *Predator 2*. It's no accident that all three of these films are about hunting. Jungle's world was one in which entities – human as well as nonhuman – stalked each other for sport as well as for sustenance. Yet darkside Jungle was about the thrill of the chased, about the videogame euphoria–anxiety of eluding ruthless predators, as much as it was about the exhilaration of running prey to ground.

At another level, darkside Jungle projected the very future that capital can only disavow. Capital can never openly admit that it is a system based on inhuman rapacity; the Terminator can never remove its human mask. Jungle not only ripped the mask off, it actively identified with the inorganic circuitry beneath: hence the android/ death's head that Rufige Kru used as their logo. The paradoxical identification with death, and the equation of death with the inhuman future was more than a cheap nihilist gesture. At a certain point, the unrelieved negativity of the dystopian drive trips over into a perversely utopian gesture, and annihilation becomes the condition of the radically new.

I was a postgraduate student in 1994, and I didn't have either the nerve or the money to hang around specialist record shops to pick up all the latest releases. So I would access Jungle tracks in much the same fitful way that I had followed American comics in the 70s. I would pick them up where and when I could, usually on CD compilations issued long after their dubplate freshness had cooled. For the most part, it was impossible to impose any narrative on Jungle's relentless flow. Fittingly for a sound that was so depersonalised and dehumanised, the names of the acts tended to be cryptic cyberpunk tags, disconnected from any biography or place. Jungle was best enjoyed as an anonymous electro-libidinal current that seemed to *pass through* producers, as a series of affects and FX that were de-linked from authors. It sounded like some audio unlife form, a ferocious, feral artificial intelligence that had been unwittingly called up in the studio, the breakbeats like genetically-augmented hounds straining to be free of the leash.

Rufige Kru were one of the few Jungle acts about which I knew a little. Because of Simon Reynolds' evangelical pieces on Jungle in the now long-defunct Melody Maker, I was aware that Rufige Kru was one of the aliases used by Goldie, who, almost uniquely in the anonymity of the Jungle scene, was already becoming a recognisable face. If there was to be a face for this faceless music, then Goldie – a mixed race former graffiti artist with gold teeth – was a strong candidate. Goldie was formed by hip-hop culture, but irrevocably altered by Rave's collective delirium. His career became a parable for a whole series of impasses. The temptation for any producer emerging from the scenius of the hardcore continuum was always to renounce the essentially collective nature of the conditions of production. It was a temptation that Goldie was unable to resist, but, tellingly, his records declined the very moment he stopped using impersonal, collective names for his projects, and started releasing them under the (albeit assumed) name Goldie. His first album,

Timeless, smoothed out the anorganic angles of Jungle with the use of analogue instruments and an alarming jazz-funk tastefulness. Goldie became a minor celebrity, took a part in the BBC soap opera *EastEnders*, and only in 2008 released the kind of album that Rufige Kru should have put out 15 years before. The lesson was clear: urban British artists can only be successful if they depart from the scenius, if they leave behind the collective.

The first records Goldie and his collaborators released under the names Rufige Kru and Metalheads were still high on Rave's carny buzz. 1992's 'Terminator' was the most epochal: jittery with excitable rave stabs, its phased and timestretched beats suggested aberrant, impossible geometries, while its vocal samples – from Linda Hamilton in *Terminator* – talked of time paradoxes and fatal strategies. The record sounded like a commentary on itself: as if the temporal anomalies that Hamilton described – 'you're talking about things that I haven't done yet in the past tense' – were made physical in the vertiginously imploding sound.

As Rufige Kru progressed their sound became sleeker. Where the early records put one in mind of an assemblage of dismembered organs that had been crudely stitched together, the later releases more closely resembled mutants that had been genetically engineered. The unruly and volatile Rave elements had gradually drained away, to be replaced by textures that were starker, moodier. The titles – 'Dark Rider', 'Fury', 'Manslaughter' – told their own story. As you listened, you felt like you were being pursued through a near-future brutalist arcade. Vocal samples were cut back, and became more subdued and ominous. 'Manslaughter' features one of the most electrifying lines from *Blade Runner*'s rogue replicant Roy Batty: 'If only you could see what I've seen, through your eyes' – the perfect slogan for Jungle's new mutants, engineered by street science to have heightened senses but a shorter life span.

I bought any Rufige Kru record that I came upon, but 'Ghosts

Of My Life' brought a special tingle of intrigue because of its title, with its suggestion of Japan's 1981 art pop masterpiece, 'Ghosts'. When I played the 'Ghosts Of My Life' 12', I quickly realised with a shiver of exhilaration that the pitched down voice repeating the title phrase did indeed belong to Japan's David Sylvian. But this wasn't the only trace of 'Ghosts'. After some atonal washes and twitchy breakbeats, the track lurched to a sudden halt, and – in a moment that still takes my breath away when I listen to it now – a brief snatch of the spidery, abstract electronics instantly recognizable from the Japan record leapt into the chasm, before being immediately consumed by viscous bass ooze and the synthetic screeches that were the sonic signatures of darkside Jungle.

Time had folded in on itself. One of my earliest pop fixations had returned, vindicated, in an unexpected context. Early 80s New Romantic synthpop, reviled and ridiculed in Britain, but revered in the dance music scenes of Detroit, New York and Chicago, was finally coming home to roost in the UK underground. Kodwo Eshun, then at work on his *More Brilliant than the Sun: Adventures in Sonic Fiction*, would argue that synthpop played the same founding role for Techno, hip-hop and Jungle as delta blues did for rock, and it was as if a disavowed part of myself – a ghost from another part of my life – was being recovered, although in a permanently altered form.

'Just when I think I'm winning'

In 1982, I taped 'Ghosts' from the radio and chain-listened to it: pressing play, rewinding the cassette, repeating. 'Ghosts' is a record which, even now, compels you to keep replaying it. Partly, that's because of the way the record teems with detail: you never feel you've fully grasped it all.

Nothing else that Japan recorded was like 'Ghosts'. It as an anomaly, not only because of its seeming confessionalism, exceptional in the work of a group which favoured aesthetic poses over emotional expression, but also because of its arrangement, its texture. Elsewhere on *Tin Drum* – the 1981 album from which 'Ghosts' came – Japan had developed a plastic ethno-funk, where electronics flitted through the elasticated rhythmic architecture created by the bass and drums. On 'Ghosts', however, there are no drums and no bassline. There is only percussion that sounds like metallic vertebrae being gently struck, and a suite of sounds so austerely synthetic that they could have come from Stockhausen.

'Ghosts' begins with chimes that make you feel like you are inside some metallic clock. The air is charged, an electrical field through which unintelligible radio-wave chitterings pass. At the same time, the track is pervaded by an immense stillness, a poise. Watch the group's extraordinary live performance of 'Ghosts' on the Old Grey Whistle Test. They look as if they are tending their instruments rather than playing them.

Only Sylvian appears animated, and then it's only his face, half-hidden by the heavy fringe, that moves. The mannered angst of his vocal sits oddly with the electronic austerity of the music. Its sense of enervated foreboding is broken by the only trace of melodrama in the song – the synth stabs which, simulating the kind of strings you'd hear on a movie thriller-score, cue in the chorus. *'Just when I think I'm win-ning/ when I've broken every door/ the ghosts of my life/ blow wild-er/ than the win-d'* . . .

What, exactly, are the ghosts that haunt Sylvian? The song derives much of its potency from declining to answer, from its lack of specificity: we can fill in the blanks with our own spectres. What's clear is that it isn't external contingencies which ruin his wellbeing. Something from his past – something he wants to have left behind – keeps returning. He can't leave it behind because he carries it with him. Is he anticipating the destruction of his happiness, or has the destruction already happened? The present tense – or rather the hesitation between past and present tense – creates an ambiguity, suggesting a fatalistic eternity, a compulsion to repeat – a compulsion that might be a self-fulfilling prophecy. The ghosts return because he fears they will . . .

It's hard not to hear 'Ghosts' as a reflection of sorts on Japan's career up to that point. The group was the culmination of a certain English take on art pop that began with Bowie and Roxy in the early 70s. They came from Beckenham, Catford, Lewisham the unglamorous conurbation where Kent joins South London – the same suburban hinterland from which David Bowie, Billy Idol and Siouxsie Sioux had come. As with most English art pop, Japan found their environment only a negative inspiration, something to escape from. 'There was a conscious drive away from everything that childhood represented,' Sylvian has remarked. Pop was the portal out of the prosaic. Music was only part of it. Art pop was a finishing school for working class autodidacts, where, by following up the clues left behind by earlier pioneers – the allusions secreted in lyrics, in track titles or in interview references – you could learn about things that weren't on the formal curriculum for working class youth: fine art, European cinema, avant-garde literature . . . Changing your name was the first step, and Sylvian had traded his given name (Batt) for one that referred to Sylvain Sylvain from the New York Dolls, the group whose style Japan had begun by imitating.

By the time of 'Ghosts', all of the ersatz Amerikan swagger of this Dolls phase is long forgotten, and Sylvian has long since perfected his plastic mass-produced copy of Bryan Ferry. In his analysis of Bryan Ferry's voice, Ian Penman argues that its peculiar quality came from an only partly successful attempt to get his Geordie accent to forge a classic, timeless Englishness. Sylvian's singing voice is the faking of a fake. The almost whinnying quality of Ferry's angst is retained, but transposed into a pure styling devoid of emotional content. It is culture(d), not natural at all; prissy, ultra-affected, and, for that very reason, strangely lacking in affect. It couldn't contrast more with

Sylvian's speaking voice at the time – awkward, tentative, strongly bearing all the traces of class and South London which his singing voice had sought to remove. *'Sons of pioneers/ are hungry men.'*

'Ghosts' was paralysed by very English anxieties: you could imagine Pip from *Great Expectations* singing it. In England, working class escape is always haunted by the possibility that you will be found out, that your roots are showing. You won't know some crucial rule of etiquette that you should. You will pronounce something wrongly – mispronunciation is a constant source of anxiety for the autodidact, because books don't necessarily tell you how to *say* words. Is 'Ghosts' the moment when art pop confronts this fear – that class will out, that one's background can never be transcended, that the rude spectres of Lewisham will return no matter how far East you travel?

Japan had pursued art pop into a sheer superficiality, which exceeded even their inspirations in its depthless aestheticism. *Tin Drum*, the 1981 album from which 'Ghosts' came, was art pop as Barthes pop, a conspicuous playing with signs for their own seductive sake. The album cover immediately drew you into their heavily confected world: Sylvian, his heavily sprayed, peroxided fringe falling artfully over his Trevor Horn specs, sits in a simulation of a simple Chinese dwelling, chopsticks in hand, as a Mao poster peels from the wall behind him. Everything is posed, every Sign selected with a fetishistic fastidiousness. Check the way his eyeshadow gives his eyelids an almost opiated heaviness – but, at the same time, everything is so painfully fragile; his face a Noh-mask, anemically ultra-white, his body posture ragdoll drained. Here he is, one of the last glam princes, and perhaps the most magnificent – his face and body rare and delicate works of art, not extrinsic to, or lesser than, the music, but forming an integral component of the overall concept. All – social, political, cultural – meaning seems to be drained from these references. When Sylvian sings 'Red Army needs you' on the closing track, 'Cantonese Boy', it is in the same spirit of semiotic orientalism: the Chinese and Japanese Empires of signs are reduced to images, exploited and coveted for their frission.

By the time of *Tin Drum*, Japan have perfected their transition from New York Dolls-trash-hounds to gentlemen connoisseurs, from working class Beckenham youth into cosmopolitan men about town. (Or they've achieved as much as is possible: 'Ghosts' suggests that the transition will never be so successful as to eliminate anxiety: the more you've disguised your background, the more it will hurt when it is exposed.) *Tin Drum*'s superficiality is the superficiality of the (glossy) photograph, the group's detachment that of the photographer. Images are decontextualised, then re-assembled to form an 'Oriental' panorama that is strangely abstract: a Far East as surrealist novelist Raymond Roussel might have reimagined it. Like Ferry, Sylvian remains Subject as well as Object: not only the frozen Image, but also he who assembles images, not in any pathological, *Peeping Tom* sense, but in a coolly detached way. The detachment, naturally, is a performance, concealing anxiety even as it sublimates it. The words are little labyrinths, enigmas with no possible solution – the appearance of enigmas, perhaps – false-fronted follies decorated with Chinese and Japanese motifs.

Sylvian's voice belongs to this masquerade. Even on 'Ghosts', Sylvian's voice does not ask to be taken at face value. It is not a voice that reveals, or even pretends to reveal, it is a voice to hide behind, just like the make-up, the conspicuously-worn sino-signs. It's not only the fixation on geography that makes Sylvian seem like a tourist, an outside observer even in his own 'inner' life. His voice seems to come entirely from his head, barely from his body at all.

And after this? Japan would fall apart, while Duran Duran were already more than half way towards taking a lumpen version of Japan's schtick into superstardom. For Sylvian, there was a pursuit of 'authenticity', which was connoted by two things: the turn away from rhythm and the embracing of 'real' instruments. The wiping away of the cosmetics, the quest for Meaning, the discovery of a Real Self. Yet, until 2003's *Blemish*, Sylvian's solo records seemed as if they were straining towards an emotional authenticity that his voice could never quite deliver, only now they lacked the alibi of aestheticism.

Tin Drum was Japan's final studio album, but it was also one of the last moments in English art pop. One future had quietly died, but others would surface.

'Your eyes resemble mine . . .'

A fragment of Japan's 'Ghosts' washed up 14 years later, on Tricky's first single, 'Aftermath'. Here it wasn't sampled, but cited, by Tricky's mentor, fellow Bristolian Mark Stewart. In the background of the track's loping-shanty rhythms, you can hear Stewart speak-sing the lines 'just when I thought I was winning, just when I thought I could not be stopped. . . ' The use of the Japan reference and the presence of Stewart – a major figure in Bristol postpunk since his time with The Pop Group in the 1970s – were already powerful clues that Tricky's positioning as a 'trip-hop' artist was reductive and misleading. Too often, the label trip-hop would be applied to what was in effect a black music with the 'blackness' muted or excised (hip-hop without rap). The 'trip' in Tricky's music had less to do with psychedelics and more to do with the fuggy indolence of marijuana. But Tricky pursued ganja inertia well beyond stoner lassitude into a visionary condition, in which rap's aggression and braggadocio weren't so much removed as refracted in the heat haze of a dreamy, hydroponic humidity.

On the face of it, Tricky's ra(s)p could be heard as the British answer to hip-hop, but, on a more subterranean level, what he was also taking up and renewing were strands in postpunk and art pop. Tricky counts postpunk acts like Blondie, The Banshees, The Cure ('the last great pop band, I think', he says) as his precursors. It's not as simple as opposing this lineage to the soul, funk and dub references which were so obvious in Tricky's earliest music. Postpunk and art pop had already drawn substantially upon funk and dub. 'I grew up in a white ghetto,' Tricky said when I interviewed him in 2008. 'My Dad's Jamaican, my grandmother is white. When I was growing up, till I was about 16, everything was normal. When I moved to an ethnic ghetto, I had friends there and my friends would say, "Why do you hang out with those skinhead guys, the white guys?" and my skinhead friends were like, "Why you hanging out with those black guys?" I couldn't get it, I couldn't understand it. I could always go to both worlds, I could go to a reggae club and then a white club and not even notice it because my family is all different colours, different shades. So at Christmas, you got a white person, black person, African looking person, Asian looking person . . . we didn't notice it, my family are colour blind. But all of a sudden things started moving around, learning bad habits, people whispering to you, like, "Why you hanging around with those white guys?" These are kids I grew up with since five years old, the guys I grew up with saying "why you hanging out with those black guys?" Then I see The Specials on TV, these white and black guys getting together.'

Tricky appeared at the very moment when the reactionary pantomime of Britpop – a rock which had whitewashed out contemporary black influences – was moving towards dominance. The phony face-off between Blur and Oasis which preoccupied the media was a distraction from the real fault lines in British music culture at the time. The conflict that really mattered was between a music which acknowledged and accelerated what was new in the 90s – technology, cultural pluralism, genre innovations – and a music which took refuge in a monocultural version of Britishness: a swaggering white boy rock built almost entirely out of forms that were established in the 1960s and 1970s. This was a music designed to reassure anxious white males at a moment when all of the certainties they had previously counted on – in work, sexual relations, ethnic identity – were coming under pressure. As we now know, Britpop would win the struggle. Tricky would slink away to become the herald of a future for British music that never materialised. (A rapprochement of sorts between Tricky and Britpop was – thankfully – missed. Blur's Damon Albarn was supposed to guest on the album Tricky recorded under the name Nearly God – alongside The Specials' Terry Hall, amongst many others – but the track that the pair recorded together was removed from the album before it was released.)

When *Maxinquaye* was released in 1995, Tricky was immediately anointed as the voice of a mute, depoliticised generation, the wounded prophet who absorbed and transmitted a decade's psychic pollution. The extent of this adulation can be gauged by the origin of the name Nearly God: a German journalist had asked him 'what's it like to be God? Well, nearly God?' Instead of taking up his assigned role as the imp of the perverse in 90s mainstream pop, though, Tricky sidled off into the sidelines, a half-forgotten figure. So much so, that when he appeared as a guest at Beyoncé's 2011 Glastonbury performance, it provoked a gasp of shock – as if, for a moment, we'd stumbled into some alternative reality where Tricky was where he deserved to be, a glamorous gargoyle on the edifice of 21st century pop. All-too-symbolically, however, Tricky's microphone didn't seem to be switched on, and he could barely be heard.

'On *Maxinquaye*,' Ian Penman wrote in his landmark March 1995 essay for *The Wire* magazine, 'Tricky sounds like ghosts from another solar system'. The spectrality of Tricky's music, the way it refused to *step up* or *represent*, the way it slurred between lucidity and inarticulacy, made for a sharp contrast with the multicoloured brashness of what Penman called 'the *Face*-cover/Talkin Loud/Jazzie B nexus of groovy One World vibery'. What's so significant about the version of multiculturalism that

Tricky and Goldie proffered was its refusal of earnestness and worthiness. Theirs was not a music that petitioned for inclusion in any kind of ordinariness. Instead, it revelled in its *other*worldliness, its science-fictional glamour. Like art pop's first pioneer, Bowie, it was about identification with the alien, where the alien stood in for the technologically new and the cognitively strange – and ultimately for forms of social relations that were as yet only faintly imaginable. Bowie was by no means the first to make this identification: loving the alien was a gesture that self-mythologizing black magi – Kodwo Eshun's 'sonic fictional' canon of Lee Perry, George Clinton, Sun Ra – had made long before Bowie first did it. Identifying with the alien – not so much speaking for the alien as letting the alien speak through you – was what gave 20th century popular music much of its political charge. Identification with the alien meant the possibility of an escape from identity, into other subjectivities, other worlds.

There was also identification with the android. 'Aftermath' includes a sample of dialogue from *Blade Runner*: 'I'll tell you about my mother', the anti-Oedipal taunt that the replicant Leon throws at his interrogator-tormentor before killing him. 'Is it merely coincidence that the Sylvian quote and the *Blade Runner* lift converge in the same song?', Penman asks.

'Ghosts'. . . Replicants? Electricity has made us all angels. Technology (from psycho-analysis to surveillance) has made us all ghosts. The replicant ('YOUR EYES RESEMBLE MINE. . . ') is a speaking void. The scary thing about 'Aftermath' is that it suggests that nowadays WE ALL ARE. Speaking voids, made up only of scraps and citations . . . contaminated by other people's memories . . . adrift . . .

When I met Tricky in 2008, he referred unbidden to the line from 'Aftermath' that Penman picks up on here. 'My first lyric ever on a song was 'your eyes resemble mine, you'll see as no others can'.

I never had any kids then, so what am I talking about? Who am I talking about? [My daughter] Maisie wasn't born. My mother used to write poetry but in her time she couldn't have done anything with that, there wasn't any opportunity. It's almost like she killed herself to give me the opportunity, my lyrics, I can never understand why I write as a female; I think I've got my Mum's talent, I'm her vehicle. So I need a woman to sing that.'

Hauntology, then, telepathy, the persistence of the *no longer*. . . You don't have to believe in the supernatural to recognise that the family is a haunted structure, an Overlook Hotel full of presentiments and uncanny repetitions, something that speaks ahead of us, instead of us . . . From the start – like all of us – Tricky was haunted, and the crepitational-texture of 21st century hauntology was already being auditioned on Tricky's earliest recordings. When I first heard *Burial* a decade later, I would immediately reach for Tricky's first album *Maxinquaye* as a point of comparison. It wasn't only the use of vinyl crackle, so much a signature of both *Maxinquaye* and *Burial*, that suggested the affinity. It was also the prevailing mood, the way suffocating sadness and mumbling melancholy bled into lovelorn eroticism and dreamspeech. Both records feel like emotional states transformed into landscapes, but where Burial's music conjures urban scenes under *Blade Runner* perma-drizzle, *Maxinquaye* feels as if it is taking place in a desert as delirial and Daliesque as the initiatory space that the characters pass through in Nic Roeg's *Walkabout*: the land is scorched, cracked and barren, but there are occasional bursts of verdant lushness (on the queasily erotic 'Abbaon Fat Tracks', for instance, we could have strayed into the ruined pastoral of Talk Talk's *Spirit of Eden*).

'Your eyes resemble mine . . .' From the very beginning, speaking in his dead mother's voice, a semi-benign Norman Bates, Tricky was conscious of his (dis)possession by female spectres. With his predilection for cosmetics and cross-dressing, he looked like one of the last vestiges of the glam impulse in

British pop: his gender ambivalence a welcome antidote to Britpop's lumpen laddishness. It's clear that gender indeterminacy is no pantomime mummery for him, but something that goes right to the core of his music. Saying that Tricky 'writes from a female point of view' fails to capture the uncanniness of what he does, since he also induces women to sing from what seems to be a male perspective. 'I like putting women in a male role, to have the woman play the strength and the man be the weak. I was brought up, one of my uncles was in jail for 30 years and the other for 15 years. I didn't see my dad, I was brought up by my grandmother and my auntie so I've seen my grandmother fight in the street. I've seen my auntie and my grandmother have fistfights, I've seen my grandmother grab my auntie's arm and close it in the door and break her arm fighting over meat. So I see women as tough. They fed me, they clothed me, my grandmother taught me to steal, my auntie taught me to fight, she sent me to boxing when I was 15. If men go to war, you stand in one field, I stand in another, we shoot each other, but what's the hardest is when you are at home and you gotta listen to kids cry and you gotta feed 'em. That's tough, I've seen no men around, I've seen my uncle go jail for seven years, then ten years, my other uncle; my Dad never rang. Women keep it together, keep the food on the table, defend us, defend the children, like if anyone fucked with us they would be down the school. I've never seen men do that for me, I've never seen men there for me like that. All I know is women.'

Gender doesn't dissolve here into some bland unisex mush; instead it resolves into an unstable space in which subjectivity is continually sliding from male to female voice. It is an art of splitting which is also an art of doubling. Through the women who sing for/as him, Tricky becomes less than one, a split subject that can never be restored to wholeness. Yet their voicing of his incompleteness also makes him more than one, a double in search of a lost other half it will never recover. Either way, what Tricky unsettles – both as a vocalist and as a writer/ producer who coaxes singing from an Other – is the idea of the voice as a rock solid guarantor of presence and identity. His own weakened, recessed voice, all those croaks, mumbles and murmurs, has always suggested a presence that was barely there, something supplementary rather than centred. But the main – usually female – voice on his songs also sounds absented and abstracted. What the voices of his female singers – flat, drained, destitute of ordinary affective cadences – most resemble is the sound of a medium, a voice being spoken by something else.

'So this is the aftermath...' It is not that Tricky possesses female singers; more that he induces them into sharing his trance states. The words that come to him from a lost female source are returned to a female mouth. 'I'm already on the other side', as Martina Topley-Bird sang on 'I Be The Prophet' from the Nearly God LP. Tricky's upbringing was particularly gothic. 'My grandmother used to keep me at home because my stepgrandfather used to be out working, and she used to watch all these black and white horror movies, vampire movies, and it was like growing up in a movie. She used to sit me in the middle of the floor, cause she lost my mum, her daughter. She'd be playing Billie Holiday, smoking a cigarette and would say things like "you look like your Mum," watching me. I was always my Mum's ghost. I grew up in a dreamlike state. One time I've seen a suicide off an NCP car park and the police took me down to see what I saw and the next day in the Evening Post there was my name in there. I woke up and it was on the fridge, my grandmother had put it on the fridge like I was famous.'

The one who is possessed is also dispossessed – of their own identity and voice. But this kind of dispossession is of course a precondition for the most potent writing and performance. Writers have to tune into other voices; performers must be capable of being taken over by outside forces – and Tricky can be a great live performer because of his capacity to work himself up into a state of head-shaking shamanic self-erasure. Like the occult, religion provides a symbolic repertoire which deals with the idea of an alien presence using the tongue, of the dead having influence on the living, and Tricky's language has always been saturated with biblical imagery. *Maxinquaye*'s purgatorial landscape was littered with religious signs, while *Pre-Millennium Tension* exhibited what seemed like religious mania: 'I saw a Christian in Christiansands, a devil in Helsinki.' 'Here come the Nazarene/look good in a magazine . . . Mary Magdalene that'll be my first sin.'

When I interviewed Tricky he had just released the single, 'Council Estate'. Here, class spectres spoke – but not for the first time in Tricky's work. Class rage could be detected smouldering in many of his tracks from the beginning. 'Master your language/and until then, I'll create my own,' he warned on 1996's 'Christiansands', casting himself as the proletarian Caliban plotting revenge on his alleged betters. He is acutely aware of the way in which class determines destiny. 'Breaking into a house or car equals locksmiths, insurance, it's all making money off me. The longer I'm in prison you're making more money. Modern-day slavery: instead of slaves, they turn them into criminals.'

Tricky called the album from which 'Council Estate' came *Knowle West*, after the area of Bristol in which he grew up. 'When I was at school, there was one certain teacher who said, when you go for a job, as soon as you put your postcode down and they know you're from Knowle West, you ain't gonna get the job. So lie, if you're going to fill in your application forms, lie.'

'Council Estate' conceived of resentment as a motivating force and success as revenge. It wasn't about leaving your past behind, as Sylvian wanted to, it is about succeeding so that your class origins can be forced back down the throat of those who said you couldn't succeed. Like so many working class pop stars before him – including Sylvian – success provided vindication for Tricky and gave him access to a world which both attracted and appalled him. 1996's 'Tricky Kid' was his take on the theme of class dislocation that has preoccupied British pop since at least as far back as The Kinks. It was the best song about a working class male projected out of their milieu into the pleasure gardens of the hyper–successful since The Associates' 'Club Country' ('A drive from nowhere leaves you in the cold . . . every breath you breathe belongs to someone there'). With its febrile, *Jacob's Ladder*–like vision of leering hedonism – 'coke in your nose . . . everyone wants to be naked and famous' – 'Tricky Kid' anticipated the way in which, in the first decade of the 21st century, working class ambitions would be bought off by the fool's gold of celebrity culture and reality TV. 'Now they call me superstar. . .,' it demonically proclaimed, a line echoed in the refrain of 'Council Estate'. Why is 'superstar' such an important word for him? 'Because it's such a stupid word in a way. What used to happen is that you make an album, and if your album's successful, fame is almost part of the game. When I was starting off, I just wanted to make a good album, I wanted to make something that no one's ever heard before – I wasn't interested in anything else.'

01: THE RETURN OF THE 70S

No Longer the Pleasures: Joy Division

Adapted from k–punk post, January 9, 2005

If Joy Division matter now more than ever, it's because they capture the depressed spirit of *our* times. Listen to JD now, and you have the inescapable impression that the group were catatonically channelling our present, their future. From the start their work was overshadowed by a deep foreboding, a sense of a future foreclosed, all certainties dissolved, only growing gloom ahead. It has become increasingly clear that 1979-80, the years with which the group will always be identified, was a threshold moment – the time when a whole world (social democratic, Fordist, industrial) became obsolete, and the contours of a new world (neoliberal, consumerist, informatic) began to show themselves. This is of course a retrospective judgement; breaks are rarely experienced as such at the time. But the 70s exert a particular fascination now that we are locked into the new world – a world that Deleuze, using a word that would become associated with Joy Division, called the 'Society of Control'. The 70s is the time before the switch, a time at once kinder and harsher than now. Forms of (social) security then taken for granted have long since been destroyed, but vicious prejudices that were then freely aired have become unacceptable. The conditions that allowed a group like Joy Division to exist have evaporated; but so has a certain grey, grim texture of everyday life in Britain, a country that seemed to have given up rationing only reluctantly.

By the early 2000s, the 70s was long enough ago to have become a period setting for drama, and Joy Division were part of the scenery. This was how they featured in Michael Winterbottom's *24 Hour Party People* (2002). The group were little more than a cameo here, the first chapter in the story of Factory records and its buffoon-genius impresario Tony Wilson. Joy Division assumed centre stage in Anton Corbijn's *Control* (2007), but the film didn't really connect. For those who knew the story, it was a familiar trip; for those not already initiated, however, the film didn't do enough to convey the group's sorcerous power. We were taken through the story, but never drawn into the maelstrom, never made to feel why any of it mattered. Perhaps this was inevitable. Rock depends crucially on a particular body and a particular voice and the mysterious relationship between the two. *Control* could never make good the loss of Ian Curtis's voice and body, and so ended up as arthouse karaoke naturalism; the actors could simulate the chords, could ape Curtis's moves, but they couldn't forge the vortical charisma, couldn't muster the unwitting necromantic art that transformed the simple musical structures into a ferocious expressionism, a portal to the outside. For that you need the footage of the group performing, the sound of the records. Which is why, of the three films featuring the group, Grant Gee's 2007 documentary, *Joy Division*, patched together from super-8 fragments, TV appearances, new interviews and old images of postwar Manchester, was most effective at transporting us back to those disappeared times. Gee's film begins with an epigraph from Marshall Berman's *All That Is Solid Melts Into Air: The Experience Of Modernity*: 'To be modern is to find ourselves in an environment that promises us adventure, power, joy, growth, transformation of ourselves and the world – and, at the same time that threatens to destroy everything we have, everything we know, everything we are.' Where *Control* tried to conjure the presence of the group, but left us only with a tracing, an outline, *Joy Division* is organised around a vivid sense of loss. It is selfconsciously a study of a time and a place, both of which are now gone. *Joy Division* is a roll call of disappeared places and people – so many dead, already: not only Curtis, but also the group's manager Rob Gretton, their producer Martin Hannett and of course Tony Wilson. The film's coup, its most electric moment, the sound of a dead man wandering in the land of the dead: a scratchy old cassette recording of Ian Curtis being hypnotised into 'a past life regression'. *I travelled far and wide through many different times.* A slow, slurred voice channelling something cold and remote. 'How old are you?' '28', an exchange made all the more chilling because we know that Curtis would die at the age of 23.

Asylums with doors open wide

I didn't hear Joy Division until 1982, so, for me, Curtis was always-already dead. When I first heard them, aged 14, it was like that moment in John Carpenter's *In the Mouth of Madness* when Sutter Cane forces John Trent to read the novel, the hyper-fiction, in which he is already immersed: my whole future life, intensely compacted into those sound images – Ballard, Burroughs, dub, disco, Gothic, antidepressants, psych wards, overdoses, slashed wrists. Way too much stim to even begin to assimilate. Even they didn't understand what they were doing. How on earth could I, then?

New Order, more than anyone else, were in flight from the mausoleum edifice of Joy Division, and they had finally achieved severance by 1990. The England world cup song, cavorting around with beery, leery Keith Allen, a man who more than any other personifies the quotidian masculinism of overground Brit bloke culture in the late 80s and 90s, was a consummate act of desublimation. This, in the end, was what Kodwo Eshun called the 'price of escaping the anxiety of influence (the influence of themselves)'. On *Movement* the group were still in post-traumatic stress, frozen into a barely communicative trance ('The noise that surrounds me/ so loud in my head...')

It was clear, in the best interviews the band ever gave – to Jon Savage, a decade and a half after Curtis's death – that they had no idea what they were doing, and no desire to learn. Of Curtis' disturbing-compelling hyper-charged stage trance spasms and of his disturbing-compelling catatonic downer words, they said nothing and asked nothing, for fear of destroying the magic. They were unwitting necromancers who had stumbled on a formula for channelling voices, apprentices without a sorcerer. They saw themselves as mindless golems animated by Curtis' vision(s). (Thus, when he died, they said that they felt they had lost their eyes...)

Above all – and even if only because of audience reception – they were more than a pop group, more than entertainment, that much is obvious. We know all the words as if we wrote them ourselves, we followed stray hints in the lyrics out to all sorts of darker chambers, and listening to the albums now is like putting on a comfortable and familiar set of clothes.... But who is this 'we'? Well, it might have been the last 'we' that a whole generation of not-quite-men could feel a part of. There was an odd universality available to Joy Division's devotees (provided you were male of course).

Provided you were male of course... The Joy Division religion was, self-consciously, a boys' thing. Deborah Curtis: 'Whether it was intentional or not, the wives and girlfriends had gradually been banished from all but the most local of gigs and a curious male bonding had taken place. The boys seemed to derive their fun from each other.' (Deborah Curtis, *Touching from a Distance*, 77) No girls allowed...

As Curtis's wife, Deborah was barred from rock's pleasure garden, and could not pass into the cult of death that lay beyond the pleasure principle. She was just left to clear up the mess.

If Joy Division were very much a boys' group, their signature song, 'She's Lost Control' saw Ian Curtis abjecting his own disease, the 'holy sickness' of epilepsy, onto a female Other. Freud includes epileptic fits – along, incidentally, with a body in the grip of sexual passion – as examples of the *unheimlich*, the unhomely, the strangely familiar. Here the organic is slaved to the mechanical rhythms of the inorganic; the inanimate calls the tune, as it always does with Joy Division. 'She's Lost Control' is one of rock's most explicit encounters with the mineral lure of the inanimate. Joy Division's icy-spined undeath disco sounds like it has been recorded inside the damaged synaptic pathways of a brain of someone undergoing a seizure, Curtis' sepulchral, anhedonic vocals sent back to him – as if they were the voice of an Other, or Others – in long, leering expressionistic echoes that linger like acrid acid fog. 'She's Lost Control' traverses Poe-like cataleptic black holes in subjectivity, takes flatline voyages into the land of the dead and back to confront the 'edge of no escape', seeing in seizures little deaths (petil mals as petit morts) which offer terrifying but exhilarating releases from identity, more powerful than any orgasm.

In this colony

Try to imagine England in 1979 now. . .

Pre-VCR, pre-PC, pre-C4. Telephones far from ubiquitous (we didn't have one till around 1980, I think). The postwar consensus disintegrating on black and white TV.

More than anyone else, Joy Division turned this dourness into a uniform that self-consciously signified absolute authenticity; the deliberately functional formality of their clothes seceding from punk's tribalised anti-Glamour, 'depressives dressing for the Depression' (Deborah Curtis). It wasn't for nothing that they were called Warsaw when they started out. But it was in this Eastern bloc of the mind, in this slough of despond, that you could find working class kids who wrote songs steeped in Dostoyevsky, Conrad, Kafka, Burroughs, Ballard, kids who, without even thinking about it, were rigorous modernists who would have disdained repeating themselves, never mind disinterring and aping what had been done 20, 30 years ago (the 60s was a fading Pathe newsreel in 1979).

Back in '79, Art Rock still had a relationship to the sonic experimentation of the Black Atlantic. Unthinkable now, but White Pop then was no stranger to the cutting edge, so a genuine trade was possible. Joy Division provided the Black Atlantic with some sonic fictions it could re-deploy – listen to Grace Jones's extraordinary cover of 'She's Lost Control', or Sleazy D's 'I've Lost Control', or even to Kanye West's *808s and Heartbreak* (with its sleeve references to Saville's 'Blue Monday' cover design, and its echoes of *Atmosphere* and 'In A Lonely Place'). For all that, Joy Division's relationship to black pop was much more occluded than that of some of their peers. Postpunk's break from lumpen punk R and R consisted in large part in an ostentatiously flagged return-reclaiming of Black Pop: funk and dub especially. There was none of that, on the surface at least, with Joy Division.

But a group like PiL's take on dub, now, sounds a little laborious, a little literal, whereas, Joy Division, like The Fall, came off as a white anglo *equivalent* of dub. Both Joy Division and The Fall were 'black' in the priorities and economies of their sound: bass-heavy and rhythm-driven. This was dub not as a form, but a methodology, a legitimation for conceiving of sound-production as abstract engineering. But Joy Division also had a relationship to another super-synthetic, artily artificial 'black' sound: disco. Again, it was they, better than PiL, who delivered the 'Death Disco' beat. As Jon Savage loves to point out, the swarming syn-drums on 'Insight' seem to be borrowed from disco records like Amy Stewart's 'Knock on Wood'.

The role in all this of Martin Hannett, a producer who needs to be counted with the very greatest in pop, cannot be underestimated. It is Hannett, alongside Peter Saville, the group's sleeve designer, who ensured that Joy Division were more Art than Rock. The damp mist of insinuating uneasy listening Sound FX with which Hannett cloaked the mix, together with Saville's depersonalising designs, meant that the group could be approached, not as an aggregation of individual expressive subjects, but as a conceptual consistency. It was Hannett and Saville who transmuted the stroppy neuromantics of Warsaw into cyberpunks.

Day in/ Day out

Joy Division connected not just because of what they were, but when they were. Mrs Thatcher just arrived, the long grey winter of Reagonomics on the way, the Cold War still feeding our unconscious with a lifetime's worth of retina-melting nightmares.

JD were the sound of British culture's speed comedown, a long slow screaming neural shutdown. Since 1956, when Eden took amphetamines throughout the Suez crisis, through the Pop of the 60s, which had been kicked off by the Beatles going through the wall on uppers in Hamburg, through punk, which consumed speed like there was no tomorrow, Britain had been, in every sense, speeding. Speed is a connectivity drug, a drug that made sense of a world in which electronic connections were madly proliferating. But the comedown is vicious.

Massive serotonin depletion.

Energy crash.

Turn on your TV.

Turn down your pulse.

Turn away from it all.

It's all getting

Too much

Melancholia was Curtis' art form, just as psychosis was Mark E Smith's. Nothing could have been more fitting than that *Unknown Pleasures* began with a track called 'Disorder', for the key to Joy

Division was the Ballardian spinal landscape, the connexus linking individual psychopathology with social anomie. The two meanings of breakdown, the two meanings of Depression. That was how Sumner saw it, anyhow. As he explained to Savage, 'There was a huge sense of community where we lived. I remember the summer holidays when I was a kid: we would stay up late and play in the street, and 12 o'clock at night there would be old ladies, talking to each other. I guess what happened in the '60s was that the council decided that it wasn't very healthy, and something had to go, and unfortunately it was my neigh- bourhood that went. We were moved over the river to a towerblock. At the time I thought it was fantastic; now of course I realise it was an absolute disaster. I'd had a number of other breaks in my life. So when people say about the darkness in Joy Division's music, by age of 22, I'd had quite a lot of loss in my life. The place where I used to live, where I had my happiest memories, all of that had gone. All that was left was a chemical factory. I realised then that I could never go back to that happiness. So there's this void.'

Dead end lives at the end of the 70s. There were Joy Division, Curtis doing what most working class men still did, early marriage and a kid . . .

Feel it closing in

Sumner again: 'When I left school and got a job, real life came as a terrible shock. My first job was at Salford town hall sticking down envelopes, sending rates out. I was chained in this horrible office: every day, every week, every year, with maybe three weeks holiday a year. The horror enveloped me. So the music of Joy Division was about the death of optimism, of youth.'

A requiem for doomed youth culture. 'Here are the young men/ the weight on their shoulders,' went the famous lines from 'Decades', on *Closer*. The titles 'New Dawn Fades' and *Unknown Pleasures* could themselves be referring to the betrayed promises of youth culture. Yet what is remarkable about Joy Division is their total acquiescence in this failure, the way in which, from the start, they set up an Antarctic camp beyond the pleasure principle.

Set the controls for the heart of the black sun

What impressed and perturbed about JD was the fixatedness of their negativity. Unremitting wasn't the word. Yes, Lou Reed and Iggy and Morrison and Jagger had dabbled in nihilism – but even with Iggy and Reed that had been ameliorated by the odd moment of exhilaration, or at least there had been some explanation for their misery (sexual frustration, drugs). What separated Joy Division from any of their predecessors, even the bleakest, was the lack of any apparent object-cause for their melancholia. (That's what made it melancholia rather than melancholy, which has always been an acceptable, subtly sublime, delectation for men to relish.) From its very beginnings, (Robert Johnson, Sinatra) 20th-century Pop has been more to do with male (and female) sadness than elation. Yet, in the case of both the bluesman and the crooner, there is, at least ostensibly, a reason for the sorrow. Because Joy Division's bleakness was without any specific cause, they crossed the line from the blue of sadness into the black of depression, passing into the 'desert and wastelands' where nothing brings either joy or sorrow. Zero affect.

No heat in Joy Division's loins. They surveyed 'the troubles and the evils of this world' with the uncanny detachment of the neurasthenic. Curtis sang 'I've lost the will to want more' on 'Insight' but there was no sense that there had been any such will in the first place. Give their earliest songs a casual listen and you could easily mistake their tone for the curled lip of spiky punk outrage, but, already, it is as if Curtis is not railing against injustice or corruption so much as marshalling them as evidence for a thesis that was, even then, firmly established in his mind.

Depression is, after all and above all, a theory about the world, about life. The stupidity and venality of politicians ('Leaders of Men'), the idiocy and cruelty of war ('Walked in Line') are pointed to as exhibits in a case against the world, against life, that is so overwhelming, so general, that to appeal to any particular instance seems superfluous. In any case, Curtis expects no more of himself than he does of others, he knows he cannot condemn from a moral high ground: he 'let them use you/ for their own ends' ('Shadowplay'), he'll let you take his place in a showdown ('Heart and Soul').

That is why Joy Division can be a very dangerous drug for young men. They seem to be presenting The Truth (they present themselves as doing so). Their subject, after all, is depression. Not sadness or frustration, rock's standard downer states, but depression: depression, whose difference from mere sadness consists in its claim to have uncovered The (final, unvarnished) Truth about life and desire.

The depressive experiences himself as walled off from the lifeworld, so that his own frozen inner life – or inner death – overwhelms everything; at the same time, he experiences himself as evacuated, totally denuded, a shell: there is nothing except the inside, but the inside is empty. For the depressive, the habits of the former lifeworld now seem to be, precisely, a mode of play-acting, a series of pantomime gestures ('a circus complete with all fools'), which they are both no longer capable of performing and which they no longer wish to perform – there's no point, everything is a sham.

Depression is not sadness, not even a state of mind, it is a (neuro)philosophical (dis)position. Beyond Pop's bipolar oscillation between evanescent thrill and frustrated hedonism, beyond Jagger's Miltonian Mephistopheleanism, beyond Iggy's negated carny, beyond Roxy's lounge lizard reptilian melancholy, beyond the pleasure principle altogether, Joy Division were the most Schopenhauerian of rock groups, so much so that they barely belonged to rock at all. Since they had so thoroughly stripped out rock's libidinal motor – it would be better to say that they were, libidinally as well as sonically, anti-rock. Or perhaps, as they thought, they were the truth of rock, rock divested of all illusions. (The depressive is always confident of one thing: that he is without illusions.) What makes Joy Division so Schopenhauerian is the disjunction between Curtis's detachment and the urgency of the music, its implacable drive standing in for the dumb insatiability of the life-Will, the Beckettian 'I must go on' not experienced by the depressive as some redemptive positivity, but as the ultimate horror, the life-Will paradoxically assuming all the loathsome properties of the undead (whatever you do, you can't extinguish it, it keeps coming back).

Accept like a curse an unlucky deal

JD followed Schopenhauer through the curtain of Maya, went outside Burroughs' Garden of Delights, and dared to examine the hideous machineries that produce the world-as-appearance. What did they see there? Only what all depressives, all mystics, always see: the obscene undead twitching of the Will as it seeks to maintain the illusion that this object, the one it is fixated upon NOW, this one, will satisfy it in a way that all other objects thus far have failed to. Joy Division, with an ancient wisdom ('Ian sounded old, as if he had lived a lifetime in his youth' – Deborah Curtis), a wisdom that seems pre–mammalian, pre-multicellular life, pre-organic, saw through all those reproducer ruses. This is the 'Insight' that stopped fear in Curtis, the calming despair that subdued any will to want more. JD saw life as the Poe of 'The Conqueror Worm' had seen it, as Ligotti sees it: an automated marionette dance, which 'Through a circle that ever returneth in/ To the self-same spot', an ultra-determined chain of events that goes through its motions with remorseless inevitability. You watch the pre-scripted film as if from outside, condemned to watch the reels as they come to a close, brutally taking their time.

A student of mine once wrote in an essay that they sympathise with Schopenhauer when their football team loses. But the true Schopenhauerian moments are those in which you achieve your goals, perhaps realise your long-cherished heart's desire – and feel cheated, empty, no, more – or is it less? – than empty, voided. Joy Division always sounded as if they had experienced one too many of those desolating voidings, so that they could no longer be lured back onto the merry-go-round. They knew that satiation wasn't succeeded by tristesse, it was itself, immediately, tristesse. Satiation is the point at which you must face the existential revelation that you didn't want really want what you seemed so desperate to have, that your most urgent desires are only a filthy vitalist trick to keep the show on the road. If you 'can't replace the fear or the thrill of the chase', why stir yourself to pursue yet another empty kill? Why carry on with the charade?

Depressive ontology is dangerously seductive because, as the zombie twin of a certain philosophical wisdom, it is half true. As the depressive withdraws from the vacant confections of the lifeworld, he unwittingly finds himself in concordance with the human condition so painstakingly diagrammed by a philosopher like Spinoza: he sees himself as a serial consumer of empty simulations, a junky hooked on every kind of deadening high, a meat puppet of the passions. The depressive cannot even lay claim to the comforts that a paranoiac can enjoy, since he cannot believe that the strings are being pulled by any one. No flow, no connectivity in the depressive's nervous system. 'Watch from the wings as the scenes were replaying', go the fatalistic lines in 'Decades', and Curtis wrote with a depressive's iron certainty about life as some pre-scripted film. His voice – from the very start terrifying in its fatalism, in its acceptance of the worst – sounds like the voice of man who is already dead, or who has entered an appalling state of suspended animation, death-within-life. It sounds preternaturally ancient, a voice that cannot be sourced back to any living being, still less to a young man barely in his twenties.

A loaded gun won't set you free – so you say

'A loaded gun won't set you free,' Curtis sang on 'New Dawn Fades' from *Unknown Pleasures*, but he didn't sound convinced. 'After pondering over the words to 'New Dawn Fades',' Deborah Curtis wrote, 'I broached the subject with Ian, trying to make him confirm that they were only lyrics and bore no resemblance to his true feelings. It was a one-sided conversation. He refused to confirm or deny any of the points raised and he walked out of the house. I was left questioning myself instead, but did not feel close enough to anyone else to voice my fears. Would he really have married me knowing that he still intended to kill himself in his early twenties? Why father a child when you have no intention of being there to see it grow up? Had I been so oblivious to his unhappiness that he had been forced to write about it?' (*Touching from a Distance: Ian Curtis and Joy Division*, Faber&Faber, 1995, p85) The male lust for death had always been a subtext in rock, but before Joy Division it had been smuggled into rock under libidinous pretexts, a black dog in wolf's clothing – Thanatos cloaked as Eros – or else it had worn pantomime panstick. Suicide was a guarantee of authenticity, the most convincing of signs that you were 4 Real. Suicide has the power to transfigure life, with all its quotidian mess, its conflicts, its ambivalences, its disappointments, its unfinished business, its 'waste and fever and heat' – into a cold myth, as solid, seamless and permanent as the 'marble and stone' that Peter Saville would simulate on the record sleeves and Curtis would caress in the lyrics to 'In a Lonely Place'. ('In a Lonely Place' was Curtis' song, but it was recorded by a New Order in a zombie state of post-traumatic disorder after Curtis' death. It sounds like Curtis is an interloper at his own funeral, mourning his own death: 'how I wish you were here with me now'.)

The great debates over Joy Division – were they fallen angels or ordinary blokes? Were they Fascists? Was Curtis' suicide inevitable or preventable? – all turn on the relationship between Art and Life. We should resist the temptation to be Lorelei-lured by either the Aesthete-Romantics (in other words, us, as we were) or the lumpen empiricists. The Aesthetes want the world promised by the sleeves and the sound, a pristine black and white realm unsullied by the grubby compromises and embarrassments of the everyday. The empiricists insist on just the opposite: on rooting the songs back in the quotidian at its least elevated and, most importantly, at its least serious. 'Ian was a laugh, the band were young lads who liked to get pissed, it was all a bit of fun that got out of hand. . .' It's important to hold onto both of these Joy Divisions – the Joy Division of Pure Art, and the Joy Division who were 'just a laff' – at once. For if the truth of Joy Division is that they were Lads, then Joy Division must also be the truth of Laddism. And so it would appear: beneath all the red-nosed downer-fuelled jollity of the past two decades, mental illness has increased some 70% amongst adolescents. Suicide remains one of the most common sources of death for young males.

'I crept into my parents' house without waking anyone and was asleep within seconds of my head touching the pillow. The next sound I heard was "This is the end, beautiful friend. This is the end, my only friend, the end. I'll never look into your eyes again. . ." Surprised at hearing the Doors' 'The End', I struggled to rouse myself. Even as I slept I knew it was an unlikely song for Radio One on a Sunday morning. But there was no radio – it was all a dream.' (*Touching From a Distance*, p132)

Smiley's Game: *Tinker, Tailor, Soldier, Spy*

Film Quarterly, Vol. 65, No. 2, (2011)

What is the allure of George Smiley? Why does Smiley beguile even left-wing viewers who, on the face of it, might be expected to see him as at one point in John le Carré's 1974 novel he describes himself: 'the very archetype of a flabby Western liberal'? The enigma of Smiley's appeal is one of many spectres that haunts Tomas Alfredson's movie adaptation of *Tinker Tailor Soldier Spy*. The ghost that most insistently refuses to be exorcised is the 1979 BBC TV version, rightly remembered as one of the greatest ever British television series. Re-adapting a novel after so accomplished a version is risky, especially when you have a mere two hours to play with, as opposed to the series' more unhurried five.

Pace – and pacing, as in moving around restively while waiting – were central to the coiling tension of the TV series, which caught the crab-like convolutions and slowly interlocking rhythms of le Carré's narrative exceptionally well. The limitations of television production actually benefited the sense of expansiveness. Sets and action were minimal; the drama was often about faces, and about Alec Guinness's face in particular, which could suggest a lifetime of regret with the slightest wince. Guinness's performance was a masterclass in concision and nuance – not words one would always associate with Gary Oldman, cast (emphatically against type) as Smiley in the new *Tinker Tailor*.

When a novel creates as rich a mythworld as le Carré's does, no single adaptation will ever completely exhaust it. There is always the possibility of uncovering hitherto underexplored angles and for those of us who are fans of the novel, a strong new version would have had the benefit of liberating the book (and

Smiley) from the Guinness portrayal – a prospect that might explain some of le Carré's enthusiasm for the film. Le Carré has said he felt that Guinness took Smiley from him, making him unable to write the character anymore. When it was announced that this was Alfredson's next directing project after the success of *Let the Right One In* (2008), hopes for something special were justifiably high. His brilliant reworking of vampire fiction had a sense of melancholy, violent lives lived in secret that could have carried over most effectively to the closed-world intrigues of British spying. It is thus all the more disappointing that this new *Tinker Tailor* fails to compellingly reimagine the story, and central to its failure is the film's inability to make Smiley alluring.

In the novel le Carré reckoned with the sensational exposures that had both traumatised and titillated British society in the 1960s when Soviet double agents Guy Burgess, Donald Maclean, and Kim Philby were revealed to be operating right at the heart of the intelligence establishment. The book begins when Smiley is called out of retirement to search for a deep-cover mole – it was in fact le Carré who popularised this term – in the Secret Intelligence Service (otherwise known as MI6). *Tinker Tailor* follows Smiley's circuitous pursuit and exposure of the traitor, who is ultimately revealed to be Smiley's friend and rival Bill Haydon – one of many men to have affairs with Smiley's semi-estranged wife, Ann. The narrative is suffused with what Paul Gilroy has called 'postcolonial melancholia'. Smiley, Haydon, and their contemporaries – notably Jim Prideaux, the former head of the 'scalphunters' section, shot in the bungled operation that ultimately leads to the mole being uncovered, and Connie Sachs, the head of intelligence, dismissed when she comes uncomfortably close to the truth – have watched all the expectations born of imperial privilege slowly disappearing. 'Trained to Empire, trained to rule the waves. All gone, all taken away,' Sachs laments (Pan Books, 1979, 102).

Postcolonial melancholia is fed more by hostility towards the

US than it is by fear of the Soviets – Haydon and Smiley's boss, the irascible Control, are united in their loathing of Americans. When Control is maneuvered out of his position by the ambitious (and very pro-US) Percy Alleline, this seems to consolidate the sense of irreversible decline which hangs over the novel. England's glory lies in the past; the future is American. In the novel and its sequels, it is clear that Smiley's victory is temporary; his world is on the brink of disappearing.

Smiley brings to mind English archetypes both ancient and modern. What is the perpetually cuckolded Smiley, returning to save his ailing kingdom, if not a Cold War King Arthur? Yet this is Arthur done in the style of T. S. Eliot's Prufrock, whose famous self-characterization as 'an attendant lord' applies all too acutely to le Carré's character as well: 'Deferential, glad to be of use, / Politic, cautious, and meticulous; / Full of high sentence, but a bit obtuse; / At times, indeed, almost ridiculous – / Almost, at times, the Fool' ('The Love Song of J. Alfred Prufrock,' *The Complete Poems and Plays of T. S. Eliot*, Faber and Faber, 1969, 16).

While in some respects a pathologically self–blinding figure, Smiley shares some of Prufrock's self–consciousness; when, in a scene that is powerfully played out in both the BBC and the film version, Smiley recalls his one face-to-face encounter with his counterpart, the Soviet spy chief Karla, he calls himself a 'fool.' Crucially, however, he adds that he would rather be his kind of fool than Karla's.

When Smiley recounts the meeting with Karla to his younger protégé Peter Guillam, he reproaches himself for having talked too much on that memorable occasion in an Indian jail cell. Karla wins the encounter by never speaking, by transforming himself into the blank screen that Smiley cannot on this occasion become – which makes it all the easier for Smiley to fall into the trap of projecting his own anxieties and preoccupations onto the impassive Karla. In the novel, Smiley affects to disdain the psychoanalytic language of 'projection' but, tellingly, he cannot resist using these terms to describe himself; appropriately, for in the normal run of things Smiley's art consists in cultivating a particular kind of silence – not the mere absence of chatter, but the authoritative, probing silence of the psychoanalyst. The face can't give anything away, yet at the same time it has to invite confidence. Those who don't want to talk must be drawn into confiding. And isn't that a large part of Smiley's appeal to those of us from a more adolescent, more compulsively loquacious time: his grownup capacity to engender respect, and to quietly solicit our need for his approval? Speaking after a London critics' screening of *Tinker Tailor* in September, Oldman said that, by contrast with the Guinness version, no-one would want to hug his Smiley. Yet the suggestion that we would want to hug Guinness's Smiley is absurd. Surely what we find ourselves craving from Smiley is a word, a gesture, the merest hint of approbation. But it is a mistake to see the avuncular seductions of Guinness's performance as if they were in opposition to the ruthlessness which Oldman emphasises in his rendition of Smiley, for Smiley's merciless, unblinking hunting down of his prey depends upon this very capacity to draw people out.

Oldman's reading of Smiley's blankness is far less sophisticated than Guinness's. Le Carré's Smiley is famously corpulent; Oldman's is angular, stiff, dyspeptic. We can't imagine ever wanting to confide in him. Oldman's Smiley is simply an inexpressive mask: forbidding, impassive, unyielding. It is as if Oldman is giving us his shallow reading of his grandparents' generation: aloof, distanced, bottled-up. They kept it all inside; they didn't know how to have a good time. For Oldman, Smiley's restraint plays as repression and a certain malicious self-satisfaction – his silence is a simple lack of demonstrativeness, or a merely inverted demonstrativeness.

Speaking on BBC Radio 4's *Today*, le Carré himself identified Oldman's performance of repression as one of the highlights of this new version. 'You couldn't really imagine Alec [Guinness] having a sex life,' he said. 'You couldn't imagine a kiss on the screen with Alec, not one that you believed in. Whereas Oldman has quite obviously a male sexuality that he represses, like all his other feelings, in this story. Oldman is a Smiley waiting patiently to explode. I think the air of frustration, of solitude that he is able to convey is something that really does take me back to a novel I wrote 37 years ago.' Sadly, this remark suggests less a new way of seeing Smiley than a certain coarsening of understanding brought about, no doubt, by the dissemination of a therapeutic wisdom which insists that the truth of a character is to be found in their (narrowly defined) sexuality.

To say that Smiley is waiting patiently to explode is a very curious take on a character defined rather by a *lack* of heat. When Oldman shouts at Haydon 'what are you then, Bill?' at the climax of the film, this is an abandonment of emotional decorum quite out of keeping with Smiley's character, for whom the English ruling-class habit of transposing aggression into the chill of superficially polite discourse comes as second nature. Anger is one of the emotions that the Smiley of the novel feels at the moment of Haydon's exposure, yet it is not the dominant one: Smiley

saw with painful clarity an ambitious man born to the big canvas, brought up to rule, divide and conquer, whose vision and vanities all were fixed, like Percy's, upon the world's game; for whom the reality was a poor island with scarcely a voice that would carry across the water. Thus Smiley felt not only disgust; but, despite all that the moment meant to him, a surge of resentment against the institutions he was supposed to be protecting' (297).

Thus, the tone of triumphalism with which the film ends – Smiley gloriously restored to his place of honour in MI6 – strikes another false note.

The Smiley in Alfredson's film is a figure who is far less *queer* than the Smiley of the novel or the television series. Homosexual desire is widespread in *Tinker Tailor* – most notably in Prideaux's betrayed love for the flamboyantly polysexual Haydon – but there is no suggestion that Smiley shared these passions. The Smiley of novel and series is queer in the more radical sense that a 'normal' sexuality cannot be assigned to him. Smiley's is not a fluid, indeterminate sexuality like, say, that of Patricia Highsmith's Tom Ripley. His perversity is renunciation itself. At the preview, Oldman referred approvingly to le Carré's comments on Guinness's lack of sexuality; but he also characterised Smiley as masochistic (repeatedly subjecting himself to adulterous humiliations) and sadistic (the way he pursues his prey goes far beyond professional duty). Yet the idea that Smiley is sadomasochistic quite clearly contradicts the idea that he is repressed. For sadomasochism entails enjoyment, not repression. Far from being repressed, it's clear that Smiley is *driven* – driven by something which will not allow him to ever recline into happy retirement any more than he could settle into the pleasures of conjugal life, were they available to him.

From his earliest appearances in le Carré's fiction – in the novels *Call for the Dead* and *A Murder of Quality* – Smiley is on the edge of things. In most of the novels which feature Smiley, he rarely appears as *officially* a member of MI6. He is called out of retirement, or pretending to be retired; and when, after *Tinker Tailor*, he is not only restored to the organization but made chief, it is in a temporary caretaker capacity. One of the paradoxes of Smiley's character is that he seems to stand for the solidity – and stolidity – ascribed to a certain model of Englishness, yet he is himself an outsider, an interloper, a voyeur. This is the spy's vocation, and le Carré repeatedly insists on it, nowhere more passionately than in the bitter outburst of the agent Alec Leamas at the end of *The Spy who Came in from the Cold*, so memorably performed by Richard Burton in the 1965 film adaptation.

'What do you think spies are, moral philosophers measuring everything they do against the word of God or Karl Marx? They're not, they're just a bunch of seedy, squalid bastards like me,' Burton's Leamas tells his lover, Liz, after it has been revealed that they were pawns in a complex plot hatched by Control and Smiley. It is the beyond-good-and-evil agent, the one who acts without performing complex moral calculations, the one who cannot belong to the 'normal' world, who allows ordinary folk to sleep easily. Yet duty is only the pretext; there is also the matter of the deep libidinal lure of this no-man's-land for outsiders like Leamas and Smiley. Like writers, they listen and observe; like actors, they play parts.

But, for spies, there are no limits to these roles; one cannot simply step out of them and return to the warm, because everything – including inner life itself, all its wounds and private shames – starts to feel like cover, a series of props. There is a revelatory passage towards the end of the second Smiley novel, A Murder of Quality, first published in 1962. At the end of the novel – a strange whodunit thriller – Smiley confronts the murderer, but, as in the later confrontation with Karla, he ends up talking about himself:

> And there are some of us – aren't there? – who are nothing, who are so labile that we astound ourselves; we're the chameleons. I read a story once about a poet who bathed himself in cold fountains so that he could recognise his own existence in the contrast of it . . . The people like that, they can't feel anything inside them: no pleasure or pain, no love or hate . . . They have to feel that cold water. Without it, they're nothing. The world sees them as showmen, fantasists, liars, as sensualists perhaps, not for what they are: the living dead (Coronet, 1994, 174).

There is a clear implication in this slide from first person ('some

of us') to third person ('people like that'): the Cold Warrior
Smiley is himself one of the 'living dead.' In psychoanalytic
terms, Smiley is less a 'sadomasochist' than an obsessional
neurotic. (Lacan in fact argues that the question posed by the
obsessional is 'am I alive or am I dead?') At the end of *Smiley's
People*, when Smiley has defeated Karla and has the possibility of
winning Ann back, Smiley is very far from being elated. There is
little sense of this in Oldman's Smiley: his 'sadomasochism' is too
crude to approximate the baroque mechanisms of self-decep-
tions and self-torturings which govern Smiley's psyche. Yet
another false note is struck in Alfredson's film when Smiley sees
Ann being embraced by Haydon at the MI6 Christmas party; he
throws himself against the wall in a spasm of agony. In other
respects, the party scene adds something which wasn't there in
the BBC version, a sense of the camaraderie within the
department, but it is hard to imagine Smiley engaging in so
public and so spontaneous display of emotion. More troublingly,
to suggest that Smiley would straightforwardly feel pain when
confronted with Ann's infidelities is to betray the very idea that
he is masochistic. When confronted about Ann in the novel and
TV adaptation, Smiley's preferred pose is one of weary resignation; but this conceals the secret satisfaction that he experiences in Ann playing her assigned role as impossible object. But
where the masochist would organise his enjoyment around this
impossible object, for Smiley, the function of Ann's unattain-
ability is to keep her at a safe distance. His enjoyment is not
organised around Ann – or sexuality – at all, and when she is
safely unattainable she cannot trouble him.

Unlike in the TV series, we never see the faces of either Ann
or Karla, Smiley's other Other, in the film. This rightly suggests
that both figures are at least partially absent for Smiley, filled in
with his fantasies. But what's missing is an account of the *way*
that Smiley fills in these fantasy screens, and any sense of
discrepancy between the fantasy figures that Smiley projects and

their real-life counterparts. In the film, Smiley cannot remember what Karla looked like; in the novel he gives a detailed description of his adversary. Defined externally by his struggle against Karla, Smiley's internal struggle consists of his necessarily thwarted attempts to refuse any identification with his Soviet counterpart. Smiley's attempts to distance himself from the 'fanatic' Karla, his attempts to position himself outside politics itself, are the exemplary gestures of a very English ideology, which appeals to a pre- or post-political notion of 'common humanity.' Yet, ironically, what Smiley and Karla have in common is their inhumanity, their exile from any sort of 'normal' world of human passions. When they meet in Delhi, Smiley is baffled, frustrated but also fascinated by Karla's refusal of the appeal, unable to fathom a commitment to an abstract ideology, especially when – in Smiley's view – it has self-evidently failed. 'The irony in le Carré's fiction,' writes Tony Barley, 'is that a sound basis for commitment is always either sought or mourned for its absence, and yet when genuine commitment appears (invariably in communism) it is treated as incomprehensible. Communism becomes fanaticism, not a strength but a weakness' (*Taking Sides: The Fiction of John le Carré* (Open University Press, 1986, 95). Barley rightly argues that Smiley cannot be read as a cipher for liberal ideology because the incoherencies and impasses of his own position are never resolved. Behind the manifest content of Smiley's entreaties to Karla – come and join us, give up your dead generalities, enjoy the particularities of the lived world – the latent message is that all Britain has to offer is disillusionment, the impossibility of belief. (Smiley tells Guillam that 'fanaticism' will be the undoing of Karla: in fact, when Karla is defeated in *Smiley's People*, it is because of his failure to be *sufficiently* 'fanatical'.) Very little of this comes out in Alfredson's depoliticised film, in which Smiley is simply a wronged hero who ultimately attains justice, Haydon is simply a traitor, and communism is simply an exotic period reference. The nickname for MI6, 'The Circus,' in fact openly acknowledges the aberrant enjoyment available to those who have crossed into this fictional Cold World. The multivalent origin of the nickname – in addition to hinting at the way the spies play their deadly game in a spirit of mordant, laconic cynicism, it is also a near homonym of 'service,' and a play on the location in the novel of MI6's offices: Cambridge Circus, central London – tells you a great deal about the world in which Smiley operates. Much of the power of the television version derived from the way it threw us directly into this world. Guinness's Smiley incarnated a model of BBC paternalism: he guided us through his world, but he had high expectations of us. Very little was explained – we had to pick up le Carré's invented nomen-clature (scalphunters, lamplighters) on the fly. The work slang invoked the exoticism of a rarefied form of labour, while also suggesting the routinisation of espionage for those involved in it on a daily basis. It all contributed to the feeling that the Circus was a lived-in world. One of the major problems with Alfredson's *Tinker Tailor*, by contrast, is that its world doesn't feel lived-in at all. Gratifyingly, the film does not talk down to audiences; just as in the TV series, we are required to orientate ourselves in the Circus's intrigues. But the combination of Oldman's inexpressiveness and the compression brought about by having to tell so complicated a story in such a short time results in something that is strangely uninvolving. The film is almost entirely lacking in tension or paranoia; in the TV series, the scene where Guillam steals a file from the Circus is almost unbearably tense. In the film, the same scene plays out in a curiously distanced way. Then there is the question of period, and the film's striving to create a sense of London in the 1970s. I was too often reminded of *Life on Mars*, which evoked the decade with a series of clumsily placed period signifiers. As with *Life on Mars*, much of Alfedson's film looks like a 1970s theme park. Rather than discreetly constituting a period background, branded goods (Trebor mints, Ajax household cleaner) are distractingly pushed to the foreground of our attention, details that we are invited to approvingly note. But where the details matter, this new version is lacking. Eras produce certain voices, certain faces. What's missing in Alfredson's version is something like the *grain* of the 1970s. Too often, the actors seem like 21st-century moisturised metrosexuals in 1970s drag – and bad drag at that. Presented with photographs of people from the 1970s, the clichéd but accurate observation is that people looked so much older then. But the preposterously fresh-faced likes of Benedict Cumberbatch (who plays Guillam) and Tom Hardy (in the role of rogue agent Ricki Tarr) aren't nearly weathered enough to convince as 1970s secret agents. The skin, the hair are too good. The faces are without the sallow, harrowed, harried look that Michael Jayston and Hywel Bennett brought to the roles in the 1970s production; their voices unable to convey any sense of the bitter and brutalising effects of the spy's life. John Hurt's Control, at least, has the right weatherbeaten complexion and cynical-playful cadences. Accents are a severe problem in the film. Oldman plays Smiley as generically posh, but at the same time he sounds like no one you've ever heard; at points there's an oddly Scottish lilt to his accent. The accent of Toby Jones's Percy Alleline, meanwhile – played as Scottish in keeping with the novel – keeps drifting southward. Kathy Burke is hopelessly miscast as Connie Sachs: she sounds like a schoolgirl taking on the part of a posh woman in the school play. The problem here isn't just one of authenticity; it's that the wayward accents once again undermine the sense of a lived-in world. There is too much conspicuous *effort* going into this 1970s simulation. Throughout, you can practically hear Gary Oldman straining to hold back the Estuary English. In the BBC version, the Circus was an unprepossessing space – functional, dreary corridors leading into cramped offices. In Alfredson's version, Control's office looks more like something from a nightclub than what you would expect to see in

MI6. One wants to escape the 1970s version, but Alfredson doesn't give us nearly enough to do that. There is much that is different, but nothing that is strong enough to displace the television version in the memory. The casting of Colin Firth as Haydon, however, at least allows us to see the character in a different way. The face of Ian Richardson – who would go onto play the Tory grandee and Machiavel in the BBC television series *House of Cards* – provided a grey-eminence image of British power in the 1970s and 80s. I don't know who it was who said that Colin Firth looks like the midway point between the current British prime minister David Cameron and his deputy Nick Clegg, but the observation is very astute. The face of the British Establishment no longer has the hawk-like puckishness of Richardson; it has the rumpled, casual youthfulness of Firth. One of the major problems with Alfredson's film is that it assumes the ruling values of the neoliberal world governed by youth and consumerism (isn't this what 'American' codes for in the Smiley novels?). Richard Sennett has argued that the chronic short-termism of neoliberal culture has resulted in a 'corrosion of character' (*The Corrosion of Character: The Personal Consequences of Work in the New Capitalism*, W. W. Norton, 1999): a destruction of permanence, loyalty, and the capacity to plan. Isn't Smiley's allure tied up with the possibilities of character itself? In the 1970s, Smiley showed up all the inadequacies, squalid compromises, and subterranean brutalities of social democracy. Then, Smiley's doubts and his failings prompted us to imagine a better world even as we struggled to resist Smiley's blankly and perversely comforting avuncularity; now, when that better world seems if anything further away, it takes all our effort to resist the lure of nostalgia for the social-democratic world of which Smiley was both the conscience and the dirty secret.

The Past is an Alien Planet: The First and Last Episodes of *Life on Mars*

k-punk post January 10, 2006

Life On Mars is symptomatic enough to be interesting. Symptomatic of what? Well, of a culture that has lost confidence not just that the future will be good, but that any sort of future is possible. And also: *Life On Mars* suggests that one of the chief resources of recent British culture – the past – is reaching the point of exhaustion.

The scenario is that Sam Tyler (John Simm), a detective from 2006, is hit by a car and finds himself back in 1973. The game that you can't help playing as you watch is: how convincing is the simulation of 1973? You're constantly on the look out for period anachronisms. The answer is that it isn't very convincing. But not because of anachronisms. The problem is that this is a 73 that doesn't feel lived in. The actual post-psychedelic, quasi-Eastern Bloc seediness of the 70s is unretrievable; kitsch wallpaper and bell bottoms are transformed instantly into Style quotations the moment the camera falls upon them.

(There must be some technical reason – maybe it's the film stock they use – that accounts for why British TV is no longer capable of rendering any sense of a lived-in world. No matter what is filmed, everything always looks as if it has been thickly, slickly painted in gloss, like it's all a corporate video. That remains my problem with the new *Dr Who* as it happens: the contemporary British scenes look like a theme park, a very stagey stage-set, too well lit.)

'Look Out There's a Thief About' public information films on black and white TV, Open University lecturers with preposterous moustaches and voluminous collars, the test card. . . Everything is so iconic, and the thing with icons, after all, is that they evoke nothing. The icon is the very opposite of the Madeleine, Chris Marker's name – rhyming Hitchcock and Proust – for those totemic triggers that suddenly abduct you into the past. The point being that the Madeleine can only manage this time-snatching function because it has avoided museumification and memorialisation, stayed out of the photographs, been forgotten in a corner. Hearing T-Rex now doesn't remind you of 73, it reminds you of nostalgia programmes about 1973.

And isn't part of our problem that every cultural object from 1963 on has been so thoroughly, forensically, mulled over that nothing can any longer transport us back? (A problem of digital memory: Baudrillard observes somewhere that computers don't really remember because they lack the ability to forget.)

k-punk post, April 13, 2007

In the end, the science fiction elements of *Life On Mars* consisted solely in an ontological hesitation: is this real or not? As such, *Life On Mars* fell squarely into Todorov's definition of the Fantastic as that which hesitates between the Uncanny (that which can ultimately be explained naturalistically) and the Marvellous (that which can only be accounted for in supernatural terms). The predicament that *Life On Mars* explored was: is Sam Tyler in a coma, and the whole 1970s world in which he is lost some kind of unconscious confabulation? Or has he, by some means not yet understood, been transported back into the real 1973? The show maintained the equivocation until the end (the final episode was ambivalent to the point of being cryptic).

Simm has wryly observed that the show's central conceit lets the production off the hook. If Tyler was in a coma, then any of *Life On Mars's* historical inaccuracies could be explained away as gaps in the character's recollections of the period. No doubt the enjoyment of *Life On Mars* derived from its imperfect recollection, not of 1973 itself, but of the television of the 1970s. The programme was mitigated nostalgia, I Love 1973 as a cop show. I say cop show, because it is clear that the SF elements of *Life On Mars* were little more than pretexts; the show was a meta-cop show rather than meta-SF. The time travel conceit permitted the showing of representations which would otherwise be unacceptable, and beneath the framing ontological question (is this real or not?), there was a question about desire and politics: do we want this to be real?

As the avatar of the present, Sam Tyler became the bad conscience of the 70s cop show, whose discontent with the past permitted us to enjoy it again. Simm, as the modern, enlightened 'good cop', was less the anti-type of antediluvian 'bad cop' Gene Hunt than the postmodern disavowal which made possible our enjoyment of Hunt's invective and violence. Hunt, played by Philip Glenister, became the show's real star, beloved of the tabloids who adored quoting his streams of abuse, carefully constructed by the writers so that they could come across as comic rather than inflammatory. Hunt's 'no-nonsense policing' was presented with enough 'grit' to make us wince, but never so much violence that it would invoke disgust. (In this respect, the programme was the cultural equivalent of a blow to a suspect that would not show up under later medical examination.)

Undoubtedly, although perhaps unintentionally, the show's ultimate message was reactionary; in the end, rather than Tyler educating Hunt, it was he would come to an accommodation with Hunt's methods. When, in the final episode, Tyler is faced with a choice between betraying Hunt or staying loyal (at this point in the narrative, it appears that Tyler's betrayal of Hunt is the requisite price Tyler must pay in order to return to 2007), this also became a choice between 1973 and the present day that amounted to a decision, not about collar lengths or other cultural preferences, but about policing styles. Audience sympathy is managed such that, however much we disapprove of Hunt, we are never supposed to lose faith in him, so that Tyler's betrayal seemed far worse than any of Hunt's many misdemeanours. Tyler's (apparent) return to 2007 underscores this by presenting the modern environment as sterile, drearily worthy, ultimately far less real than the rough justice of Hunt's era. Modern wisdom ('how can you maintain the law by breaking the law?') is set against Hunt's renegade-heroic identification of himself with the law ('I am the law, so how can I break it?') The deep libidinal appeal of Hunt derives from his impossible duality as upholder of the Law and he who enjoys unlimited jouissance. The two faces of the Father, the stern lawgiver and Pere Jouissance, resolved: the perfect figure of reactionary longing, a charismatic embodiment of everything allegedly forbidden to us by 'political correctness'.

'Can The World Be as Sad as It Seems?': David Peace and his Adapters

David Peace's four Red Riding novels were acts of exorcism and excavation of the near-past, a bloody riposte to I Love The 1970s clipshow nostalgia. They stalk the West Yorkshire that Peace grew up in, transforming real events – the framing and intimidation of Stefan Kisco; the incompetent police operation to catch the Yorkshire Ripper – into background for brutal and unrelenting fictions that possess an apocalyptic lyricism.

Peace has always been dogged by comparisons with James Ellroy. There's no doubt that encountering Ellroy liberated something in Peace, but in the end Peace is the better writer. Peace has called the experience of reading Ellroy's *White Jazz* his 'Sex Pistols moment'. But Peace builds upon what Ellroy achieved much in the way that the postpunk groups leapt into the space that the Pistols had blown open. Peace extrapolates a pulp modernist poetics from Ellroy's experiments in telegraphic compression, and while Ellroy's pugilistic prose has a pump-action amphetamine drive, Peace's writing is hypnotic and oneiric; its incantatory repetitions delaying and veiling plot revelations rather than rushing headlong towards resolution. Despite presenting seemingly similar worlds – in which the police are routinely corrupt, journalists are venal and co-optable, and the wealthy are vampiric exploiters – their political orientations are very different. Ellroy is a Hobbesian conservative, who evinces a macho pragmatism that accepts violence, exploitation and betrayal as inevitable. The same phenomena are oppressively omnipresent in Peace's world, but there is no sense of acceptance: instead, his novels read like howls of agony and calls for retribution, divine or otherwise.

Peace, who has said that he aimed to produce a Crime fiction which is no longer entertainment, has written Crime works that are hauntological in a triple sense. The Crime genre is of course well suited to explore the (moral, existential, theological) problems posed by what Quentin Meillassoux called 'odious deaths': the deaths 'of those who have met their end prematurely, whose death is not the proper conclusion of a life but its violent curtailment'; and as they moved away from the uneasy combination of fanciful genre trappings, period signifiers, Angry Young Man homage and brutality that characterised *1974*, the novels of the Red Riding Quartet were simultaneously drawn towards actuality and theology, as if the proximity of the one entailed the other. Readers are put into the position of spectral mourners by the voices of those who have died odiously, the Ripper's victims, heard in the visionary 'Transmissions' which preface each of the chapters in *1980*, sections which combine the actual (gleaned from reportage and biography) with the spectral.

The novels are hauntological in another sense, a sense that is closer to the way in which we have used it in relation to music, but not quite the same. Peace is not at all interested in the problems of degraded memory which preoccupy The Caretaker, Burial or Basinski. His is a past without crackle, rendered in the first person and in a tense that is very nearly present. The occlusions in the narrative are due, not to faulty recording devices or memory disorders (cultural or personal) but to the self-blindings of his characters, who see themselves (and the events of which they are a part) only through a glass darkly. In the end, everything – narrative, intelligibility – succumbs to total murk; as the characters begin to disassociate, it becomes difficult to know what is happening, or what has happened; at a certain point, it is unclear as to whether we have crossed over into the land of the dead.

Hunter, the senior Manchester detective assigned to investigate the West Yorkshire police force in *1980*, finds himself caught in a world in which *things don't add up; they don't fit together*. It's a Gnostic terrain. The Gnostics thought that the world was made of a corrupt matter characterised by heavy weight and impenetrable opacity: a murky, muddy mire in which fallen angels – one of the persistent images in the Red Riding books – are trapped. There is no question of Hunter, or solicitor John Piggott in *1983* – or even Peace – being able to completely illuminate what has happened. This is a world in which, as Tony Grisoni, the screenwriter who adapted the novels for Channel 4, puts it, 'narratives disappear into the dark'.

The libidinal orientation towards the past is also markedly different in the case of Peace and sonic hauntology: whereas hauntological music has emphasised the unexplored potentials prematurely curtailed in the periods it invokes, Peace's novels are driven by the unexpiated suffering of Yorkshire at the end of the 70s. And Peace's writing is also hauntological in its intuition that particular places are stained by particular occurrences (and vice versa). As he has insisted in many interviews, it is no accident that Sutcliffe was the *Yorkshire* Ripper. Peace's books are avowedly anti-nostalgic, the anti-*Life On Mars*, with its ambivalence towards police brutality (and its media representation). There is no such vindication in Peace's novels, no suppressed yearning for a time in which coppers could beat suspects with impunity. After all, it is corruption, rather than criminality per se, that is the focus of the Red Riding Quartet.

Music in Peace's books functions as a hauntological trigger. He's remarked that he uses music, including music he doesn't like, to take him back to the feel, the grain, of a period. Musical references are embedded in the text either diegetically, as background sound, or more esoterically, as cryptic-epigraphic ciphers and repeated incantations: a portal effect that gratifyingly echoes (in reverse) the way in which music of the 1970s, especially postpunk, would direct listeners to fiction. *1980* is haunted in particular by Throbbing Gristle, especially the phrase that they took from another killer, Charles Manson: 'can the world be as sad as it seems?' In Peace's hands, this question becomes an urgent theological enquiry, the very relentlessness of the sadness and misery he recounts calling forth an absent God, a God who is experienced as absence, the great light eclipsed by the world's unending tears. The world, the sad, desolated world, is full of angels whose wings have either been shorn off, reduced to stubble, or which have grown into gigantic, dirty monstrosities . . . addict angels hooked on alcohol, casual but incessant lusts, and the trash of the consumer society that is struggling to be born out of the wreckage of the social democratic consensus . . . angels whose ultimate response to the world is puking (everyone pukes in Peace's books), throwing up the whiskies and the undercooked crispy pancakes, but never being able to purge any of it, never being able to take flight.

The religious elements in the books become increasingly foregrounded as the Quartet develops, until the deeply ambiguous, hallucinatory ending of *1983* becomes a quasi-Gnostic treatise on evil and suffering. The final section of the novel, 'Total Eclipse Of The Heart' (that transfiguration of pop cultural reference into epigraph being one of Peace's signature techniques), explicitly posits the idea that, far from undermining the existence of God, evil and suffering entail that God must exist. Eclipse implies something that is eclipsed, a hidden source of light that produces all this shadow. In the philosophy of religion, the problem of evil maintains that suffering, particularly suffering visited upon the innocent, means that the theistic God could not exist, since a benevolent, omnipotent and omniscient being would not countenance undeserved suffering. With his inventory of wretched child abuse cases, Dostoyevsky's Ivan Karamazov makes the most famous, and most passionate, statement of this position. Yet if there is no God, the suffering remains, only now there is no possibility of its expiation; if there can be no justice to come, the universe is permanently blighted, irrevocably scarred by atrocity, abuse and torture.

The Red Riding novels inspired Channel 4 into making the kind of television dramas that some of us had long since ceased hoping could ever be made in Britain again. The three films, broadcast in 2009, were the most striking British dramas of the first decade of the 21st century, towering above all the facile costume epics, routine police procedurals and emotional pornography which clogged the schedules. Moreover, in their use of setting and landscape, in the epiphanic power of their images, the Red Riding films attained a visual poetry and an expressionist naturalism that exceeded practically anything British cinema has achieved in the past 30 years.

As Nick James observed in his preview of the Red Riding films for Sight & Sound, nothing in the previous career of the Red Riding's three directors – Julian Jarrold for *1974*, James Marsh for *1980*, and Anand Tucker for *1983* – gave any hints that they could produce work of this quality. In many ways, it is as if the auteur of these films was Peace himself, and the three directors succeed so consummately because they allowed themselves to be channels of his infernal vision. It was inevitable that some compression occurred in the transition from page to screen; indeed, one whole novel from Peace's Red Riding sequence – *1977* – was never filmed, but Tony Grisoni deserves immense credit for the way that he weaved the three films into a symphonic coherence that nevertheless refused easy closure and intelligibility.

Peace's equivalent of Ellroy's anti-hero Dudley Smith, the corrupt detective who justifies his own running of drugs and vice operations as 'containment', is Maurice Jobson, the whey-faced policeman who features in all three of the films. Where Smith (as masterfully played by James Cromwell in the best Ellroy adaptation to date, *LA Confidential* [1997]) is charming, charismatic and flamboyantly loquacious, Jobson (as played by David Morrissey in the C4 adaptations) is taciturn, abstracted, immobile, blank, in a semi-fugue state of disassociation from the atrocities he participates in. Morrissey's is one of many excellent performances in the trilogy: all of them masterpieces of measure and controlled power, proper television/ film acting, far from the braying thespery that the British theatrical tradition often turns out. Rebecca Hall is damaged and dangerous as Paula Garland, Maxine Peake, angular yet vulnerable as Helen Marshall. Sean Harris manages to make Robert Craven plausibly loathsome without tripping over into grand guignol grotesquerie; while Paddy Considine brings a flinty resolution to the role of Peter Hunter, one of the few lightbringers in the Red Riding's North, an inverted world in which evil enjoys carnivalesque licence and the police and the powerful are free to 'do what they want'.

The film adaptation of Peace's extraordinary novel *The Damned Utd* lived down to expectations to just about the same extent that the Channel 4 films exceeded them. The team tasked with adapting the novel looked unpromising. Before *The Damned Utd*, Director Tom Hooper (drafted in after Stephen Frears left the project) had a background in fairly unremarkable television (he would later go on to make *The King's Speech*), while the shtick of screenwriter Peter Morgan and lead actor Michael Sheen – as established in *The Queen* and *Frost/ Nixon* – didn't have any obvious fit with Peace's fractured and abrasive modernism. In the end, Hooper and Morgan didn't adapt Peace; they eliminated him. Hooper's film returns us to the found object-narrative – Brian Clough's bitter 44-day stint as manager of Leeds United in 1974 – that Peace used as the raw material for his 'fiction based on a fact'. What's missing is everything that Peace brought to the facts: the bite of a Real that will always elude (bourgeois) realism; and the shaping power of a Gnostic mythography, in which the most malign entity is the cursed land of Yorkshire itself.

It can be tiresome to criticise a film adaptation simply for the ways it differs from its source novel. In this case, however, a close comparison of the two versions of *The Damned Utd* is instructive, for two reasons. First, because, in erasing Peace's signature, the film in effect *competes* with his rendition of the Clough/ Leeds story; and second, because Peace's pulp modernism precisely offers British culture an escape from the kind of good humoured, well balanced, middle of the road, middlebrow realism that Hooper and Morgan trade in.

At the press screening, Morgan said that when he read *The Damned Utd*, it brought a nostalgia rush 'like eating Farley's rusks'. Yet surely even the most guileless of the readers of Peace's novel could see that it tastes not of the warm mush of baby food but of bile, scotch and refluxed stomach acid. In Hooper and Morgan's hands, Clough's story is reduced to all of the givens, all the off-the-shelf narrative and thematic pegs: he was a 'misunderstood genius', struggling against an establishment represented by puffed-up provincial patriarchs like the Derby County chairman, Sam Longson (well played by Jim Broadbent); he was self-destructive, and he needed his partner Peter Taylor (Timothy Spall) to curb his excesses; he was locked into an oedipal struggle with the man he replaced at Leeds, Don Revie. Even this is told more than it is shown, and throughout, the audience treated as if it is witless: dialogue is too often used for clumsy plot exposition or to crudely telegraph Themes. Not only do Hooper and Morgan fail to evoke Peace's existential terrain, his blighted vision of Yorkshire, they also convey little of his intense sense of territoriality. In the novel, Leeds's Elland Road ground is the site of a struggle over space in which Clough is up against both the spectre of Don Revie and the animal aggression of the players he has left behind. (A striking image from the novel – of Clough chopping up and burning Revie's desk in an attempt to exorcise the absent father's ghost – inexplicably never made it to screen.) The film also misses the purgatorial rhythm of sport which Peace caught so acutely. As every sports fan – never mind about coach – knows, the jouissance of sport is essentially masochistic. '*The Damned Utd* shows what Clough's tragedy was,' Chris Petit put in his review of the novel, 'deep down, he knew that winning was only loss deferred.' The intense fear that colours everything in Peace's novel is dissolved in a tone that is frequently *jaunty*.

Then there is Michael Sheen. The problem with Sheen's now well established approach to historical characters is that it deprives the film's world of any autonomous reality – everything is indexed to a reality external to the film, judged only by how well it matches our already existing image of the character, whether that be Clough, Kenneth Williams, Blair or Frost. (And there are bizarre bleed-throughs between the characters – at one point, it felt as if Sheen's campy Clough had morphed into Kenneth Williams.) Certainly, Peace has an advantage over the film-makers here: written fiction can move beyond received television images of figures from recent history far more quickly than film can but an actor with more courage and presence than Sheen might have reached beyond physical appearances to reach a truth of Clough not accessible via the TV footage. Instead, Sheen offers his usual tracing of mannerisms and verbal tics, competent enough as far as it goes, but devoid of any of the tortured inner life that Peace gave to his Clough. Even if the acting were uniformly superb, it would have needed far more than Hooper provides in order to summon the dread and misery of Peace's world; but the indifferent photography and the often appalling soundtrack make Hooper's *The Damned Utd* feel more like a dramatisation of actual events than a film of Peace's novel.

Now Then, Now Then: Jimmy Savile and 'the 70s On Trial'

July 2013

The turn that events took had all the look of some kind of ritual assassination. The killing not of a body – the body was already dead – but of a name. It was as if some kind of deal had been struck – you'll get to live out your life with your reputation intact (or as intact as it could be), but a year after your death, it will all be destroyed. Nothing, absolutely nothing, will survive. Your headstone will be dismantled. The penthouse in which you lived will be demolished. Your name will become synonymous with evil.

September 2012, and it all starts to come up. Like a build-up of effluent that could no longer be contained, first seeping, then surging out. Jimmy Savile, the nation's favourite grotesque, the former DJ and children's entertainer, is exposed as a serial sex abuser and paedophile. You can't say it comes as a surprise, and that's one of the most unsettling aspects of the whole affair. How out in the open it all was . . . We all read the text purporting to be the transcript of an unbroadcast scene from the BBC's satirical programme, *Have I Got News For You*, in which Savile is openly accused of being a child sex abuser, and took it at face value (it seems now that the transcript was a fake, but it was an astonishingly convincing simulation . . . The rhythm of the interaction between the panellists . . . The way the verbal sparring escalates into aggression . . . The name of the supposed victim, Sarah Cornley . . . it all had a ring of authenticity – the signature of a Real, perhaps, that could not at then be recognised except in fiction . . .)

Yes, in a certain way, it was all out in the open – *we all knew*, or felt that we knew – but it mattered that the abuse was never acknowledged in his lifetime. For while the story remained unofficial Savile would not only go unpunished, he could continue to comport himself as a celebrated entertainer, a knight of the realm, stalwart charity fundraiser. No doubt Savile took a sociopathic delight in being able to get away with it in plain sight. In his 1974 autobiography, *As It Happens*, Savile had boasted about having sex with an underage runaway. The police wouldn't dare touch him, he taunted. Neither, it seemed, would the media. Occasionally, a journalist would attempt to breach his defences. Louis Theroux did his trademark gentle probing of Savile about the paedophilia allegations in 2000 BBC documentary, but of course there was no question of the old man cracking.

By the end of 2012, the 70s was returning, no longer as some bittersweet nostalgia trip, but as a trauma. The phrase *it's like something out of David Peace* has become something of a commonplace in the past few years. Strangely for fiction that is about the past, Peace's work has actually gained in prophetic power since its publication. Peace wasn't predicting the future – how could he be, when he was writing about the 70s and the 80s? – so much as he had fixated on those parts of the past which were about to resurface. The Fritzl case had echoes of the underground lair in which children are kept prisoner in the Red Riding novels. And everything that came to light about conspiracies amongst the English power elite – all the murk and tangle of Murdoch and Hillsborough – seemed to throw us back into Peace's labyrinths of corruption and cover-up. Murdoch, Hillsborough, Savile . . . Pull on one thread and it all started to connect, and, wherever you looked, there was the same grim troika – police, politicians, media . . . Watching each other's backs (partly for fear that they will be stabbed in their own back) . . . Having the goods on each other, the best kind of insurance policy, the ruling class model of solidarity . . .

After his death, Savile increasingly started to look like

something Peace had dreamt up. We were drawn to a certain kind of fiction because consensual reality, the commonsense world that we like to think we live in, wasn't adequate to a figure like Savile. At the same time, it became clear that the elements in Peace's writing that previously seemed most melodramatically excessive were those which ended up rhyming with the new revelations. It's as if melodramatic excess is built into the Real itself, and the sheer implausibility of corruption and abuse itself forms a kind of cloak for the abuser: *surely this can't be happening?*

Savile's stomping ground was right in the heart of Peace's territory . . . in Leeds . . . where the entrepreneur-DJ started to build his empire, and where, knowing that abuse is easier to get away with when it comes disguised as care, he volunteered as a hospital porter . . . *A spoonful of sugar helps the medicine go down* . . . Incredibly, Savile was for a time a suspect in the Yorkshire Ripper investigation – members of the public had named Savile, and the body of one of the Ripper's victims, Irene Richardson, had been found very near to his flat. Then there was the infamous photograph of Savile, Peter Sutcliffe and Frank Bruno at Broadmoor in 1991 – Savile, toting his signature cigar, brokering a meeting between a serial killer and a troubled former celebrity boxer. The grinning Sutcliffe looks like he's wearing one of Savile's shell-suits. The insanity of a society and of an era – all their occult complicities between celebrity, psychosis and criminality – is screamingly exposed here. Ritual inversion: light (entertainment) transforming into the darkest horror. By the end of 2012, Savile's name was so irretrievably sullied that his old friend Peter Sutcliffe felt the need to speak up for him.

Savile was the kind of figure who came to dominate popular culture without inspiring much affection. You couldn't say he was ever loved. Someone writing in to the London Review of Books dug up the BBC's audience research reports on Savile's first appearances on Top of the Pops. '*10 December 1964.* Jimmy Savile, who introduced the programme on this occasion, was obviously disliked by a large number of the sample audience. Many indicated their aversion to this artist by remarking that anything they had to say about him would be "quite unprintable", whilst comment by those who freely expressed their feelings was liberally larded with such terms as "this nutcase"; "this obnoxious 'thing'"; and "this revolting spectacle".' You don't have to be loved, or even liked, to be a *popular figure*. Savile didn't even have the love-to-hate appeal of a national pantomime villain such as Simon Cowell. His ticket to fame was his grotesquerie itself (and this grotesquerie meant that one of the most initially unnerving things about the revelations was being forced to think of Savile as *any* kind of sexual being). As Andrew O'Hagan argued in his piece on Savile for the London Review of Books, what mattered in the new world of television light entertainment was not likeability, or talent, but a certain larger-than-life aura – call it eccentricity, or call it derangement – which Savile easily possessed as his birthright. Even those who found Savile creepy could accept that he 'belonged' on television. After all, where else could he possibly belong? The problem was that, after the 60s, if you belonged on television, there was nowhere that wasn't open to you. We now know that Savile was given keys to the Broadmoor hospital for the criminally insane, so that he could wander around the institution – just one example of the freedoms that Savile's celebrity and power would acquire for him. We hear that Savile molested paraplegic patients in their hospital beds, and I'm reminded of Dennis Potter's 1976 television play, *Brimstone and Treacle*, in which the lead character, the unctuous Martin, rapes a severely brain-damaged young woman while pretending to care for her. The BBC withdrew the play just before it was due to be broadcast – presumably at around the same time that Savile was appearing on Saturday night kids' TV while raping helpless patients in private.

As Savile's reputation descended into the mire, it pulled others' with it. The police investigation prompted by the scandal,

Operation Yewtree, went after a whole slew of former household names with (surely) more to come. Someone, I don't remember who, says *it's like the 70s have gone on trial.* Yes, but it's a very particular strand of the 70s that is under investigation – not the officially debauched rock 'n' roll 70s, not Zeppelin or Sabbath, but the family entertainment 70s.

As the stories mounted up, Savile came to seem more and more unbelievable. Taken together, even facts that were already known about Savile before his death came to look as if they couldn't possibly be true. Could it really be the case, for instance, that Savile had taken part in negotiations between the Israeli and the Egyptian governments in the 70s? That he had mediated between Prince Charles and Princess Diana as their marriage started to fail? (And how mad, how desperate, would you have to be to take *Jimmy Savile's* advice on your marriage?) That he had spent Christmas after Christmas with Margaret Thatcher? (Thatcher had tried four times to ennoble Savile, but was repeatedly rebuffed by her advisers, and only succeeded in knighting him at the fag-end of her period as Prime Minister.)

Murdoch and the Daily Mail wasted no time in pushing the idea that the abuse was an institutional pathology – it was the BBC, and, more broadly, the paternalistic media culture of the 60s and 70s, which had incubated Savile's corruption. The BBC, now in a permanent state of confusion about its role in a neoliberal world, duly went into a neurotic, narcissistic collapse. Its judgement was shot; it had failed to broadcast a report about Savile's abuse, and the crisis over Savile would push it into moving too hastily when, a few months later, a Tory peer was wrongly named in another abuse scandal. Murdoch and the Mail crowed on about how the Savile revelations demonstrated the importance of press freedom – but the question that they neatly evaded was, where were *their* brave hacks? Why didn't they expose Savile when it mattered, when he was alive?

When the question started to be asked about how he'd got

away with it, we already knew the answer. He had connections at the very top. The very top. And he took care to make friends with those in power and authority at lower levels, too. Police officers regularly attended Savile's now notorious Friday Morning Club meetings at his home in Leeds.

Savile's ascent to his unlikely position of power and influence required immense amounts of hard work. One thing you could never accuse him of was slacking. A forensically researched post on the Sump Plug blog details how infernally busy Savile was in the early days of his career:

> The Plaza [Ballroom in Manchester] was just one of many dance halls and clubs that Savile oversaw, managed, disk-jockeyed at, wielded shadowy control over or had some kind of undeclared stake in, not only in Manchester but also on the other side of the Pennines — in Bradford, in Wakefield, in Halifax, over on the coast in Scarborough and Whitby, and especially in Leeds. In his hometown the joints he presided over included the Cat's Whiskers and the Locarno Ballroom in the County Arcade, known by locals simply as 'the Mecca' (later rebranded as the Spinning Disc). That's where, in 1958, his predilection for underage girls first came to the attention of the police. The matter was swiftly resolved by peeling a few hundred quid off the big roll of twenties that he always carried, right up until he died.
>
> Meanwhile, in Manchester on any given night in the late 50s and early 60s, if you couldn't find Savile at the Plaza at lunchtime, he'd surely be at the Ritz later on. Or, if not, try the Three Coins in Fountain Street. He didn't even rest on Sundays; that was when he span the platters for upwards of two thousand jivers and twisters at his Top Ten Club at Belle Vue.
>
> The man was everywhere — at practically every major dance hall and nightclub in the North's heaving conurbations,

as much of a fixture as the rotating mirror ball.

Savile's empire quickly spread down south too, down to the Ilford Palais, and to Decca Records, who would pay him to play their latest releases. Up North, Savile's rackets were protected by a gang of bodybuilders, boxers, and wrestlers, including – improbably for those of us who came to know him as the comically fat wrestler Big Daddy, cuddly mainstay of Saturday afternoon television – Shirley Crabtree. The roots of 70s television were here, in these ballrooms and dancehalls, their seediness waiting to be transubstantiated into light entertainment.

But, a year after Savile's death, the transubstantiation would go into extreme reverse. *Now then, now then* – one of Savile's catchphrases started to assume an ominous significance. Only a few months previously, the BBC had broadcast a number of programmes celebrating his life and work. Now, condemnation is not enough: all traces of his existence must be removed. Not only is the headstone taken away, but we hear – can this possibly be true? It's impossible to tell in the fevered atmosphere – that the family of a child buried near to Savile had requested that Savile's remains be disinterred – as if he were some medieval devil, a noxious cloud of malignancy that can corrupt even the dead. More farcically, CBeebies, one of the BBC's children's channels, was censured because it broadcasted a repeat of an episode of the programme the Tweenies, in which one of the characters impersonated Savile.

Now then, now then . . .

At the time when Savile was abusing, the victims were faced, not with Jimmy Savile *the monster*, Jimmy Savile *the prolific abuser of children*, but with Jimmy Savile *OBE* – *Sir* Jimmy Savile – Jimmy Savile, *Knight Commander of the Pontifical Equestrian Order of Saint*

Gregory the Great. When we ask how Savile got away with it all, we must remember this. Naturally, fear played a part in keeping Savile's victims quiet. *Who's going to believe your word against the word of a television entertainer, someone who has raised millions for charity?* But we also need to take seriously the way that power can warp the experience of reality itself. Abuse by the powerful induces a cognitive dissonance in the vulnerable – *this can't possibly be happening.* What has happened can be pieced together only in retrospect. The powerful trade on the idea that abuse and corruption used to happen, but not any more. Abuse and cover–up can be admitted, but only on condition that they are confined to the past. That was *then*, things are different *now* . . .

02: HAUNTOLOGY

London After the Rave: Burial

k-punk post April 14, 2006

Burial is the kind of album I've dreamt of for years; literally. It is oneiric dance music, a collection of the 'dreamed songs' Ian Penman imagined in his epochal piece on Tricky's *Maxinquaye*. *Maxinquaye* would be a reference point here, as would Pole – like both these artists, Burial conjures audio-spectres out of crackle, foregrounding rather than repressing sound's accidental materialities. Tricky and Pole's 'cracklology' was a further development of dub's materialist sorcery in which 'the seam of its recording was turned inside out for us to hear and exult in' (Penman). But rather than the hydroponic heat of Tricky's Bristol or the dank caverns of Pole's Berlin, Burial's sound evokes what the press release calls a 'near future South London underwater. You can never tell if the crackle is the burning static off pirate radio, or the tropical downpour of the submerged city out of the window.'

Near future, maybe . . . But listening to Burial as I walk through damp and drizzly South London streets in this abortive Spring, it strikes me that the LP is very London Now – which is to say, it suggests a city haunted not only by the past but by lost futures. It seems to have less to do with a near future than with the tantalising ache of a future just out of reach. *Burial* is haunted by what once was, what could have been, and – most keeningly – what could still happen. The album is like the faded ten year-old tag of a kid whose Rave dreams have been crushed by a series of dead end jobs.

Burial is an elegy for the hardcore continuum, a *Memories From the Haunted Ballroom* for the Rave generation. It is like walking into the abandoned spaces once carnivalised by Raves and finding them returned to depopulated dereliction. Muted air horns flare like the ghosts of Raves past. Broken glass cracks underfoot. MDMA flashbacks bring London to unlife in the way that hallucinogens brought demons crawling out of the subways in *Jacob's Ladder*'s New York. Audio hallucinations transform the city's rhythms into inorganic beings, more dejected than malign. You see faces in the clouds and hear voices in the crackle. What you momentarily thought was muffled bass turns out only to be the rumbling of tube trains.

Burial's mourning and melancholia sets it apart from dubstep's emotional autism and austerity. My problem with dubstep has been that in constituting dub as a positive entity, with no relation to the Song or to pop, it has too often missed the spectrality wrought by dub's subtraction-in-process. The emptying out has tended to produce not space but an oppressive, claustrophobic flatness. If, by contrast, Burial's schizophonic hauntology has a 3D depth of field it is in part because of the way it grants a privileged role to voices under erasure, returning to dub's phono-decentrism. Snatches of plaintive vocal skitter through the tracks like fragments of abandoned love letters blowing through streets blighted by an unnamed catastrophe. The effect is as heartbreakingly poignant as the long tracking shot in Tarkovsky's *Stalker* (1979) that lingers over sublime objects-become trash.

Burial's London is a wounded city, populated by ecstasy casualties on day release from psychiatric units, disappointed lovers on night buses, parents who can't quite bring themselves to sell their Rave 12 inches at a carboot sale, all of them with haunted looks on their faces, but also haunting their interpassively nihilist kids with the thought that things weren't always like this. The sadness in the Dem 2 meets *Vini Reilly*-era Durutti Column 'You Hurt Me' and 'Gutted' is almost overwhelming. 'Southern Comfort' only deadens the pain. Ravers have become deadbeats, and Burial's beats are accordingly undead – like the tik-tok of an off-kilter metronome in an abandoned Silent Hill school, the klak-klak of graffiti-splashed ghost trains idling in sidings. 10 years ago, Kodwo Eshun compared the 'harsh, roaring noise' of No U-Turn's 'hoover bass' with 'the sound of a thousand car alarms going off simultaneously'. The subdued bass on Burial is the spectral echo of a roar, burned-out cars remembering the noise they once made. Burial reminds me, actually, of paintings by Nigel Cooke. The morose figures Cooke graffitis onto his own paintings are perfect visual analogues for Burial's sound. A decade ago, jungle and hip hop invoked devils, demons and angels. Burial's sound, however, summons the 'chain-smoking plants and sobbing vegetables' that sigh longingly in Cooke's painting. Speaking at the Tate, Cooke observed that much of the violence of graffiti comes from its velocity. There's something of an affinity between the way that Cooke re-creates graffiti in the 'slow' medium of oil paints and the way in which Burial submerges (dubmerges?) Rave's hyperkinesis in a stately melancholia. *Burial*'s dilapidated Afro NoFuturism does for London in the 00s what Wu Tang did for New York in the 90s. It delivers what Massive Attack promised but never really achieved. It's everything that Goldie's *Timeless* ought to have been. It's the Dub City counterpart to Luomo's *Vocalcity*. *Burial* is one of the albums of the decade. Trust me.

Downcast Angel: Interview with Burial

The Wire 286, December 2007

With his self-titled debut LP last year, Burial established himself as an extraordinary sonic mythographer, a sound poet capable of articulating the existential malaise of an era and a place using only sampled voices, broken breakbeats and musique concrète sound effects. *Burial* was a vivid audio portrait of a wounded South London, a semi-abstract sound painting of a city's disappointment and anguish. Burial's was a sound saturated in dance music, but his unsequenced beats were too eccentric to dance to. His sound was too out of step to fit into dubstep, the genre his records were most likely to be filed under because they were released on Kode9's Hyperdub label. Burial's sound might have fallen between the cracks, but it wasn't some eclectic melange of existing forms. What was most impressive about it – and no doubt one of the reasons that it was *The Wire*'s Record Of The Year for 2006 – was the consistency of its sonic concept. There was an impersonal quality to Burial's desolate elegies, a quality reinforced by his doing only a few interviews and refusing to allow a photograph of his face to be used in any promotion. Swarming rumours filled the hype-vacuum. Many didn't believe he actually existed, attributing the record's production to Basic Channel, The Bug, Kode9 himself – a massive backhanded compliment to how fully realised Burial's (syn)aesthetic was. In fact, his sound has been gestating slowly, semi-secretly, for at least half a decade. The tracks on the first album had been selected from recordings Burial had made since 2001. His first appearance on vinyl was the track 'Broken Home' on Wasteland's Vulture Culture Mix 2 in 2004. And the 12' EP *South London Boroughs*, which trailed some of the most potent tracks from the first LP, followed a year later.

Burial's refusal to 'be a face', to constitute himself as a subject of the media's promotional machine, is in part a temperamental preference, and in part a resistance to the conditions of ubiquitous visibility and hyper-clarity imposed by digital culture – 'It's like a ouija board, it's like letting someone into your head, behind your eyes. It lets randoms in,' he says of the internet.

'I'm just a well low key person,' he admits. 'I want to be unknown, because I'd rather be around my mates and family, but there's no need to focus on it. Most of the tunes I like, I never knew what the people who made them looked like, anyway. It draws you in. You could believe in it more.' Burial doesn't DJ or play live, so photographs of him can't even be surreptitiously taken and circulated. 'I just want to be in a symbol, a tune, the name of a tune,' he explains. 'It's not like it's a new thing. It's one of the old underground ways and it's easier.' Burial is more sensitive than most to the way in which people are shaped by impersonal forces. 'When you are young you are pushed around by forces that are nothing to do with you,' he says. 'You're lost; most of the time you don't understand what's going on with yourself, with anything.' He knows that his sound does not come from anything with a face.

Without being chauvinistic, Burial is fiercely loyal to the British Hardcore continuum from which his sound has emerged. 'If you're well into tunes, your life starts to weave around them,' he says. 'I'd rather hear a tune about real life, about the UK, than some US hip-hop 'I'm in the club with your girl'-type thing. I love R&B tunes and vocals but I like hearing things that are true to the UK, like drum 'n' bass and dubstep. Once you've heard that underground music in your life, other stuff just sounds like a fucking advert, imported.' Indeed, one track on his new album *Untrue* is called 'UK'; another, one of the most sorrowful, is called 'Raver'. Burial's London seems to be a city populated by dejected Ravers, returning to the sites of former revels and finding them derelict, forced to contrast the quotidian compromises of their post-Rave life with the collective ecstasy they once lived out. Burial's is a re-dreaming of the past, a condensation of relics of abandoned genres into an oneiric montage. His sound is a work of mourning rather than of melancholia, because he still longs for the lost object, still refuses to abandon the hope that it will return. 'A lot of those old tunes I put on at night and I hear something in the tune that makes me feel sad,' he says. 'A few of my favourite producers and DJs are dead now too – and I hear this hope in all those old tracks, trying to unite the UK. But they couldn't, because the UK was changing in a different direction, away from us. Maybe the feeling of the UK in clubs and stuff back then, it wasn't as artificial, self-aware or created by the Internet. It was more rumour, underground folklore. Anyone could go into the night and they had to seek it out. Because you could see it in people, you could see it in their eyes. Those Ravers were at the edge at their lives, they weren't running ahead or falling behind, they were just right there and the tunes meant everything. In the 90s you could feel that it had been taken away from them. In club culture, it all became like superclubs, magazines, Trance, commercialised. All these designer bars would be trying to be like clubs. It all got just taken. So it just went militant, underground from that point. That era is gone. Now there's less danger, less sacrifice, less journey to find something. You can't hide, the media clocks everything.' He checks his pessimism: 'But [dubstep nights] DMZ and FWD have that deep atmosphere and real feeling. The true underground is still strong, I hear good new tunes all the time.'

After a statement as definitive as his first LP, it was difficult to imagine where Burial would go next. But *Untrue* substantially modifies the sound auditioned on *Burial*. The most obvious difference from the first record is the amount and type of vocal on the new LP. His mentor Kode9 describes it as 'weird soul' and, if the reference points for the debut were early to mid-90s Rave and Jungle, the touchstones on *Untrue* are late 90s Garage and 2-

step. The cut-up and pitchshifted voices – looped fragments of longing – make *Untrue* even more addictive and even more keeningly moving than *Burial*. Burial had in fact produced a whole album's worth of material in another style – 'more technical, all the tunes sounded like some kind of weapon that was being taken apart and put back together again' – but he scrapped it. 'I was worrying,' he recalls, 'I'd made all these dark tunes and I played them to my mum, and she didn't like them. I was going to give up, but she was sweet, telling me, 'Just do a tune, fuck everyone off, don't worry about it.' My dog died and I was totally gutted about that. She was just like, 'Make a tune, cheer up, stay up late, make a cup of tea.' And I rang her mobile 20 minutes later and I'd made that 'Archangel' tune [on Untrue], and I was like, 'I've made the tune, the tune you told me to make.''

Burial's treatment of voice has always been crucial to his sound. Too much dub-influenced music is content to simply erase the voice and turn up the echo, but Burial instinctively knew that dubbing is about veiling the song, about reducing it to a tantalising tissue of traces, a virtual object all the more beguiling because of its partial desubstantialisation. The drizzly crackle that has become one of his sonic signatures is part of the veiling process. Self-deprecatingly, he claims that he initially used the crackle to conceal 'the fact that I wasn't very good at making tunes'. But he is not so much influenced by dub as by the 'vocal science' developed by Jungle, Garage and 2-step producers. When he and his brothers would listen to darkside Jungle, Burial found himself increasingly drawn to the vocal tracks. 'I'd love these vocals that would come in, not proper singing but cut-up and repeating, and executed coldly. It was like a forbidden siren. I was into the cut-up singing as much as the dark basslines. Something happens when I hear the subs, the rolling drums and vocals together. So when I started doing tunes, I didn't have the kit and I didn't understand how to do it properly, so I couldn't make the drums and bass sound massive, so as long as it had a bit of singing in it, it forgave the rest of the tune. Then I couldn't believe that I'd done a tune that gave me that feeling that proper records used to, and the vocal was the one thing that seemed to take the tune to that place. My favourite tunes were underground and moody but with killer vocals: 'Let Go' by Teebee, 'Being With You Remix' by Foul Play, Intense, Alex Reece, Digital, Goldie, Dillinja, EL-B, D-Bridge, Steve Gurley. I miss being on the bus to school listening to DJ Hype mixes.'

New Labour Britain is intoxicated by consensual sentimentality, hooked on disposable simulated emotion. With the ubiquity of TV talent shows, religiose emoting has become a fast track to media recognition, secular UK's equivalent of sanctification and salvation. In this process, singing has become almost incidental – it's lachrymose back stories that the media really hungers for. Burial's strategy with singing is exactly contrary to this: he removes voices from biography and narrative, transforming them into fluttering, flickering abstractions, angels liberated from the heavy weight of personal history. 'I was listening to these Guy Called Gerald tunes,' he says. 'I wanted to do vocals but I can't get a proper singer like him. So I cut up a cappellas and made different sentences, even if they didn't make sense, but they summed up what I was feeling.' In the process of changing the pitch of the vocals, buried signals come to light. 'I heard this vocal and it doesn't say it but it sounds like 'archangel',' says Burial. 'I like pitching down female vocals so they sound male, and pitching up male vocals so they sound like a girl singing.' This is apt, as angels are supposed to be without gender. 'Well that works nice with my tunes, kind of half boy half girl,' he enthuses. 'I understand that moody thing, but some dance music is too male. Some Jungle tunes had a balance, the glow, the moodiness that comes from the presence of both girls and boys in the same tune. There's tension because it's close, but sometimes perfect together. I look like her. I am her.'

Kode9 describes the album as 'downcast euphoria', and that seems to fit. 'I wanted to make a half euphoric record,' Burial agrees. 'That was an older thing that UK underground music used to have. Old Rave tunes used to be the masters of that, for a reason, to do with the Rave, half human endorphins and half something hypnotised by drugs. It was stolen from us and it never really came back. Mates laugh at me because I like whale songs. But I love them, I like vocals to be like that, like a night cry, an angel animal.'

Angels, again. On *Untrue*, Burial's Ravers appear as downcast angels, beings of light exiled into the dull weight of the worldly. *Untrue* is like German director Wim Wenders's *Wings Of Desire* (1987) relocated to the UK: an audio vision of London as a city of betrayed and mutilated angels, their wings clipped. But angels also hover above the hopeless and the abandoned here. 'My new tunes are about that,' Burial agrees, 'wanting an angel to be watching over you, when there's nowhere to go and all you can do is sit in McDonalds late at night, not answering your phone.'

As you might expect, Burial's attunement to angels, demons and ghosts goes back to childhood. 'My dad when I was really little,' he says, 'sometimes he used to read me MR James stories. On the South Bank last year, I bunked off from my day job and I found a book of MR James ghost stories. The one that fucked me up when I was little was "Oh, Whistle And I'll Come To You, My Lad". Something can betray how sinister it is even at a distance. Something weird happens with MR James, because even though it's in writing, there'll be a moment when the person meets the ghost, where you can't quite believe what you've read. You go cold, just for those few lines when you glimpse the ghost for a second, or he describes the ghost face. It's like you're not reading any more. In that moment it burns a memory into you that isn't yours. He says something like, "There's nothing worse for a human being than to see a face where it doesn't belong." But if you're little, and you've got an imagination which is always messing you up and darking you out, things like that are almost comforting to read.

'Also,' he continues, 'there is nothing worse than not recognising someone you know, someone close, family, seeing a look in them that just isn't them. I was once in a lock-in in a pub and the regulars there and some mates started telling these fucked-up ghost stories from real life, maybe that had happened to them, and I swear if you heard them. . . One girl told me the scariest thing I ever heard. Some of these stories would stop a few words earlier than seemed right. They don't play out like a film, they're too simple, too everyday, slight. Those stories ring true and I never forgot them. Sometimes maybe you see ghosts. On the underground with an empty Costcutters plastic bag, nowhere to go, they are smaller, about 70 per cent smaller than a normal person, smaller than they were in life.'

Burial makes the most convincing case that our zeitgeist is essentially hauntological. The power of Derrida's concept lay in its idea of being haunted by events that had not actually happened, futures that failed to materialise and remained spectral. Burial craves something he never actually experienced firsthand. 'I've never been to a festival, a Rave in a field, a big warehouse, or an illegal party,' he says, 'just clubs and playing tunes indoors or whatever. I heard about it, dreamed about it. My brother might bring back these records that seemed really adult to me and I couldn't believe I had them. It was like when you first saw Terminator or Alien when you're only little. I'd get a rush from it, I was hearing this other world, and my brother would drop by late and I'd fall asleep listening to tunes he put on.' It was his older brother who made Rave a kind of 'present absence' in Burial's life, a space to be filled with yarns and yearnings. 'He loved tunes, Rave tunes, Jungle,' Burial tells me. 'He lived all that stuff, and he was gone, he was on the other side of the night. We were brought up on stories about it: leaving the city in a car and finding somewhere and hearing these tunes. He would sit us down and play these old tunes, and later on he'd play us 'Metropolis', Reinforced, Paradox, DJ Hype, Foul Play, DJ Crystl, Source Direct and Techno tunes.'

The Rave relics feed a hunger for escape. 'I respect working hard but I dread a day job,' asserts Burial. 'Or a job interview. I've got a truant heart, I just want to be gone. I'd be in the kitchens, the corridors at work, and I'd be staring at the panels on the roof, clocking all the maintenance doors, dreaming about getting into the airducts. A portal. As a kid I used to dream about being put in the bins, escaping from things, without my mum knowing she'd put me out in the bins. So I'm in a black plastic bag outside a building and hearing the rain against it, but feeling all right, and just wanting to sleep, and a truck would take me away.' A too quick psychoanalytic reading would hear this as a thinly coded wish to return to the womb – and Burial's warm bass certainly feels enwombing – but that would be to ignore the desire to flee that is also driving this fantasy. Burial wants out, but he cannot positively characterise what lies beyond. 'We all dream about it,' he says. 'I wish something was there. But even if you fight to see it, you never see anything. You don't have a choice. You'd be on the way to a job, but you're longing to go down this other street, right there, and you walk past it. No force on Earth could make you go down there, because you've got to traipse to wherever. Even if you escape for a second, people are on your case, you can't go down old Thames side and throw your mobile in.'

But there are always flickers and flashes of the other side. After-images. 'I used to get taken away to the middle of nowhere, by the sea,' concludes Burial. 'I love it out there, because when it's dark, it's totally dark, there's none of this ambient light London thing. We used to have to walk back and hold hands and use a lighter. See the light, see where you were and then you'd walk on, and the image of where you've just been would still be on your retina.

Sleevenotes for The Caretaker's
Theoretically Pure Anterograde Amnesia

May 2006

Could it be said that we *all* now suffer from a form of theoretically pure anterograde amnesia?

Oliver Sacks' *The Man who Mistook his Wife for a Hat* and Christopher Nolan's *Memento* (2000) have made the features of the condition – referred to, misleadingly, as short-term memory loss – well-known. In fact, sufferers *do* produce new memories, but they are not retained. There is no long-term encoding. This type of amnesia is anterograde rather than retrograde because it does not affect any memories formed before the onset of condition. *Theoretically*: in practice, it is likely that even the old memories will undergo some degradation.

On *Theoretically Pure Anterograde Amnesia* the album, a tendency in the Caretaker's music has reached a kind of culmination. The theme was once homesickness for the past. Now, it is the impossibility of the present.

Selected Memories From The Haunted Ballroom was a kind of replicant mnemonic implant, a false memory of the tearoom pop of the twenties and thirties. For those of us haunted by the lambent ache of Al Bowlly's croon in *The Shining* and *Pennies From Heaven*, that kind of Total Recall trip was irresistible. The ghosts were so glamorous, their bob haircuts and pearls glistening in the candlelight, their dance moves oh so elegant.

An occulted reference might have been *The Invention of Morel* (an influence upon *Last Year at Marienbad* (1961) and therefore also upon *The Shining* (1980)), Adolfo Bioy Casares' science fictional lovesong to Louise Brooks. Casares imagined a world we live in it where the spectres of the beautiful and the damned are preserved forever, their little gestures and banal conversations transformed, by repetition, into holy artefacts. The simulation machine on Morel's island is film, of course, and who has not at some time wanted to do as Casares' hero does and pass beyond the screen, so as to finally be able to talk with the ghosts you have for so long mooned over? It is the same temptation that Jack yields to in *The Shining* when he enters into the consensual hallucination of The Overlook. The Gold Room, in which the Scott Fitzgerald-era elite forever cavort in a ceaseless whirl of wit, cocaine and wealth, is perfectly heavenly. But you know what the price of the ticket to heaven is, don't you Jack?

Don't you?

It is that grave-damp, mildewed odour which the perfume and the preservative never quite covered up which has always made The Caretaker's music uneasy, rather than easy, listening. Queasy listening, actually. It has never been possible to ignore the shadows lurking at the periphery of our audio-vision; the trip down memory lane was deliciously intoxicating but there was a bitter undertaste. A faint horror, something like the dim but insistent awareness of plague and mortality that must have nagged at the entranced-dancers in Poe's 'The Masque of the Red Death'.

That's not all.

Something else was wrong.

The sepia and the soft focus were photoshopped in, we knew that. These thick carpets and china tea-sets weren't really there. And they never were, not for us. We were in a simulation of *another's* mind's eye. The mottled, honeyed, slurred and reverbed quality of the sound alerted us to the fact that this was not the object itself but the object as it is for someone else's memory.

On *Theoretically Pure Anterograde Amnesia*, things have worsened immeasurably. It is as if the Overlook simulation has run out of steam. The lights have gone out. The hotel is rotten, a burned out wreck long since gutted, the band is pale and very nearly translucent.

The threat is no longer the deadly sweet seduction of nostalgia. The problem is not, any more, the longing to get *to* the past, but the inability to get *out* of it. You find yourself in a grey black drizzle of static, a haze of crackle. Why is it always raining here? Or is that just the sound of the television, tuned to a dead channel?

Where were we?

You suppose that you could be in familiar territory. It's difficult to know if you've heard this before or not. There's not much to go on. Few landmarks. The tracks have numbers, not names. You can listen to them in any order. The point is to get lost. That's easy in this ill-seen, late Beckett landscape. You extemporise stories they call it confabulation – to make sense of the abstract shapes looming in the smoke and fog.

Who is editing the film, and why all the jump–cuts?

By now, very little a few haunting refrains lingering at the back of your mind separates you from the desert of the real.

Let's not imagine that this condition afflicts only a few unfortunates. Isn't, in fact, theoretically pure anterograde amnesia the postmodern condition par excellence? The present – broken, desolated is constantly erasing itself, leaving few traces. Things catch your attention for a while but you do not remember them for very long. But the old memories persist, intact. . . Constantly commemorated . . . *I love 1923. . .*

Do we really have more substance than the ghosts we endlessly applaud?

The past cannot be forgotten, the present cannot be remembered.

Take care. It's a desert out there. . .

Memory Disorder: Interview with The Caretaker

The Wire 304, June 2009

'I have always been fascinated by memory and its recall especially where sound is concerned,' writes James Kirby via email. 'Some things we remember easily and others we never seem to grasp. That idea was developed more on the boxset I did [2006's *Theoretically Pure Anterograde Amnesia*] which was based around a specific form of amnesia where sufferers can remember things from the past but are unable to remember new things. To recreate that in sound was a challenge that I relished really. I realised the only way was to make a disorientating set with very few reference points. Fragments of melody breaking out of this monotonous tone and audio quagmire. Even if you listen over and over to all the songs you still can't remember when these melodies will come in. You have no favourite tracks, it's like a dream you are trying to remember. Certain things are clear but the details are still buried and distant.'

Kirby's description perfectly captures the unsettling experience of listening to *Theoretically Pure Anterograde Amnesia*. With the release of the six CD boxset, his project The Caretaker crossed over from being an exercise in atmospheric nostalgia to being a harrowing investigation of memory disorder. The box set is more like a sonic installation than a record, a work whose conceptual and textural richness puts much sound art to shame. The first three Caretaker records – *Selected Memories From The Haunted Ballroom* (1999), *A Stairway To The Stars* (2001) and *We'll All Go Riding On A Rainbow* (2003) – swathed sampled British tearoom pop in a gaslit halo of reverb and crackle. On *Theoretically Pure Anterograde Amnesia* the effects and the surface noise take over, so that instead of a gently dub–dilapidated pop, there is an unnavigable murk, as abstract and minimal as a Beckett landscape. Echoes and reverberations float free of any originating sound source in a sea of hiss and static. If the earlier records suggested spaces that were mildewed but still magnificent – grand hotels gone to seed, long abandoned ballrooms – *Theoretically Pure Anterograde Amnesia* invokes sites that have deteriorated into total dereliction, where every unidentified noise is pregnant with menace. The 72 tracks – all of them numbered rather than named – simulate the amnesiac condition, and the few fragments of well known tunes that occasionally flare in the gloom are intermittent islands of familiarity in a world that has become hostile and unrecognisable.

'Maybe it's a dark humour, a kind of an audio black comedy,' Kirby says of The Caretaker, but the solemnity of the project belies Kirby's reputation as a prankster. His label V/Vm notoriously released a version of Lieutenant Pigeon's 'Mouldy Old Dough' just after appearing on the cover of *The Wire* 176 under the headline 'Harder! Faster! Louder!', one of a series of manglings of mainstream music – tracks by Chris de Burgh, John Lennon and Elton John were also butchered and reassembled – that V/Vm issued.

It is the focus on cultural memory that holds together all of Kirby's work, including the V/Vm mash–ups. If the V/Vm (sub)versions of pop come from the brash side of postmodern pastiche, then The Caretaker is about the dark side of cultural retrospection. *Theoretically Pure Anterograde Amnesia* was in many ways an act of diagnosis of a cultural pathology. It might seem strange to describe a culture that is so dominated by past forms as being amnesiac, but the kind of nostalgia that is now so pervasive may best be characterised not as a longing for the past so much as an inability to make new memories. Fredric Jameson described one of the impasses of postmodern culture as the inability 'to focus our own present, as though we have become incapable of achieving aesthetic representations of our own current experience.' The past keeps coming back because the present cannot be remembered. Memory disorders have recurred as themes in the popular cinema in the past decade or so: it is theoretically pure anterograde amnesia that afflicts Leonard, the lead character in *Memento*, while the massively successful Bourne films were preoccupied with memory loss. It is not surprising that anxieties about memory should continually surface in late capitalism, where, as Jameson and others have argued, perpetual economic instability and the rapid turnover of ephemeral images leads to a breakdown in any coherent sense of temporality.

Kirby has approached the failure of the future from a different angle on another of his projects, 2006's *The Death Of Rave*. Here, Rave is desubstantialised, stripped of all bass weight and drum propulsion, reduced to shimmer and haze. The tracks sound like they are being heard from outside a club: a horribly accurate sonic metaphor, perhaps, of our current state of exile from the future-shocking rate of innovation that dance music achieved in the 80s and 90s. 'Yeah, that project really is in its infancy,' Kirby says. 'It came about as part of the V/Vm 365 project where the aim was to make one audio track a day. I used to go Raves when I was younger, went through that whole explosion in electronic music from 1987 to around 1992-93 when it seemed like there was a new genre every single week. It was an amazing time in music to hear so many things happening and so many new possibilities opening up and to see and feel the energy of new music exploding on dancefloors and in clubs. I think *The Death Of Rave* is about the loss in that spirit and a total loss of energy in most electronic musics across the board. I feel sorry these days for people when I go to clubs as that energy isn't there any more. I mean we have some so called very cool clubs in Berlin such as Watergate and Berghain, but you compare them to those back in the late 80s and early 90s in Manchester and it really is no comparison. Of course new things pop up but the difference now really is that if something explodes then before it can grow naturally people have strangled it to death with parodies online and often a scene or new style is dead before it even surfaces. House and Techno for instance took a long time to mature in Chicago and Detroit, now there is no time, once an idea is out of the rabbit's hat it's copied ad infinitum until the energy is gone. That is the key word – 'energy', it's the one thing I have always been inspired by. For me those *Death Of Rave* tracks are about stripping Rave music from all its energy and spirit of fun – taking the audio from the Rave to the grave, if you like.' The tracks are like energy flashbacks, frail figments of Rave reconstructed in a serotonin-depleted brain.

Kirby's other project The Stranger is organised around space rather than time. 'The Stranger really is a darker version of The Caretaker,' Kirby says, 'and is its closest relative. The Stranger is about creating a physical location in sound. The last album for example [2008's *Bleaklow*] was about the site of Bleaklow which is in the Peak District, it can be a grim place on the dark grey days but also beautiful on sunny days. Weirdly I had a few people get in touch with me who walk up there and they told me I captured the atmosphere perfectly and they used it as they were walking up there. I guess the odd glint of sunshine coming through that slate northern grey sky could be heard aurally.'

Kirby himself now lives in Berlin. 'I moved to Berlin as it has the atmosphere and opportunities of the big city but also there's a lot of space here to think more and also it's easy to hide away on the dark streets here. Also it's not as brutal as Manchester here, there is more of an openess as people don't follow the media and news so much.' Like The Stranger, though, The Caretaker remains a project rooted in Britishness – 'it's often only British music which has been used as source material.' A parallel for The Caretaker's excavation of pre-rock British pop is Dennis Potter's musical drama for television, *Pennies From Heaven*. 'The use of audio in *Pennies From Heaven* is amazing along with its vibrancy and colour and of course the way Dennis Potter uses the sadness in the lyrics to keep telling the story is also special as these songs really are stories in themselves. John Clifford and Herk Harvey's film *Carnival of Souls* (1962) was also a point of reference, the closing scenes in that film could even be audio from *A Stairway To The Stars*. I only saw that film after people had mentioned it to me. It works a lot that way, people will draw a line to something and I will then investigate that too.'

But of course the main initial impetus for The Caretaker was Kubrick's *The Shining*. The name 'the caretaker' was taken from the role that Jack Torrance is condemned to forever play in the haunted Overlook hotel ('you've always been the caretaker', Torrance is told in one of the film's most chilling moments). The conceit was simple: inspired by 'the haunting sequences which feature the ballroom music which is playing only in Jack's mind', Kirby thought, why not make a whole album of material that might also have played in the Overlook? *The Shining* soundtrack includes two tracks by Al Bowlly, the between-the-wars crooner whose songs features in many of Potter's dramas, and Kirby sought out music in a similar vein. 'I spent a lot of time searching out music from that era over a two or three year period and constantly started to play around with this source material. The interesting thing for me is the fact that most of that music is about ghosts and loss as it was recorded between both the world wars. It's of a totally different era and had more or less been forgotten. Titles inspired new ideas as did the audio itself. I was fortunate as there was a great record shop near where I was in Stockport which was ran by two old guys and it specialised in 78s. I would take in audio and ask then what was similar and they would scuttle off into the back of the shop and dig out some old catalogue from the 1930s and then pull out vinyls for me. It was an amazing resource sadly which is no longer there as one of the guys passed away and the other decided to close the shop. It was like a timewarp in there, like going back 30 or 40 years. They would hand write receipts and half of their stock was in this backroom you were denied access too. They had no idea what I was doing in there buying these records, though one of them told me one time 'You were born in the wrong era as nobody is interested in this music who is your age.''

Kirby has tuned to more recent history for an upcoming project. 'It has been in my mind for a while to work on a Scragill/Thatcher project and this is the perfect time for this now as we approach the 25th anniversary of the Miners Strike. A lot has been written elsewhere about this conflict and its outcome and legacy, I have been scouring online and also have picked up some amazing footage to reprocess. It will link closely to The Caretaker in terms of its style as it will be like watching a half remembered version due to the processing. Some of the footage is totally ghostlike as it was recorded on VHS tapes from Miners back in 1984, so there is a real loss in quality and the sound fails to match the visuals. It's looking like a dream version maybe. This will be mainly video work with also an incredibly limited vinyl release featuring audio from these videos and some exclusive audio work.' This will fit into a series of re-stagings of the Miners Strike this decade, including Jeremy Deller and Artangel's *The Battle Of Orgreave* and David Peace's *GB84*.

Kirby decided to close V/Vm down last year. 'V/Vm was a vehicle for a lot of the work I have done but I think now as music consumers we have reached a point where labels are not so important, what is more important is delivery and availability of work.' It is partly the possibilities for the online distribution of music, which Kirby has always been enthusiastic about, that led him to end V/Vm, but he 'also found I was using the name V/Vm less and less when it comes to new works. I've been working on a very personal album in terms of moods I want to convey and I guess I may use my own name for that.' In fact, the album, entitled *History Always Favours The Winners*, will come out under the name Leyland Kirby ('Leyland is my grandather's and my middle name. There are already too many James Kirby's making music out there, if I believe Google. Now I'm only competing with a glamour model from Sheffield in the Google search.') The Leyland Kirby music was made without the use of samples, but it has clearly been informed by Kirby's time in the vaults. The tracks have an eerily untimely quality, a stately grace, a filmic scope. On 'When Did Our Dreams And Futures Drift So Far Apart', a doleful, echo-refracted piano desolately tracks through subdued electronic textures. 'The Sound Of Our Music Vanishing' is a more violent exercise in thwarted recall – here it as if the memories are rushing in and being obliterated at the same time, like Basinski if the tapes were being violently shredded instead of gently disintegrating. The epic 'When We Parted My Heart Wanted To Die', meanwhile, has a swelling, magisterial melancholy that recalls Angelo Badalamenti.

The Caretaker project continues, however. 'I have started to play shows finally as The Caretaker, usually I just like to let the music just creep out of the speakers as if it's actually the venue playing the audio or that the sounds are in your own mind. I played in Athens last week in a pitch black room which worked well, maybe I can work some visuals into the live process but they would have to add to the audio and not distract the listening process. I am always of course interested in playing more relevant locations, so for instance Blackpool Tower would be amazing as the ballroom there is a great Victorian example and perfect for this particular audio recall.'

'More than anything it's all about research and mood when making the albums,' Kirby replies when I ask him how he makes The Caretaker records. 'Knowing the source material, maybe hearing a lyrical phrase which opens up an idea in my mind or indeed just reading something, such as with the *Anterograde* boxset which sparked off another idea and offered a different tangent and possibility. Without going into the specifics, things are reworked totally in a digital realm until the right mood surfaces. It's very important too that I am in the right mood mentally to make that music which I think comes across certainly in the later albums, as opposed maybe to the first album. I am getting better at realising the days when I get the best results now when working on a specific project. It's strange really because there is a full range of emotions in the music when I listen back, from loss to happiness, dislocation, regret, longing. Maybe it's the source music itself which inspires this, but there are still for me a lot of personal moments in amongst those albums. Maybe even some of my own memories are intertwined in there.'

The word 'research' keeps coming up in Kirby's discussion of The Caretaker project. 'I have been doing a lot of online research in the last couple of years and also have been watching a lot of documentaries about people who suffer from brain disorders and memory problems. The last release [2008's *Persistent Repetition of Phrases*] was based around a lot of conditions where the sufferer just repeats themselves, so the audio featured a lot of loops and microloops, it was a lot warmer and more gentle than the boxset release. Not all memories are necessarily bad or disturbing memories.' On *Persistent Repetition of Phrases*, one of *The Wire*'s top ten records of last year, there was accordingly a return of the some of the prettiness that was absent from *Theoretically Pure Anterograde Amnesia*, but there was also an icy lucidity, an exquisite poise, about the record. It felt like a distillation and a consolidation. 'The challenge now is to move the sound somewhere else brainwise and memory wise, that will take time to find the new direction. More research will have to be done before I find the best pathway for future exploration. I would also love to use this music on film as it would be perfect for this, so maybe a door will open somewhere.'

Home is Where The Haunt is:
The Shining's Hauntology

k-punk post, January 23, 2006

I. The sound of hauntology

Conjecture: hauntology has an intrinsically sonic dimension. The pun – hauntology, ontology – works in spoken French, after all. In terms of sound, hauntology is a question of hearing what is not here, the recorded voice, the voice no longer the guarantor of presence (Ian P: 'Where does the Singer's voice GO, when it is erased from the dub track?') Not phonocentrism but phonography, sound coming to occupy the dis-place of writing. Nothing here but us recordings...

2. Ghosts of the Real

Derrida's neologism uncovers the space between Being and Nothingness.

The Shining – in both book and film versions, and here I suggest a side-stepping of the wearisome struggle between King fans and Kubrickians and propose treating the novel and the film as a labyrinth-rhizome, a set of interlocking correspondences and differences, a row of doors – is about what lurks, unquiet, in that space. Insofar as they continue to frighten us once we've left the cinema, the ghosts that dwell here are not supernatural. As with *Vertigo* (1958), in *The Shining* it is only when the possibility of supernatural spooks has been laid to rest that we can confront the Real ghosts . . . or the ghosts of the Real.

3. The haunted ballroom

Mark Sinker: 'ALL [Kubrick's] films are fantastically 'listenable' (if you use this in sorta the same sense you use watchable)'
Where does

The conceit of The Caretaker's *Memories from the Haunted Ballroom* has the simplicity of genius: a whole album's worth of songs that you might have heard playing in the Gold Room in The Shining's Overlook Hotel. *Memories from the Haunted Ballroom* is a series of soft-focus delirial-oneiric versions of 20s and 30s tearoom pop tunes, the original numbers drenched in so much reverb that they have dissolved into a suggestive audio-fog, the songs all the more evocative now that they have been reduced to hints of themselves. Thus Al Bowlly's 'It's All Forgotten Now', for instance, one of the tracks actually used by Kubrick on The Shining soundtrack, is slurred down, faded in and out, as if it is being heard in the ethereal wireless of the dreaming mind or played on the winding-down gramophone of memory. As Ian Penman wrote of dub: 'It makes of the Voice not a self-possession but a dispossession – a 're' possession by the studio, detoured through the hidden circuits of the recording console.'
the singer's voice
GO?

4. In the Gold Room

Jameson: 'it is by the twenties that the hero is haunted and possessed. . .'

Kubrick's editing of the film does not allow any of the polyvalencies of that phrase, 'It's All Forgotten Now', to go un(re)marked. The uncanniness of the song, today and 25 years ago when the film was released, arises from the (false but unavoidable) impression that it is commenting on itself and its period, as if were an example of the way in which that era of beautiful and damned decadence and Gatsby glamour were painfully, delightfully aware of its own butterfly's wing evanescence and fragility. Simultaneously, the song's place in the film – it plays in the background as a bewildered Jack speaks to Grady in the bathroom about the fact that Grady has killed himself after brutally murdering his children – indicates that what is forgotten may also be preserved: through the mechanism of repression.

I don't have any recollection of that at all.

Why does this Gold Room Pop, all those moonlight serenades and summer romances, have such power? The Caretaker's spectralised versions of those lost tunes only intensifies something that Kubrick, like Dennis Potter, had identified in the pop of the 20s and 30s. I've tried to write before about the peculiar aching quality of these songs that are melancholy even at their most ostensibly joyful, forever condemned to stand in for states that they can evoke but never instantiate.

For Fredric Jameson, the Gold Room revels bespeak a nostalgia for 'the last moment in which a genuine American leisure class led an aggressive and ostentatious public existence, in which an American ruling class projected a class-conscious and unapologetic image of itself and enjoyed its privileges without guilt, openly and armed with its emblems of top-hat and champagne glass, on the social stage in full view of the other classes'. But the significance of this genteel, conspicuous hedonism must be construed psychoanalytically as well as merely historically. The 'past' here is not an actual historical period so much as a fantasmatic past, a Time that can only ever be retrospectively – retrospectrally – posited. The 'haunted ballroom' functions in Jack's libidinal echonomy (to borrow a neologism from Irigaray) as the place of belonging in which, impossibly, the demands of both the paternal and the maternal superegos can be met, the honeyed, dreamy utopia where doing his duty would be equivalent to enjoying himself. . . Thus, after his conversations with bartender Lloyd and waiter Grady (Jack's frustrations finding a blandly indulgent blank mirror sounding board in the former and a patrician, patriarchal voice in the latter), Jack comes to believe that he would be failing in his duty as a man and a father if he didn't succumb to his desire to kill his wife and child.

White man's burden, Lloyd . . . white man's burden . . .

If the Gold Room seems to be a male space (it's no accident that the conversation with Grady takes place in the men's room), the place in which Jack – via male intermediaries, intercessors working on behalf of the hotel management, the house, the house that pays for his drinks –faces up to his 'man's burdens', it is also the space in which he can succumb to the injunction of the maternal super-ego: 'Enjoy'.

Michel Ciment: 'When Jack arrives at the Overlook, he describes this sensation of familiarity, of well-being ('It's very homey'), he would 'like to stay here forever', he confesses even to having 'never been this happy, or comfortable anywhere', refers to a sense of dèja vu and has the feeling that he has 'been here before'. 'When someone dreams of a locality or a landscape,' according to Freud, 'and while dreaming thinks "I know this, I've been here before", one is authorised to interpret that place as substituting for the genital organs and the maternal body.'

5. Patriarchy/hauntology

Isn't Freud's thesis – first advanced in *Totem and Taboo* and then repeated, with a difference, in *Moses and Monotheism*, simply this: patriarchy is a hauntology? The father – whether the obscene Alpha Ape Pere-Jouissance of *Totem and Taboo* or the severe, forbidding patriarch of Moses and Monotheism – is inherently spectral. In both cases, the Father is murdered by his resentful children who want to re-take Eden and access total enjoyment.

Their father's blood on their hands, the children discover, too late, that total enjoyment is not possible. Now stricken by guilt, they find that the dead Father survives – in the mortification of their own flesh, and in the introjected voice which demands its deadening.

6. A History of Violence

Ciment: 'The camera itself – with its forward, lateral and reverse tracking shots . . . following a rigorously geometric circuit – adds further to the sense of implacable logic and an almost mathematical progression.'

Even before he enters the Overlook, Jack is fleeing his ghosts. And the horror, the absolute horror, is that he – haunter and the hunted – flees to the place where they are waiting. Such is *The Shining*'s pitiless fatality (and the novel is if anything even more brutal in its diagramming of the network of cause–and–effect, the awful Necessity, the 'generalized determinism', of Jack's plight than the film).

Jack has a history of violence. In both novel and film of *The Shining*, the Torrance family is haunted by the prospect that Jack will hurt Danny. . . again. Jack has already snapped, drunkenly attacked Danny. An aberration, a miscalculation, 'a momentary loss of muscular coordination. A few extra foot-pounds of energy per second, per second': so Jack tries to convince Wendy, and Wendy tries to convince herself. The novel tells us more. How has it come to this, that a proud man, an educated man, like Jack, is reduced to sitting there, false, greasy grin plastered all over his face, sucking up everything that a smarmy corporate non-entity like Stuart Ulman serves up? Why, because he has been sacked from his teaching job for attacking a pupil, of course. That is why Jack will accept, and be glad of, Ulman's menial job in Overlook.

The history of violence goes back even further. One of the things missing from the film but dealt with at some length in the novel is the account of Jack's relationship with his father. It's another version of patriarchy's occult history, now not so secret: abuse begetting abuse. Jack is to Danny as Jack's father was to him. And Danny will be to his child. . .?

The violence has been passed on, like a virus. It's there inside Jack, like a photograph waiting to develop, a recording ready to be played.

Refrain, refrain. . .

7. Home is where the haunt is

The word 'haunt' and all the derivations thereof may be one of the closest English word to the German 'unheimlich', whose polysemic connotations and etymological echoes Freud so assiduously, and so famously, unravelled in his essay on 'The Uncanny'. Just as 'German usage allows the familiar (das Heimliche, the 'homely') to switch to its opposite, the uncanny (das Unheimliche, the 'unhomely')' (Freud), so 'haunt' signifies both the dwelling-place, the domestic scene and that which invades or disturbs it. The OED lists one of the earliest meanings of the word 'haunt' as 'to provide with a home, house.'

Fittingly, then, the best interpretations of The Shining position it between melodrama and horror, much as Cronenberg's *History of Violence* (2005) is positioned between melodrama and the action film. In both cases, the worst Things, the real Horror, is already Inside. . .. (and what could be worse than that?)

You would never hurt Mommie or me, would ya?

8. The house always wins

What horrors does the big, looming house present? For the women of Horrodrama, it has threatened non-Being, either because the woman will be unable to differentiate herself from the domestic space or because – as in Rebecca (itself an echo of Jane Eyre) – she will be unable to take the place of a spectral-predecessor. Either way, she has no access to the proper name. Jack's curse, on the other hand, is that he is nothing but the carrier of the patronym, and everything he does always will have been the case.

I'm sorry to differ with you, sir. But you are the caretaker. You've always been the caretaker. I should know, sir. I've always been here.

9. I'm right behind you Danny

Metz: 'When Jack chases Danny into the maze with ax in hand and states, 'I'm right behind you Danny', he is predicting Danny`s future as well as trying to scare the boy.'

Predicting Danny`s future Jack might be, but that is why he could equally well say 'I'm just ahead of you Danny. . .' Danny may physically have escaped Jack, but psychically. . .? The Shining leaves us with the awful suspicion that Danny may become (his) Daddy, that the damage has already been done (had already been done even before he was born), that the photograph has been taken, the recording made; all that is left is the moment of development, of playing back.

Unmask!

(And how does Danny escape from Jack? By walking backwards in his father's footsteps).

10. The No Time of trauma

Jack: Mr. Grady. You were the caretaker here. I recognise ya. I saw your picture in the newspapers. You, uh, chopped your wife and daughters up into little bits. And then you blew your brains out.

Grady: That's strange, sir. I don't have any recollection of that at all.

What is the time when Jack meets Grady?

It seems that the murder – and suicide – has already happened, Grady tells Jack that he had to correct his daughters. Yet – not surprisingly – Grady has no memory – Bowlly's 'It's All Forgotten Now' wafting in the background – of any such events. 'I don't have any recollection of that at all.'

(And you think, well, it's not the sort of thing that you'd forget, killing yourself and your children, is it? But of course, it's not the sort of thing that you could possibly remember. It is an exemplary case of that which must be repressed, the traumatic Real.)

Jack: Mr. Grady. You were the caretaker here.

Grady: I'm sorry to differ with you, sir. But you are the caretaker. You've always been the caretaker. I should know, sir. I've always been here.

11. Overlooked

Overlook:

To look over or at from a higher place.

To fail to notice or consider; miss.

Hauntological Blues: Little Axe

k-punk post, October 3, 2006

Since we're talking about hauntology, we ought to have mentioned *Beloved* by now: not only Morrison's novel, but also Demme's astonishing film. It's telling that Demme is celebrated for his silly grand guignol, *The Silence of the Lambs*, while *Beloved* is forgotten, repressed, screened out. Hopkins' pantomime ham turn as Lecter surely spooks no-one, whereas Thandie Newton's automaton-stiff, innocent-malevolent performance as Beloved is almost unberable: grotesque, disturbing, moving in equal measure.

Like *The Shining* – a film that was also widely dismissed for nigh on a decade – *Beloved* (1998) reminds us that America, with its anxious hankerings after an 'innocence' it can never give up on, is haunted by haunting itself. If there are ghosts, then what was supposed to be a New Beginning, a clean break, turns out to be a repetition, the same old story. The ghosts were meant to have been left in the Old World . . . but here they are . . .

Whereas *The Shining* digs beneath the hauntological structure of the American family and finds an Indian Burial Ground, *Beloved* pitches us right into the atrocious heart of America's *other* genocide: slavery and its aftermath. No doubt the film's commercial failure was in part due to the fact that the wounds are too raw, the ghosts too Real. When you leave the cinema, there is no escape from these spectres, these apparitions of a Real which will not go away but which cannot be faced. Some viewers complain that *Beloved* should have been reclassifed as Horror. . . well, so should American history. . .

Beloved comes to mind often as I listen to *Stone Cold Ohio*, the outstanding new LP by Little Axe. Little Axe have been releasing records for over a decade now, but, in the 90s, my nervous system amped up by jungle's crazed accelerations, I wasn't ready to be seduced by their lugubrious dub blues. In 2006, however, the haunted bayous of *Stone Cold Ohio* take their place alongside Burial's phantom-stalked South London and Ghost Box's abandoned television channels in hauntological Now. Since I received *Stone Cold Ohio* last week, I've listened to little else; and when I wasn't immersed in *Stone Cold Ohio* I was re-visiting the other four Little Axe LPs. The combination of skin-tingling voices (some original, some sampled) with dub space and drift is deeply addictive. Little Axe's world is entrancing, vivid, often harrowing; it's easy to get lost in these thickets and fogs, these phantom plantations built on casual cruelty, these makeshift churches that nurtured collective dreams of escape. . .

Shepherds. . .

Do you hear the lambs are crying?

Little Axe's records are wracked with collective grief. Spectral harmonicas resemble howling wolves; echoes linger like wounds that will never heal; the voices of the living harmonise with the voices of the dead in songs thick with reproach, recrimination and the hunger for redemption. Yet utopian longings also stir in the fetid swamps and unmarked graveyards; there are moments of unbowed defiance and fugitive joy here too.

I know my name is written in the Kingdom. . ..

Little Axe is Skip McDonald's project. Through his involvement with the likes of Ohio Players, the Sugarhill Gang and Mark Stewart, McDonald has always been associated with future-orientated pop. If Little Axe appear at first sight to be a retreat from full-on future shock – McDonald returning to his first encounter with music, when he learned blues on his father's guitar – we are not dealing here the familiar, tiresome story of a 'mature' disavowal of modernism in the name of a re-treading of Trad form. In fact, Little Axe's anachronistic temporality can be seen as yet another rendering of future shock; except that this time, it is the vast unassimilable trauma, the SF catastrophe, of slavery that is being confronted. (Perhaps it always was. . .)

Even though Little Axe are apt to be described as 'updating the blues for the 21st century' they could equally be seen as downdating the 21st century into the early 20th. Their dyschronia is reminiscent of those moments in Stephen King's *It* where old photographs come to (a kind of) life, and there is a hallucinatory suspension of sequentiality. Or, better, to the time slips in Octavia Butler's *Kindred*, where contemporary characters are abducted back into the waking nightmare of slavery. (The point being: the nightmare never really ended. . .)

There is no doubt that blues has a privileged position in pop's metaphysics of presence: the image of the singer-songwriter alone with his guitar provides rockism with its emblem of authenticity and authorship. But Little Axe's return to the supposed beginnings unsettles this by showing that there were ghosts at the origin. Hauntology is the proper temporal mode for a history made up of gaps, erased names and sudden abductions. The traces of gospel, spirituals and blues out of which *Stone Cold Ohio* is assembled are not the relics of a lost presence, but the fragments of a time permanently out of joint. These musics were vast collective works of mourning and melancholia. Little Axe confront American history as a single 'empire of crime', where the War on Terror decried on *Stone Cold Ohio*'s opening track – a post 9/11 re-channelling of Blind Willie Johnson's 'If I had My Way' – is continuous with the terrordome of slavery.

When I interviewed Skip, he emphasised that Little Axe tracks always begins with the samples. The origin is out of joint. He has described before the anachronising Method-ology he uses to transport himself into the past. 'I like to surf time. What I like to do is study time-periods – get right in to 'em, so deep it gets real heavy in there.' McDonald's deep immersion in old music allows him to travel back in time and the ghosts to move forward. It is a kind of possession (recalling Winfrey's claim that she and the cast were 'possessed' when they were making *Beloved*). Little Axe's records skilfully mystify questions of authorship and attribution, origination and repetition. It is difficult to disentangle sampling from songwriting, impossible to draw firm lines between a cover version and an original song. Songs are texturally-dense palimpsests, accreted rather than authored. McDonald's own vocals, by turns doleful, quietly enraged and affirmatory, are often doubled as well as dubbed. They and the modern instrumentation repeatedly sink into grainy sepia and misty trails of reverb, falling into a dyschronic contemporeanity with the crackly samples.

In his landmark piece on Tricky (the piece, really, in which sonic hauntology was first broached), Ian Penman complained about Greil Marcus' 'measured humanism which leaves little room for the UNCANNY in music'. Part of the reason Little Axe are intriguing is that their use of dub makes it possible for us to encounter blues as uncanny and untimely again. Little Axe position blues not as part of American history, as Marcus does, but as one corner of the Black Atlantic. What makes the combination of blues and dub far more than a gimmick is that there is an uncanny logic behind the superimposition of two corners of the Black Atlantic over one another.

Adrian Sherwood's role in the band is crucial. Sherwood has said that Little Axe take inspiration from the thought that there is a common ground to be found in 'the music of Captain Beefheart and Prince Far I, King Tubby and Jimi Hendrix'. In the wrong hands, a syncresis like this could end up as a recipe for stodgy, Whole Earth humanism. But Sherwood is a designer of OtherWorld music, an expert in eeriness, a kind of anti-Jools Holland. What is most pernicious about Holland is the way in which, under his stewardship, pop is de-artificialised, re-naturalised, blokily traced back to a facialised source. Dub, evidently, goes in exactly the opposite direction – it estranges the voice, or points up the voice's inherent strangeness. When I interviewed Sherwood, he was delighted by my description of his art as 'schizophonic' – Sherwood detaches sounds from sources, or at least occults the relationship between the two. The tyranny of Holland's *Later* . . . has corresponded with the rise of no-nonsense pop which suppresses the role of recording and production. But 'Dub was a breakthrough because the seam of its recording was turned inside out for us to hear and exult in; when we had been used to the "re" of recording being repressed, recessed, as though it really were just a re-presentation of something that already existed in its own right.' (Penman)

Hence what I have called dubtraction; and what is subtracted, first of all, is *presence*. Pierre Schaeffer's term for a sound that is detached from a source is 'acousmatic'. The dub producer, then, is an acousmatician, a manipulator of sonic phantoms that have been detached from live bodies. Dub time is unlive, and the producer's necromantic role – his raising of the dead – is doubled by his treating of the living as if dead. For Little Axe, as for the bluesmen and the Jamaican singers and players they channel, hauntology is a political gesture: a sign that the dead will not be silenced.

I'm a prisoner
Somehow I will be free

Nostalgia for Modernism: The Focus Group and Belbury Poly

'Myself and my friend Jim Jupp had been making music, independently and together for a while, and also obsessing over the same things – the cosmic horror of Machen, Lovecraft, the Radiophonic Workshop, weird folk and the occult. We realised that we wanted to put our music out, but also create our own world where we could play with all these reference points. Starting our own label was the only way to do it.' Julian House is describing how he and his school-friend Jim Jupp came to found the Ghost Box label.

Off-kilter bucolic, drenched in an over-exposed post-psyche-delic sun, Ghost Box recordings are uneasy listening to the letter. If nostalgia famously means 'homesickness', then Ghost Box sound is about unhomesickness, about the uncanny spectres entering the domestic environment through the cathode ray tube. At one level, the Ghost Box is television itself; or a television that has disappeared, itself become a ghost, a conduit to the Other Side, now only remembered by those of a certain age. No doubt there comes a point when every generation starts pining for the artefacts of its childhood – but was there something special about the TV of the 1970s which Ghost Box releases obsessively reference?

'I think there definitely was something powerful about the children's TV from that period,' House maintains. 'I think it was just after the 60s, these musicians and animators, film makers had come through the psychedelic thing and acid folk, they had these strange dark obsessions that they put into their TV programmes. Also, someone like Nigel Kneale had obviously come from a tradition of HP Lovecraft – 20th century science used as a background to cosmic horror and the occult. The themes he explored in the Quatermass series eventually found their way into Doctor Who, *Children of the Stones, Sapphire and Steel*. If you look at the BBC Radiophonic workshop, people like David Cain also studied medieval music, and he did a great dark folky electronic album called *The Seasons*. And a few of Paddy Kingsland's arrangements bring to mind Pentangle. It's like there was this strange past/future thing which had come through psychedelia.'

The affect produced by Ghost Box's releases (sound *and* images, the latter absolutely integral) are the direct inverse of irritating postmodern citation-blitz. The mark of the postmodern is the extirpation of the uncanny, the replacing of the unheimlich tingle of unknowingness with a cocksure knowingness and hyper-awareness. Ghost Box, by contrast, is a conspiracy of the half-forgotten, the poorly remembered and the confabulated. Listening to sample-based sonic genres like Jungle and early hip-hop you typically found yourself experiencing *déjà vudu* or *déjà entendu*, in which a familiar sound, estranged by sampling, nagged just beyond recognisability. Ghost Box releases conjure a sense of *artificial* déjà vu, where you are duped into thinking that what you are hearing has its origin somewhere in the late 60s or early 70s: not false, but simulated, memory. The spectres in Ghost Box's hauntology are the lost contexts which, we imagine, must have prompted the sounds we are hearing: forgotten programmes, uncommissioned series, pilots that were never followed-up.

Belbury Poly, The Focus Group, Eric Zann – names from an alternative 70s that never ended, a digitally-reconstructed world in which analogue rules forever, a time-scrambled Moorcockian near-past. This return to the analogue via the digital is one of the ways in which Ghost Box records are not straight-up simulations of the past. 'We like to confuse the boundaries between analogue and digital. Jim uses a combination of analogue synths and digital technology. In the Focus Group stuff there are samples of old percussion albums and digital effects, electronic sounds generated on the computer and processed found sounds. I think it's do with this space between what happens in the computer and what happens outside of it. The recording of space, real reverb/room sound and the virtual space on the hard drive. Like different dimensions.'

'It was bang on 1980 when Fairlights and DX7s appeared in electronic music,' Jupp points out. 'I suppose that digital technology is a tipping point in culture in general, even in the way that television is made.' Yet Belbury Poly's sound relies on digital equipment. 'At the heart of it is a computer and we don't hide that fact. Having said that, I'm sitting in the studio now and it's mostly analogue synths and a pile of acoustic instruments, what we do couldn't exist without hip-hop and sampling culture and the access to cheap electronic instruments. It's revisiting old textures and old imagined worlds with new tools.'

Jupp laughs when I suggest that there was a certain *grain* to 70s British culture that got smoothed away by 80s style culture gloss. 'It's almost as if we became totally Americanised, got our teeth fixed and had a proper wash. I was talking to someone the other day whose girlfriend can't stand him watching old sitcoms, she always calls it grot TV. I know what she means. But maybe in TV, radio and records then there was a feel that was washed clean in the 80s when everything was angular, digital, American, upbeat and colourful.'

Ghost Box explore a sonic continuum which stretches from the quirkily cheery to the insinuatingly sinister. The most obvious predecessors lie in 'functional music', sounds designed to hover at the edge of perceptibility, not to hog centre-stage: signature tunes, incidental music, music that is instantly recognizable but whose authors, more often (self-)styled as technicians rather than artists, remain anonymous. The Radiophonic Workshop (whose two 'stars', Delia Derbyshire and Daphne Oram, became widely recognised only after their deaths) would be the obvious template. House agrees: 'I think the key reference is the Radiophonic Workshop, which is wildly experimental (Britain's electronic avant garde, the equivalent of GRM Pierre Schaeffer in France etc.) but it's also incredibly evocative of radio and television with which we grew up. It's got a sort of duality to it, it's haunting in its own right but also serves as a memory trigger. I think this dim, half remembered aspect of old Hammer films, Doctor Who, Quatermass is important – it's not like an I Love 1974 reminiscence. Rather than being just nostalgia, it's triggering something darker, you're remembering the strange ideas in these programmes, the stuff under the surface, rather than just knowing the theme tune. I think this is why Library music is such an influence – you listen to the albums divorced from context and it operates on an unconscious level, like musical cues for missing visuals.

When I grew up Doctor Who episodes like *The Sea Devils* haunted me, the way slightly shaky monsters and sets have their own uncanny horror. The loud blasts of Atonal music. The first time I saw the Hammer film of *Quatermass and the Pit* really affected me. And those dimly remembered eastern European animations had a certain quality. Also, certain public information films and adverts.'

Ghost Box preside over a (slightly) alternative world in which the Radiophonic Workshop were more important than the Beatles. In a sense that is our world, because the Workshop rendered even the most experimental rock obsolete even before it had happened. But of course you are not comparing like with like here; the Beatles occupied front stage in the Pop Spectacle, whereas the Radiophonic Workshop insinuated their jingles, idents, themes and special FX into the weft of everyday life. The Workshop was properly unheimlich, unhomely, fundamentally tied up with a domestic environment that had been invaded by media.

Naturally, Ghost Box have been accused of nostalgia, and of course this plays a part in their appeal. But their aesthetic in fact exhibits a more paradoxical impulse: in a culture dominated by retrospection, what they are nostalgic for is nothing less than (popular) modernism itself. Ghost Box are at their most beguiling when they foreground dyschronia, broken time – as on Belbury Poly's 'Caermaen' (from 2004's *The Willows*) and 'Wetland' (from 2006's *The Owl's Map*) where folk voices summoned from beyond the grave are made to sing new songs. Dyschronia is integral to the Focus Group's whole methodology; the joins are too audible, the samples too jagged, for their tracks to sound like refurbished artefacts.

In any case, at their best, Ghost Box conjure a past that never was. Their artwork fuses the look of comprehensive school text books and public service manuals with allusions to weird fiction, a fusion that has more to do with the compressions and conflations of dreamwork than with memory. House himself talks of 'a strange dream of a school textbook'. The implicit demand for such a space in Ghost Box inevitably reminds us that the period since 1979 in Britain has seen the gradual but remorseless destruction of the very concept of the public. At the same time, Ghost Box also remind us that the people who worked in the Radiophonic Workshop were effectively public servants, that they were employed to produce a *weird* public space – a public space very different from the bureaucratic dreariness invoked by neoliberal propaganda.

Public space has been consumed and replaced by something like the third place exemplified by franchise coffee bars. These spaces are uncanny only in their power to replicate sameness, and the monotony of the Starbucks environment is both reassuring and oddly disorientating; inside the pod, it's possible to literally forget what city you are in. What I have called nomadalgia is the sense of unease that these anonymous environments, more or less the same the world over, provoke; the travel sickness produced by moving through spaces that could be anywhere. My, I. . . what happened to Our Space, or the idea of a public that was not reducible to an aggregate of consumer preferences?

In Ghost Box, the lost concept of the public has a very palpable presence-in-absence, via samples of public service announcements. (Incidentally one connection between rave and Ghost Box is the Prodigy's sampling of this kind of announcement on 'Charly'.) Public service announcements – remembered because they could often be disquieting, particularly for children – constitute a kind of reservoir of collective unconscious material. The disinterment of such broadcasts now cannot but play as the demand for a return of the very concept of public service. Ghost Box repeatedly invoke public bodies – through names (Belbury Poly, the Advisory Circle) and also forms (the tourist brochure, the textbook).

Confronted with capital's intense semiotic pollution, its encrustation of the urban environment with idiotic sigils and imbecilic slogans no-one – neither the people who wrote them nor those at whom they are aimed – believes, you often wonder: what if all the effort that went into this flashy trash were devoted to a public good? If for no other reason, Ghost Box is worth treasuring because they make us pose that question with renewed force.

The Ache of Nostalgia:
The Advisory Circle

'The Advisory Circle – helping you make the right decisions.' With its suggestions of a benevolent bureaucracy, The Advisory Circle was always the perfect name for a Ghost Box act. On *Mind How You Go* (2005), producer and vinyl archivist Jon Brooks produced a kind of Anglo-analogue pastoralism that is as affecting as anything that the label has released. In what has since been established to be the customary Ghost Box fashion, Brooks's analogue synthesizer doodles – all the more powerful, somehow, for their unassuming slightness – gently trigger drifts down (false) memory lanes, inducing you to recall a mass mediated past which you never quite experienced. *Mind How You Go* frequently invokes that talisman of 1970s paternalism, the Public Information Film, and it's perhaps no accident that the rise of Ghost Box has coincided with the emergence of YouTube, which has made public information films and other such street furniture of 1970s audio–visual experience widely available again.

What Brooks captures extremely poignantly is the conflicted cluster of emotions involved in nostalgic longing . 'Mind How You Go' and 'Nuclear Substation' summon remembered sunlight from childhood summers even as their doleful melodies are laced with a deep sense of loss. Yet there's a very definite but subdued joy here, too, in the way that a track such as 'Osprey' achieves a kind of faltering soaring. It's not for nothing that the word *ache* is often associated with nostalgia; and The Advisory Circle's music positively aches with a sadness that is simultaneously painful and enjoyable. 2011's *As The Crow Flies* felt folkier than The Advisory Circle's previous releases, with acoustic guitars creeping over the analogue synthesizers like ivy spreading over the frontage of a brutalist building. The album's closing track, 'Lonely Signalman', brings these different textures together beautifully: its vocodered refrain (*'signalman lives all alone/ signalman is all alone'*) is simultaneously playful and plangent, a combination that is typical of Brooks's work. I asked Brooks about the roots of the exquisite sadness that colours his music.

'A lot of it stems from my childhood. Without wishing to go too far down the 'tortured artist' path, I will say that my upbringing was a cyclic period of safety, security, contentment, anxiety, despair and sadness. As an adult, I've managed to work through a lot of these childhood feelings and channel them into what I'm doing musically. Thankfully, I can now make sense of a lot of stuff that happened back then; I can balance this against any residual scars I might be left with. I'm not saying I'm glad that I had a turbulent childhood, but for what it's worth, it has shaped my art, quite indelibly.'

A paradoxical impulse lies behind Brooks's work. He is fascinated by functional culture – that which we don't consciously hear or see but which shapes our experience of environments – yet the attention on what was background necessarily pushes it into the foreground. 2011's *Music For Dieter Rams*, a homage to the designer best known for his work with Braun released under Brooks's name, was an attempt to bring functional music together with functional design. Rams's slogan 'less, but better' could equally apply to the original conception of Ambient music. After all, What was the ambition for Ambient if not that music attain the unassuming ubiquity of many of Rams's products – all those radios, coffee makers and calculators which were embedded into everyday life, their designer unknown to the general public? Perhaps for that reason, Brooks isn't the first artist to dedicate music to Rams: Alva Noto devoted two wonderfully eerie tracks on his *For 2* album to the designer. It's those things lurking at the background of attention, things that we took for granted at the time, which now evoke the past most powerfully.

'With hindsight,' Brooks says, 'the fact that these things are so evocative of the past, accentuates and crystallises my interest in them; but actually, I've always been interested in things 'in the background' – for me, that's where the really interesting stuff has always been. As a kid, I was equally fascinated by library music used on TV (or TV themes) as I was about pop music; things that we weren't supposed to take any real notice of. I used to look out for TV test transmissions, for example, and of course Public Information Films. Open University broadcasts held the same fascination; these broadcasts weren't targeted at an eight-year-old child, but I was drawn towards them nonetheless. I was also drawn to logos, branding and so forth. I remember being particularly entranced by certain record labels' logos – Polydor, Decca and Pye were my favourites. I loved the way they looked on the records and would quite often sit at the turntable and watch them go round, as the record played. There was something very elegant about them. Again, these things were presented as 'functional', in their own way. So, the fascination was always there. It's just stayed with me.'

Those objects and spaces are also functional. Is Brooks particularly fascinated by culture that operates in this ostensibly functional way?

'I am absolutely fascinated by that aspect. At the risk of being slightly tangential, taking the concept of Muzak as an example, I very much enjoyed reading Joseph Lanza's *Elevator Music*. This is a great example of bringing the background to the foreground, in the form of strictly 'functional' music. It goes a step further in this respect than even Library music does. I have always been fascinated by the cultural aspect of this – how we can have small speakers installed in ceilings in shops and the music just filters through and no-one is really supposed to notice; they called it 'non-entertainment music' at the time. Muzak gained a really bad reputation in the 1970s, but if you go back and listen to some of the music that was produced for the system, you'll find some very tight, compact arrangements hidden in there. Composers that are highly regarded by record collectors now, for example Sven Libaek and Syd Dale, did a lot of work for Muzak. In much the same way, I apply this fascination to domestic design or motorway service stations. Dieter Rams was interested in creating something that just worked, with elegance and simplicity. I love the fact that he wasn't searching for fame with his designs, but now we can celebrate those designs publicly and hand him the spotlight, as it were, in much the same way as we have discovered composers like Sven Libaek.'

Someone Else's Memories: Asher, Philip Jeck, Black To Comm, G.E.S., Position Normal, Mordant Music

In 2009, an artist known as Asher released an album called *Miniatures* on the Sourdine label. The only information on the sleeve was the following terse statement: 'recorded in Somerville, MA, winter 2007'. Rumours and mysteries proliferate in a data vacuum, and *Miniatures* puts the listener into a state of suspension and suspicion: what exactly are we listening to? Who made it? What does 'making' it mean in this context? And what sense of 'recorded' is being used?

Let's consider the audio facts, such as they are. Even here there is veiling – all the tracks are covered in a fog of crackle. What we hear is mostly piano, although occasionally strings can also be detected. The piano is contemplative, reflective, exquisitely sad: the lugubrious tempo seems to literalise the notion of longing. The haze of the crackle and the quietness of the playing mean that you have to 'lean in' to hear the music – played on ipod headphones, it practically disappears into the background noise of the street.

How were the tracks made? At least two theories circulated online. One, the closest there seems to be to any official story, maintains that the tracks on *Miniatures* were all short sections recorded by Asher from the radio and then digitally looped. (If so, he should buy himself a radio with better reception.) The other theory is that the piano pieces were played by Asher on poor quality tape, then subjected to further processes of digital distortion to give the impression that they are found sound objects. The tracks' unresolved status is not some dry conceptual riddle detracting from the experience of listening to them; instead, the enigma actually heightens the music's fragile, fragmentary beauty, its uncanny intimacy.

Miniatures was one of a number of records from the 00s whose sound centred on crackle. Why should crackle resonate now? The first thing we can say is that crackle exposes a temporal pathology: it makes 'out of joint' time audible. Crackle both invokes the past and marks out our distance from it, destroying the illusion that we are co-present with what we are hearing by reminding us we are listening to a recording. Crackle now calls up a whole disappeared regime of materiality – a tactile materiality, lost to us in an era where the sources of sound have retreated from sensory apprehension. Artists like Tricky, Basic Channel and Pole started to foreground vinyl crackle at the very moment when records were becoming superseded. Back then, it was the CD that was making vinyl obsolete. Now, the MP3 can neither be seen nor touched, still less manipulated by the hand in the way that the vinyl record could be.

The digital seems to promise nothing less than an escape from materiality itself, and the story of Willam Basinski's 2002 album *Disintegration Loops* – a recording of tapes that destroyed themselves in the very process of their transfer to digital – is a parable (almost too perfect) for the switch from the fragility of analogue to the infinite replicability of digital. What we have lost, it can often seem, is the very possibility of loss. Digital archiving means that the fugitive evanescence that long ago used to characterise, for instance, the watching of television programmes – seen once, and then only remembered – has disappeared. Indeed, it turns out that experiences which we thought were forever lost can – thanks to the likes of YouTube – not only be recovered, but endlessly repeated.

Crackle, then, connotes the return of a certain sense of loss. At the same time, it is also the sign of a found (audio) object, the indication that we are in a scavenger's space. That is why crackle is a stock-in-trade of someone like turntable artist Philip Jeck. Jeck's first record had appeared in 1999, but his work gained a new currency because of its convergence with what Burial and

The Caretaker were doing. Jeck had been inspired by hearing mixers like Walter Gibbons, Larry Levan and Grandmaster Flash in the 80s, but his montages reconceive DJing as the art of producing sonic phantasmagoria. Using Dansette turntables, FX units and records found in charity shops, Jeck defamiliarises the vinyl source material to the point of near-abstraction. Occasionally, recognizable fragments (60s rock, Mantovani-like lite classical kitsch) thrillingly bob up out of the whooshing delirium-stream.

Jeck began the extraordinary 2008 version of Gavin Bryars' *The Sinking of the Titanic* (which he performed in collaboration with Italian ensemble Alter Ego and Bryars himself) with nearly 14 minutes of crackle. In this audio-fog, threatening objects loom, barely perceived. As we listen, we come to distrust our own hearing, begin to lose confidence in our ability to distinguish what is actually there from audio hallucinations. Ominous strings and a solitary bell produce an atmosphere of quiet foreboding, and the ensemble – at first indistinct shadows in a Turner-esque squall – only gradually emerge from the cloud of crepitation. Here, as in Asher's *Miniatures*, crackle suggests radio static. The sinking of the Titanic in fact prompted the first use of wireless in sea rescue. As Bryars points out in his sleevenotes, Marconi had conceived of telegraphy as a spectral science. He 'became convinced that sounds once generated never die, they simply become fainter and fainter until we no longer perceive them. Marconi's hope was to develop sufficiently sensitive equipment, extraordinarily powerful and selective filters I suppose, to pick up and hear these past sounds. Ultimately, he hoped to be able hear Christ delivering the Sermon on the Mount.'

Jeck has referred to the sonic sources he uses as 'fragments of memory, triggering associations' but it is crucial that the memories are not necessarily his; the effect is sometimes like sifting through a box of slides, photographs and postcards from anonymous people, long gone. This same feeling of coming upon other people's orphaned memories could be heard in the 2009 album *Circulations* by G.E.S. (Gesellschaft zur Emanzipation des Samples/ Society For The Emancipation Of Sampling). There is some mystery about who is behind G.E.S., but the project appears to be a front for genre-hopping dilettante Jan Jelinek, best known for his *Loop-finding Jazz Records*, which constructed a version of minimal Techno out of minuscule jazz samples; Jelinek has also produced microhouse under the name Farben and Ambient as Gramm. G.E.S.'s idea was to take micro-samples, loop and collage them, play them in public spaces, and record the results. Would the ordinary laws of copyright apply if music was sampled in these conditions? The tracks are like unsigned audio-postcards, recorded sometimes in named places (Mount Zermatt and Hong Kong are mentioned in the track titles), sometimes in places we can only guess at, using the voices and background noises to orientate ourselves. 'Birds Of Heraklion' begins with distorted electronic pulses before being swept up by a backwards rush of very cinematic strings that sound like they might have come from a black and white film extolling the benefits of train travel. 'Orinoco, Bullerbü, (Crossfade)' is initially built from the violent juxtaposition of crazed bird noises with what could be a sample from some forgotten film noir or a highly strung melodrama, but it ends with echoes, and strange, abstract whistles. 'Im Schilf' puts one in mind of the kind of alien piping noises you would hear in an Oliver Postgate animation or an early Cabaret Voltaire tape experiment, while 'Farnballett' and 'Farnballett (In Dub)' recall a Binatone tennis game having a HAL-like nervous breakdown. The random sounds, the passing conversations, make you feel like you are witnessing stray frames from a film no whole version of which exists anywhere. This sense that action is continuing beyond what we are hearing, together with the record's travelogue-cosmopolitanism, remind me of nothing so much as the cold, dislocated beauty of Antonioni's *The Passenger*.

The closing track, 'Schlaf (Nach Einführung Der Psychoanalyse)' – which sounds like windchimes on some dust-blown alien planet – is like a memory of a Cold War science fiction that never quite happened. What stops this being a dry exercise or a disparate mélange is the inescapable sense of anonymous sadness which pervades the whole record.

This same sense of depersonalised tragedy hung over *Alphabet 1968*, the 2010 album by Black to Comm, aka Marc Richter, the man behind the 'death Ambient' genre and the Hamburg-based Dekorder label. Richter mischievously described *Alphabet 1968* – on which the only human voices are on field recordings at the edge of audibility – as an album of *songs*. What if we were to take Richter's provocation seriously – what would a song without a singer be like? What would it be like, that is to say, if objects themselves could sing? It's a question that connects fairy tales with cybernetics, and listening to *Alphabet 1968*, I'm fittingly reminded of a filmic space in which magic and mechanism meet: J F Sebastian's apartment in *Blade Runner*. The tracks on the album are crafted with the same minute attention to detail that the genetic designer and toymaker Sebastian brought to his plaintive automata, with their bizarre mixture of the clockwork and the computerised, the antique and the ultra-modern, the playful and the sinister. Richter's pieces have been built from similarly heterogeneous materials – record crackle, shortwave radio, glockenspiels, all manner of samples, mostly of acoustic instruments. Except on 'Void' – a steampunk John Carpenter-like track with susurrating voices conspiring in the background – the music does not feel very electronic. As with Sebastian's talking machines, you get the impression that Richter has used the latest technology in order to create the illusion of archaism. This is a record in which you feel that you can smell the dust coming off the retrieved objects. But so intricately are these sonic palimpsests layered that it's impossible to determine what Richter and his collaborators have played and what has been conjured from the archives. The sounds are treated, reversed and slowed down in a way that makes their original sources mysterious. There is a sense of subtle but constant movement, of sound shadows flitting in and out of earshot.

Richter so successfully effaces himself as author that it is as if he has snuck into a room and recorded objects as they played (to) themselves. On the opening track, 'Jonathan', crackle, a field recording of drizzle and cut-aways to white noise set the scene for a pensive piano. Children's voices can be heard in the distance, and it is like we are being ushered out of the human world into the mysterious world of objects-amongst-themselves, a world just adjacent to ours, yet utterly foreign to it. It is as if Richter has attuned himself to the subterranean raptures and sadnesses of objects in unoccupied rooms, and it is these 'songs' that he hears. It's not for nothing that the theme of objects coming to life was taken up so often in cinema animation (for, as its name suggests, what is animation if not a version of this process?), and most of the tracks on *Alphabet 1968* could be tunes for cartoon sequences – the 'song' an object sings as it stirs itself into motion, or declines back into inertia.

In fact, the impression of things winding down is persistent on *Alphabet 1968*. Richter has made an enchanted sound-world, but one from which entropy has not been excluded. It feels as if the magic is always about to wear off, that the enchanted objects will slip back into the inanimate again at any moment – an effect which only heightens the tracks' poignancy. The labouring, looped double bass on 'Rauschen' has all the mechano–melancholy of a phonograph winding down – or perhaps of one of Sebastian's automata running out of power. On 'Trapez', reverbed wind chimes create a gentle Narnian snowfall. As so often on this album, the track recalls a running-down music box – one parallel might be Colleen's 2006 album *Boîtes à Musique*, except that, where Colleen restricted herself to actually using music boxes, Richter loops and sequences his sonic material so that it *simulates* clockwork. But it's an uncanny clockwork, running to a crooked time. On 'Amateur' – with its hints of artificial respiration, as if the walls themselves are breathing – the piano loop seems bent out of shape.

Entropy is everywhere in the work of Position Normal, an act whom Simon Reynolds once called 'the godfathers of hauntology', but it is a very English kind of entropy. In Position Normal's music, it is like London has finally succumbed to the entropy that always threatens to engulf the city in Michael Moorcock's Jerry Cornelius mythos. Except there's something attractive about the deep daydreamy lassitude that reigns here: entropy isn't a threat so much as a lysergic promise, a chance to uncoil, unwind, unspool. Gradually, you are made to forget all of your urgencies as your brain is lulled and lured into the sunny Sunday afternoon when all Position Normal tunes seem to take place. The allure of this indolent London was touched upon by a certain trajectory in 60s' rock: the sunny daze of The Kinks' 'Sunny Afternoon', The Small Faces 'Lazy Sunday Afternoon', The Beatles' 'Tomorrow Never Knows' and 'I'm Only Sleeping'. Yet this particular strand of Anglo-languor didn't originate here, in the acid and weed reveries of rockers in repose. You can look even further back for antecedents, to moments in *Great Expectations* – the airless, inertial stasis of Satis House – or to *Alice's Adventures in Wonderland* (especially well captured in the hookah-hazes and fugues of Jonathan Miller's 1968 BBC television version).

Position Normal's London is a city far distant from the corporate gloss of busy/ business London as it is from the tourist London of pageantry. The tour guide for this anachronistic city would be the James Mason in *The London That Nobody Knows*, the 1969 film directed by Norman Cohen and based on the book by Geoffrey Fletcher. It's a palimpsest city, a space where many times are layered. Sometimes, when you walk down an unfamiliar street, you might stumble into aspects of it. Street markets that you'd imagined had closed long ago, shops that (so you think) couldn't possibly survive into the 21st century, ripe old voices fit only for the Victorian music hall . . . Position Normal's tracks are Dadaist dub-doodles, disarming in their seeming slightness. They feel like skits or sketches; unwilling to be seen taking themselves too seriously, but at the same time entirely lacking in knowing smirks. There's a daydreamy quality to the way the music is constructed: ideas waft in but trail off inconclusively while still half-baked. It can be frustrating, at least initially, yet the effect is accretive and seductive. A Position Normal album comes off like an anglo-*Fantasia* scavenged out of charity shops, all the detritus of the English 20th century made to sing. For the most part, you are left to guess the sources of all the funny voices. Who are they, this cheery gang – children's radio presenters, comedians, character actors, light entertainers, newsreel announcers, jazz trumpeters (mutes always at the ready), ragpickers, costermongers, chancers, idlers, thespians gone to seed, frothy coffee café proprietors . . .? And where have they come from – scratchy old shellac, unmarked tapes, soundtrack LPs? The tracks bleed into one another, and so do the albums, like failing memories.

It turns out that decaying memory is at the heart of Position Normal's music. In an interview with Joakim Norling for *Friendly Noise* magazine, Position Normal's Chris Bailiff has said that the roots of the PN sound lay in his father's Alzheimer's disease. 'My dad went into hospital and had to sell the family home, I had to move out and whilst doing this I found so many old records of his and records that he bought for me. Nursery rhymes, documentaries and jazz. I didn't want to throw anything away so took them with me. I started to listen to all of them and recorded on to tape my favourite sounds and made incredibly varied mix tapes. I then edited them down and down until there were what I suppose are called samples.' It's as if Bailiff was simultaneously attempting to simulate Alzheimer's and counteract it.

Position Normal can be fitted into the venerable English tradition of Nonsense. (Another Small Faces parallel: Stanley Unwin provided some of his trademark gobbledygook for *Ogden's Nut Gone Flake*, the album which included 'Lazy Sunday Afternoon'.)

This same sense of lyrical dementia is at work on Mordant Music's 2006 masterpiece *Dead Air*. Mordant explicitly affirm decay and deliquescence as productive processes, and on *Dead Air* it is as if the mould growing on the archives is the creative force behind the sound. The album sounds like an electro/Rave version of *The Disintegration Loops*, except what was disintegrating here was a moment in British broadcasting history. The loose concept behind the album was a dead television studio, and what's crucial to its unnerving allure is the presence of former Thames TV continuity announcer Phillip Elsmore. There's a lunatic calm about the way that Elsmore reading Baron Mordant's Nonsense (best heard in its own right on his collaboration with Ekoplekz, eMMplekz). Listening to *Dead Air* is like stumbling into an abandoned museum 200 years into the future where old Rave tracks play on an endless loop, degrading, becoming more contaminated with each repetition; or like being stranded in deep space, picking up fading radio signals from a far distant earth to which you will never return; or like memory itself re-imagined as an oneiric television studio, where fondly recalled continuity announcers, drifting in and out of audibility, narrate your nightmares in reassuring tones.

'Old Sunlight From Other Times and Other Lives': John Foxx's *Tiny Colour Movies*

k-punk post, June 19, 2006

He was in the market crowds, wearing a shabby brown suit. Trying to find me through all the years. My ghost coming home. How do you get home through all the years? No passport, no photo possible. No resemblance to anyone living or dead. Tenderly peering into windows

John Foxx's *Tiny Colour Movies* is a welcome addition to this decade's rich cache of hauntological releases.

Foxx's music has always had an intimate relationship with film. Like sound recording, photography – with its capturing of lost moments, its presentation of absences – has an inherently hauntological dimension. It wouldn't be an exaggeration to say that Foxx's entire musical career has been about relating the hauntology of the visual with the hauntology of sound, transposing the eerie calmness and stillness of photography and painting onto the passional agitation of rock.

In the case of *Tiny Colour Movies*, the relationship between the visual and the sonic is an explicit motivating factor. The inspiration for the album was the film collection of Arnold Weizcs-Bryant. Weizcs-Bryant collects only films that are short – no movie in his collection is longer than eight minutes long – and that have been 'made outside commercial consideration for the sheer pleasure of film. This category can include found film, the home movie, the repurposed movie fragment.' The album emerged when, a few weeks after he attended a showing of some of Weizcs-Bryant films in Baltimore, Foxx found himself unable to forget 'the beauty and strangeness' of Weizcs-Bryant's movies – 'juxtapositions of underwater automobiles, the highways of Los

Angeles, movies made from smoke and light, discarded surveillance footage from 1964 New York hotel rooms' – so he decided 'to give in to it – to see what would happen if [he] made a small collection of musical pieces using the memory of those Tiny Colour Movies.'

The result is Foxx's most (un)timely LP since 1980's *Metamatic*. *Tiny Colour Movies* fits right into the out of joint time of hauntology. Belbury Poly's Jim Jupp cites *Metamatic* as a major touchstone, and time has bent so that the influence and the influenced now share an uncanny contemporaneity. Certainly, many of the tracks on *Tiny Colour Movies* – synthetic but oneiric, psychedelic but artificial – resemble Ghost Box releases. This is an electronic sound removed from the hustle and bustle of the present. An obvious comparison for a track like the majestically mournful 'Skyscraper' would be Vangelis' *Blade Runner* soundtrack, but, in the main, the synthetic textures are relieved from the pressure of signifying the Future. Instead, they evoke a timeless Now where the urgencies of the present have been suspended. Some of the best tracks – especially the closing quartet of 'Shadow City', 'Interlude', 'Thought Experiment' and 'Hand Held Skies' – are slivers of sheer atmosphere, delicate and slight. They are gateways to what Heronbone used to call 'slowtime', a time of meditative detachment from the commotions of the current.

I constantly feel a distant kind of longing. The longest song, the song of longing. I walk the same streets like a fading ghost. Flickering grey suit. The same avenues, squares, parks, colonnades, like a ghost. Over the years I find places I can go through, some process of recognition. Remnants of other almost forgotten places. Always returning.

Tiny Colour Movies is a distillation of an aesthetic Foxx has dedicatedly explored since Ultravox's *Systems of Romance*.

Although Foxx is most associated with a future-shocked amnesiac catatonia ('I used to remember/ now it's all gone/ world war something/ we were somebody's sons'), there has always been another trance-mode – more beatific and gently blissful, but no less impersonal or machinic – operative in Foxx's sound, even on the McLuhanite *Metamatic*.

Psychedelia had explicitly emerged as a reference point on *Systems of Romance* (1978) – particularly on tracks such as 'When You Walk Through Me' and 'Maximum Acceleration', with their imagery of liquifying cities and melting time ('locations change/ the angles change/ even the streets get re-arranged'). There might have been the occasional nod to the psychedelia of the past – 'When You Walk Through Me' stole the drum pattern from 'Tomorrow Never Knows' for instance – but *Systems of Romance* was remarkable for its attempt to repeat psychedelia 'in–becoming' rather than through plodding re-iteration. Foxx's psychedelia was sober, clean-shaven, dressed in smartly anonymous Magritte suits; its locale, elegantly overgrown cities from the dreams of Wells, Delvaux and Ernst.

The reference to Delvaux and Ernst is not idle, since Foxx's songs, like Ballard's stories and novels, often seemed to take place inside Surrealist paintings. This is not only a matter of imagery, but also of mood and tone (or, *cata*tone); there is a certain languor, a radically depersonalised serenity on loan from dreams here. 'If anything,' Ballard wrote in his 1966 essay on Surrealism, 'Coming of the Unconscious', 'surrealist painting has one dominant characteristic: a glassy isolation, as if all the objects in its landscapes had been drained of their emotional associations, the accretions of sentiment and common usage.' It's not surprising that Surrealism should so often turn up as a reference in psychedelia's 'derangement of the senses'.

The derangement in Foxx's psychedelia has always been a gentle affair, disquieting in its very quietude. That is perhaps because the machinery of perceptual re-engineering seemed to be painting, photography and fiction more than drugs per se. One suspects that the psychotropic agent most active on/in Foxx's sensibility is *light*. As he explained in an interview from 1983: 'some people at certain times seem to have a light inside them, it's just a feeling you get about someone, it's kind of radiance – and it's something that's always intrigued me – it's something I've covered before in songs like 'Slow Motion' and 'When You Walk Through Me'. I like that feeling of calm. . . It's like William Burroughs summed it up perfectly – "I had a feeling of stillness and wonder."'

There is a clear Gnostic dimension to this. For the Gnostics, the World was both *heavy* and *dark,* and you got a glimpse of the Outside through *glimmers* and *shimmers* (two recurrent words in Foxx's vocabulary). Around the time of *Systems of Romance,* Foxx's cover art shifted from harsh Warhol/Heartfield cut/paste towards gentle detournements of Renaissance paintings. What Foxx appeared to discover in Da Vinci and Botticelli is a Catholicism divested not only of pagan carnality but of the suffering figure of Christ, and returned to an impersonal Gnostic encounter with radiance and luminescence.

What is suppressed in postmodern culture is not the Dark but the Light side. We are far more comfortable with demons than angels. Whereas the demonic appears cool and sexy, the angelic is deemed to be embarrassing and sentimental. (Wim Wenders' excruciatingly cloying and portentous *Wings of Desire* is perhaps the most spectacular failed contemporary attempt to render the angelic.) Yet, as Rudolf Otto establishes in *The Idea of the Holy,* encounters with angels are as disturbing, traumatic and overwhelming as encounters with demons. After all, what could be more shattering, unassimilable and incomprehensible in our hyper-stressed, constantly disappointing and overstimulated lives, than the sensation of *calm joy*? Otto, a conservative Christian, argued that all religious experience has its roots in what is initially misrecognised as 'daemonic dread'; he saw encounters with ghosts, similarly, as a perverted version of what the Christian person would experience religiously. But Otto's account is an attempt to fit the abstract and traumatic encounter with 'angels' and 'demons' into a settled field of meaning. Otto's word for religious experience is the numinous. But perhaps we can rescue the numinous *from* the religious. Otto delineates many variants of the numinous; the most familiar to us now would be 'spasms and convulsions' leading to 'the strangest excitements, to intoxicated frenzy, to transport, and to ecstasy'. But far more uncanny in the ultra-agitated, present is that mode of the numinous which 'come(s) sweeping like a gentle tide,' pervading the mind with a tranquil mood of deepest worship.' Foxx's instrumental music – on *Tiny Colour Movies* and on the three *Cathedral Oceans* CDs, and with Harold Budd on the *Transluscence* and *Drift Music* LPs – has been eerily successful in rendering this alien tranquillity. On *Transluscence* in particular, where Budd's limpid piano chords hang like dust subtly diffusing in sunlight, you can feel your nervous system slowing to a reptile placidity. This is not an inner but Outer calm; not a discovery of a cheap New Age 'real' self, but a positive alienation, in which the cold pastoral freezing into a tableau is experienced as a release from identity.

Dun Scotus' concept of the haecceity – the 'here and now' – seems particularly apposite here. Deleuze and Guattari seize upon this in *A Thousand Plateaus* as a depersonalised mode of individuation in which everything – the breath of the wind, the quality of the light – plays a part. A certain use of film – think, particularly, of the aching stillness in Kubrick and Tarkovsky – seems especially set up to attune us to haecceity; as does the polaroid, a capturing of a haecceity which is *itself* a haecceity.

The impersonal melancholy that *Tiny Colour Movies* produces is similar to the oddly wrenching affect you get from a website like Found Photos. It is precisely the decontextualised quality of these images, the fact that there is a discrepancy between the importance that the people in the photographs place upon what is happening and its complete irrelevance to us, which produces a charge that can be quietly overwhelming. Foxx wrote about this effect in his deeply moving short story, 'The Quiet Man'. The figure is alone in a depopulated London, watching home movies made by people he never knew. 'He was fascinated by all the tiny intimate details of these films, the jerky figures waving from seaside and garden at weddings and birthdays and baptisms, records of whole families and their pets growing and changing through the years.'

'Here you see old sunlight from other times and other lives', Foxx observes in his evocative sleevenotes for *Tiny Colour Movies*. To leaf through *other people's* family photos, to see moments that were of intense emotional significance for them but which mean nothing to you, is, necessarily, to reflect on the times of high drama in your own life, and to achieve a kind of distance that is at once dispassionate and powerfully affecting. That is why the – beautifully, painfully – dilated moment in Tarkovsky's *Stalker* where the camera lingers over talismanic objects that were once saturated with meaning, but are now saturated only with water is for me the most moving scene in cinema. It is as if we are seeing the urgencies of our lives through the eyes of an Alien–God. Otto claims that the sense of the numinous is associated with feelings of our own fundamental worthlessness, experienced with a 'piercing acuteness [and] accompanied by the most uncompromising judgment of self-depreciation'. But, contrary to today's ego psychology, which hectors us into reinforcing our sense of self (all the better to 'sell ourselves'), the awareness of our own Nothingness is of course a pre-requisite for a feeling of grace. There is a melancholy dimension to this grace precisely because it involves a radical distanciation from what is ordinarily most important to us.

He stood in the soft beams of sunshine diffused by the

curtains, caught for a moment in the stillness of the room, watching the dust swirling slowly golden through patches of light that fell across the carpets and furniture, feeling a strange closeness to the vanished woman. Being here and touching her possessions in the dusty intimacy of these rooms was like walking through her life, everything of her was here but for the physical presence, and in some ways that was the least important part of her for him.

Longing and *aching* are words that recur throughout Foxx's work. 'Blurred Girl' from *Metamatic* – its lovers 'standing close, never quite touching' – would almost be the perfect Lacanian love song, in which the desired object is always approached, never attained, and what is enjoyed is suspension, deferral and circulation *around* the object, rather than possession of it – 'are we running still? or are we standing still?' On *Tiny Colour Machines*, as on *Cathedral Oceans* and the albums with Budd, where there are no words, this feeling of enjoyable melancholy is rendered by the minimally disturbed stillness and barely perturbed poise of the sounds themselves.

I can detect tiny edges of time leaking through. I feel nothing is completely separate. At some point everything leaks into everything else. The trick is in finding the places. They are slowly moving. Drifting. You can only do this accidentally. If you set out to do it deliberately you will always fail.

It is only when you remember, only then will you realise that you caught a glimpse. While you were talking to someone, or thinking of something else. When your attention was diverted. Just a hint, a glimmer, a shade.

Much later, you will remember. Without really knowing why. Vague peripheral sensations gather. Some fraction of a long rhythm is beginning to be recognised. The hidden frequencies and tides of the city. Geometry of coincidence.

Listening to *Tiny Colour Movies*, as with all of Foxx's best records, one has a sense of returning to a dream-place. Foxx's shifting or shadow city, with its Ernst-like 'green arcades' and De Chirico colonnades, is urban space as seen from the unconscious on a derive; an intensive space in which elements of London, Rome, Florence and other, more secret places are given an oneiric consistency.
I lost myself in that city more than 20 years ago.

Sleeping in cheap boarding houses. A ghost with leaves in his pocket and no address. The good face half blind. A nebula of songs and memories slipping in and out of focus. Someone told me he was there but it didn't register at the time. The voice came unfocussed from all around. Still and quiet like the shadows of an ocean in the moving trees.

Indented text from John Foxx's 'Quiet Man' and 'Shifting City' texts and the Cathedral Oceans *booklet.*

Electricity and Ghosts: Interview with John Foxx

k-punk post, September 23, 2006

MF: Which films were most influential on you early on?

JF: Oh, very cheap science fiction films mostly. There was one particularly memorable movie called *Robot Monster*, so bad it was surreal, it had the quality of a dream, an exceptional movie.

I now think it's one of the best films I've ever seen, partly because it had no regard for plot or anything else recognizable as conventional cinema of the time. This of course made it an event of inestimable importance to me, because, as a child I took it all literally – swallowed it whole, like Alice's potion.

And like that potion, it allowed entry to an unexpected universe. One which had unfathomable logic and laws which were endlessly flexible. A deeply exhilarating experience. I still dream sequences from it, or rather I seem to have permanently incorporated sections of it into my dream grammar.

Growing up with movies as a child and being subjected to them before I could understand the adult preoccupations and motivations involved in the plots, pitched me into conscripting these films as a personal grammar. I had no choice, so I ended up with this Lynchian reservoir of sequences that carried every dread and joy and everything in between.

These events are still imbued with unfathomable, inexplicable, tantalizing mystery, because I couldn't really understand them at all. It was hallucinogenic and vivid, and provided me with an image bank and a gorgeous range of emotional tones I still haven't managed to exhaust.

Much later, when I got to 'Cinema' – or the official critical view of it – the more intellectual, often French aspect. I didn't recognise it at all.

Later, I ended up enjoying this sort of perspective a little, but in a rather disengaged, sceptical way. To me, it seems a method of criticism which is often marvelously baroque and can be engaging, but has little to do with my own experience of Cinema.

I can only deal with it as a marvelous fictional construct, like medieval religion or quantum physics – a consensual social hallucination developed by a priesthood. In the end it's as tangential as my own individual one.

But that very crude, improvisational, amateurish side of cinema or filmmaking, I continue to find deeply fascinating. Take for example Ed Wood's films. He made them simply because he was in a place where it could be done.

I think of Ed Wood as a sort of advanced naive artist. He was among the first to make cut-up movies. He achieved this by using props he came across in warehouses and stock footage he discovered in the film vaults of Hollywood cutting rooms, then he built movies around these fragments.

This is the art of collage and sampling. It is art as found object, as coincidence, as accident, as Surrealism, as Dada, as Situationism. All made possible and motivated also by the dynamo of American opportunism, but with great love and inadequacy and tenderness.

Ed Wood was doing, fifty years ago, what the avant garde are only now beginning to do with film.

(This is also very similar to the way rock 'n' roll often manages to parallel or prefigure avant garde concepts, by arriving at them from a totally different direction. Pop is such a virile mongrel it's capable of effortlessly demonstrating, realising, manifesting, absorbing, remaking any sort of academic intellectual concept. It can do this so well, it often makes any parallel or previous version appear weak or even redundant).

An admiration for that sort of visceral, sensual, opportunistic, native intelligence led to an interest in, and respect for, home video and super-8 – very low grade domestic ways of making films – I suddenly realised there was a whole other world there, one which hadn't been properly discussed, but as real, in fact more real and potentially at least as powerful, as official cinema.

MF: The film collection you refer to in the sleeve notes to *Tiny Colour Movies* – you write about it very beautifully. Are there any plans for those films to be shown in the UK?

JF: Thanks. I'd like to – there are some problems with these fragments, because they're so small. They're physically difficult things, and they're unique irreplaceable and very fragile, so you can only ever show digital copies of them. But it would be interesting to do something like that. I'm beginning to look at some possibilities now, working with Mike Barker, who has accumulated a marvellous archive, and we're discussing this with some film festivals.

MF: I noticed you thanked Paul Auster in the sleeve notes, why was that?

JF: Paul Auster has is very interesting to me, because I wrote this thing called 'The Quiet Man' years ago, in the 80s, in fact I'm still writing it. Then I read the *New York Trilogy*, and it struck so many chimes. It was as if I'd written it, or it was the book I should have written. I have to be very careful to find my way around it now.

Such occurrences are simultaneously rewarding and terrifying. They illustrate the fact that there is something in the air, which is tremendously heartening after working alone for years, yet they scare you because it feels as if someone has published first, and therefore registered their claim to where you discovered gold.

I simply wanted to acknowledge the effect, and the odd sort of encouragement of recognised themes, as well as a continuing parallel interest in the idea of lost movies and fragments

MF: There's a certain kind of London affect that's interesting, of stillness, and the city being overgrown, which is sort of recurrent in your work – where's that come from do you think?

JF: When I first came to London it seemed a great deal like Lancashire, where I'd come from. But Lancashire had fallen into ruin. The factories had closed, the economy had faltered. We felt like the Incas after the Spaniards had passed. Helpless, nostalgic savages adrift in the ruins.

I grew up playing in empty factories, huge places which were overgrown. I remember trees growing out of the buildings. I remember a certain moments of looking at it all and thinking what it would have been like when it was all working. What life might be like, if it were all working still.

All of my family worked in mills and factories and mines. And all this was gently subsiding, spinning away.

Coming to London, I couldn't help but wonder if it might also fall into dissolution. Then I saw a picture a friend had. It was a realistic painting of what appeared to be a view over a jungle from a high place. Gradually you came to realise that it was a view of an overgrown city from a tower, then you realised that this panorama was from a ruined Centre Point and you could see Tottenham Court Road, Oxford Street, Charing Cross road in the undergrowth. It felt like a revelation. It manifested so perfectly this vision I'd had of everything becoming overgrown, an overgrown London. A vision of longing and nostalgia tinged with fear.

I would often experience a feeling of stillness and wonder as I walked through certain parts of London. I often walked through empty buildings and neglected, overlooked places and they would replay that sensation very strongly.

I went to Shoreditch, in 1982, and made a studio there. When we first went into the studio building it had trees growing out of the windows on the upper stories. It was very like Lancashire, that whole area was derelict, had been abandoned, because that had been the industrial bit of the East End. Now there was no-one there, it was empty. It gave me that calm drifting feeling of recognition. There was some kind of collective image of overgrown and abandoned cities at that time. Perhaps it's always there. Such images were present in Ballard, Burroughs, Philip K Dick. In those science fiction authors writing about the near future – conducting thought experiments, exploring likely consequences and views of the unrecognised present, which I think is very valuable. They offer perspectives and meditations on our vanity and endeavours. As such they maintain continuity with a long line of imagery, from religious myths and folk stories to science fiction.

MF: It seems to have a real unconscious resonance, this idea of overgrown cities, it's obviously there in surrealist paintings, which seem to be a constant reference, especially in your early work –

JF: Yes, there's that side of it too. In science fiction films you often get those recurrent images, which I think are very beautiful, of someone walking through an abandoned city.

We have accumulated a range of such images all along the line, from folk and fairytales, to the actual construction of follies and romantic overgrown gardens, to the truly dislocated, such as Piranesi's ruins and prisons, to Max Ernst's paintings, or Breughel's *Tower of Babel*, or the background urban locations in Bosch, as well as De Chirico's townscapes and shadows.

Planet of the Apes has one of the most shocking and resonant – the end of original movie, where we see the Statue of Liberty tilted in the sand. A real jolt, the first time you see it. A modern take on Shelley's *Ozymandias*.

The radiance I sometimes refer to occupies this sort of area. I often see people as if in a frozen moment and they seem to have an internal glow inside them. Their skin seems translucent and they carry their own time. I feel calm and distant and warm from this. It can happen in an instant. In very mundane urban situations. You realise you are not looking at a single person, but at a sort of stream or cascade.

It happened yesterday in a supermarket. I happened to glance at a young woman who looked like a transfigured hidden Madonna. She wore jeans and a teeshirt, an ordinary woman. But equally, she was a continuity, a lovely genetic physical thread to other times, both previous and ahead and still unformed. She simply glowed. Quietly and unknowingly luminous. The Eternal Woman.

MF: The sort of feelings you deal with are more abstract; it's like you go to those states without reference to the way they've traditionally been coded, really. You often use the word 'angelic', or 'angel'. . .

JF: Yes, very perilous territory, especially since these terms have since been co-opted by New Agers. I'll put on the grey suit to dispel all that.

Many of these spring from what I think of as 'thought experiments' – things I employ all the time, as a tool to get at half buried or emerging realisations. If you're at all interested, I'll try to outline a few.

Firstly, the idea interested me – still does – of parallel evolutions – imagine something that may have evolved alongside us, something we're not quite aware of yet, that we haven't yet discovered.

That may include things which exist in other planes or by other means, or things which resemble human beings so well that we assume them to be human, but they may not be. Yet they live among us undetected – the possibility that other forms of life may have evolved alongside us, but invisible because of their proximity.

'Hiding in plain sight' is a great idea, something that's very interesting in itself – on one level connected with sleight of hand and parlour tricks and conmen, but on the other hand, very subtle, intuition led perceptions. It could give rise to situations that are tremendously moving, fragile, tender. Metaphorically very resonant.

Another one – I'm also very interested in the concept of a singularity. An event that only happens once, or once every thousand or million years.

There may be rhythms which extend over tens of millions of years and are therefore unrecognisable to us, except as single unconnectable and unexplainable events.

But the fact that we have no context to fit them into doesn't mean they don't happen.

Yet another thought experiments posits the concept of Angels as a connection between things. An entity that only exists between. A sort of web or connection. They arise purely as an intrinsic, invisible and unsuspected component of the evolution of the ecology that supports whatever they exist between. They cannot exist on their own.

Many of us have these little incidents – everything from coincidences onward – things that we can't explain using the references we commonly employ.

I'm very interested in those things, always have been. Through those odd things, we glimpse something that's outside the way we usually look at the world, and realise there might be another way of looking at it, an alternate perception to the one we have, and I think that's a very valuable possibility to keep hold of. The awareness that maybe there are gaps in our perception that we aren't able to fill yet.

MF: Yes, because I think one of the most powerful things – which comes out in *Tiny Colour Movies* but in retrospect has always been there –is that you're able to deal with positive, affirmatory feelings that are eerie and uncanny, and possess a certain kind of calm serenity.

JF: Good, somehow that's always been a vital component of that sort of experience, for me. A sensation of utter calm and stillness. Miles away from any agitation. It seems deeply positive.

It's an opposite to the excitement you get from, say, rock and roll. . . I think in general we like to stir ourselves up in various ways, using art or using media or whatever, and I think it's just as valid to move against the norm, and the norm at the moment is to speed everything up.

I mean, that's what we're trying to attain, aren't we, through media? – That awful maximisation of time and efficient transmission of 'information'. Some of this is economic – time equals money – and some is simply done because it can be done, and has become an unquestioned convention.

If you could time-jump to show the average TV ad of today to someone 20 or 30 years ago, they wouldn't understand it. The ad would depend on the viewer's perception speed and also on a series of recent references. Our parents simply weren't fast enough, they hadn't been accelerated as we have been by media and the pace of modern life, and they also don't have the inculcated, busy reference chain.

Acceleration is also kind of exciting and interesting, I mean I really enjoy it, sometimes – but it equally leads you to think 'what happens if you do the opposite?'– it might be just as pleasurable and just as valid to do that.

So, one of the things I want to try to do is work on the other end of this spectrum – see what happens when you slow things down.

I was surprised when I was doing the first music for *Cathedral Oceans*, using echoes that were 30 seconds long, so the rhythms were 30 seconds between the beats.

It was very interesting slowing down enough to work with that intuitively. You had to do it, you had to synchronise with the track in order to be able to work with it. And it's very interesting what kind of state you get into – intense, yet calm and tranquil. A sort of trance state.

MF: I think it's particularly on the LPs with Harold Budd, where you get that sort of aching plateau, where you slow down so much that any peturbation has a massive effect really.

Harold was one of the first people who got that right, I think. One of the very first to have sufficient courage to leave enough space in the music and not fill spaces unnecessarily. Not decorate. Takes an awful lot of quiet courage to do that.

When this is done, it allows an alternative ecology to emerge – one based on events that are much less frequent. And that, of course, affects their significance. You are drawn to them in a sort of smiling fascination, rather than the usual pop music method of lapel grabbing bombardment.

MF: It seems to be something similar to what you get in Tarkovsky films – where either people say 'oh, this is too slow I can't stand it', or they enter into the slow time of the film and anything that happens almost becomes too much.

JF: Exactly, you can concentrate on any event very thoroughly, when that mode of perception is made available. Events become stately and welcome and valued and significant, and their arrival and departure can be fully experienced. The lack of jostling allows that sort of elegant notional space to open up.

It functions at the other end of the spectrum from commercial TV and cinema, and of rock & roll. Both ends can be equally interesting, I think.

MF: It seems to me that you've always imposed the stillness and calmness of painting and photography or a certain type of film onto the agitation of rock, really. Certain kind of dreams - the dreams we're most familiar with – are hyper-agitated, full of urgency etc, but there's another type of dream quality you seem to get to where those urgencies are suspended and you're out of that everyday life push-and-pull, really. I wondered - there seems to be a certain aching, or longing quality - these are words you seem to use a lot in your music...

JF: Well, dreams are a very important component. I realised that it is not simply the image you present yourself with, in a dream, which is important – it's also the emotional tone of the scene. You can see a cloud, but this will be accompanied by a sense of wonder or by a sense of dread, and it is that accompaniment which determines its meaning.

The employment of these images and tones are some of the things that everyone shares, aren't they? They're composed of bits of unique personal events and references and memories, such as longings that you might have had when you're a child.

When your parents are away even for an hour it feel as though it goes on forever and you really deeply miss them – and the abstraction, the tone component of that just carries on through life. Gets applied to different situations. These longings – and all other emotional parts of the spectrum – join the repertoire of tones we carry and apply. Some moments last forever.

MF: But there's almost a positive side, almost an enjoyment of longing and ache.

JF: Oh yes, where the observer part of you acknowledges an emotional connection with the rest. Simultaneously you feel as though you are very integrated, yet you are being gently pulled away from yourself. Gently disengaged.

MF: Isn't the 'emotionless' quality of your music more to do with a certain kind of calm?

JF: Yes, it's quite a complex thing, a compound. There are states where there's a sensation of time passing, things changing, knowing the world is changing, falling in on itself, and reforming. And you may even be in the process of doing just that yourself.

But there are moments where you just stand by and watch it all, where you're aware of it, in a moment that seems to go on forever. So it's something of standing in a still place and watching the patterns in passing crowds and even in your own life. It can be a very powerful experience.

That stillness, and the maintenance of a quiet dignity in the face of insurmountable circumstances can be immensely moving to witness.

It can be much more effective and moving if someone tells the story in an unemotional or undramatic way. You find that in Ishiguro. *Remains of the Day* or *Never Let Me Go* are good examples of that kind of writing, where the most important components remain unstated. *The Leopard* is suffused with, and is dependent on a variant of this.

It's also allied to a device used in different ways by Charlie Chaplin, Buster Keaton and Cary Grant. – An archetypical figure attempts to retain dignity in the face of the worldly chaos while remaining ever hopeful of romance.

And with Ballard and Burroughs, you get an almost gentlemanly, middle class version of a similar sort of stance – mayhem of all kinds observed from a disengaged viewpoint.

Another Grey World: Darkstar, James Blake, Kanye West, Drake and 'Party Hauntology'

'It's a really grey-sounding synth, really organic and grainy. We call them "swells" – where synthesisers start quite minimal and then develop into a huge chord, before progressing. I felt like it wouldn't be right if we just carried on with that dayglo Hyperdub sound of a couple of years ago. I mean I love those songs, but it already feels like a lifetime away.' I felt vindicated when I read these remarks of Darkstar's James Young in an interview with Dan Hancox. When I first heard the album about which Young is talking – 2010's *North* – the phrase that came to my mind was 'Another Grey World'. The landscape of *North* felt like the verdant Max Ernst forest of Eno's *Another Green World* become ash.

. . . with winter ahead of us

The depressive's world is black and/ or white, (you only have to remember the covers of Joy Division's *Unknown Pleasures* and *Closer*), but *North* does not (yet) project a cold world entirely swathed in snow. North is the direction that the album is heading towards, not a destination it has reached. Its landscape is colourless rather than black, its mood tentative – it is grey as in unresolved, a grey area. This is an album defined by its negative capability of remaining in doubts, disquiet and dissatisfactions that it unable to name. It is grey as in The Cure's 'All Cats Are Grey' from *Faith*, a record that stood between the spidery psyche-delia of *Seventeen Seconds* and the unrelieved darkness of *Pornography*. Yet *North* is ultimately too jittery to muster the glacial fatalism of *Faith* but what *North* has in common with The Cure's great records is the sense of total immersion in a mood. It is a work that came out of method immersion: Young told Dan Hancox that, as they recorded *North*, the group had listened obsessively to Radiohead, Burial, the Human League and the first album by Orchestral Manouevres in the Dark. The record demands the same kind of involvement, which is perhaps why some found it unengaging. On a casual listen, the very unresolved quality of the tracks could seem simply undercooked. James Buttery's vocals could come off as limp, anaemic. In addition, many were disappointed by Darkstar's failure to provide an album full of the 'robotic 2-step' that they had invented on 'Aidy's Girl is a Computer'. In fact, they made the robotic 2-step album but ditched it, dissatisfied with its lack of ambition. (This wholly completed album that was never released is one of several parallels with Burial.) 'Aidy's Girl is a Computer' apart, if you heard *North* without knowing the history, you wouldn't assume any connection with dubstep. At the same time, *North* isn't straightforwardly a return to a pre-dance sound. It is more a continuation of a certain mode of electronic pop that was prematurely terminated sometime in the mid-80s: like New Order if they hadn't abandoned the sleek cybernetic mausoleum that Martin Hannett built for them on *Movement*.

Except, of course, that it is not possible to simply continue that trajectory as if nothing had happened. Darkstar acknowledge the present only negatively. It impinges on their music in perhaps the only way it can, as a failure of the future, as a temporal disorder that has infected the voice, causing it to stutter and sibilate, to fragment into strange slithering shards. Part of what separates Darkstar from their synthpop forebears is the fact that the synthesiser no longer connotes futurity. But Darkstar are not retreating from a vivid sense of futurity – because there is no such futurity from which they could retreat. This becomes clear when you compare the Darkstar cover of 'Gold' to the Human League original. It's not just that one is no more futuristic than the other; it's that *neither* are futuristic. The Human League track is clearly a superseded futurism, while the Darkstar track seems to come after the future. It's this sense of living in an interregnum, that makes *North* so (un)timely. Where Burial made contact with the secret sadness underlying the boom, Darkstar articulate the sense of foreboding that is everywhere after the economic crash of 2008. *North* is certainly full of references to lost companionship: the album can be read as an oblique take on a love affair gone wrong.

Our fate's not to share . . ..

The connection between us gone . . ..

But the very focus on the love couple rather than the rave massive is itself symptomatic of a turn inward. In a discussion that Simon Reynolds and I had about *North* shortly after it was released, Reynolds argued that it was a mistake to talk as if rave was bereft of emotion. Rave was a music saturated with affect, but the affect involved wasn't associated with romance or intro- spection The introspective turn in 21st century (post)dance music was therefore not a turn towards emotion, it was a shift from collectively experienced affect to privatised emotions. There was an intrinsic and inevitable sadness to this inward turn, regardless of whether the music was officially sad or not. The twinning of romance and introspection, love and its disappoint- ments, runs through 20th century pop. By contrast, dance music since disco offered up another kind of emotional palette, based in a different model of escape from the miseries of individual selfhood.

The 21st century has often felt like the comedown after a speed binge, or the exile back into privatised selfhood, and the songs on *North* have the jittery clarity of Prozac withdrawal.

It's significant that most of the digital interference on *North* is applied to James Buttery's voice. Much of the vocal sounds as if it has been recorded on a shaky mobile phone connection. I'm reminded of Franco Berardi's arguments about the relationship between informational overload and depression. Berardi's argument is not that the dot.com crash caused depression, but the reverse: the crash was caused by the excessive strain put on people's nervous systems by new informational technologies. Now, more than a decade after the dot.com crash and the density of data has massively increased. The paradigmatic labourer is now the call centre worker – the banal cyborg, punished whenever they unplug from the communicative matrix. On *North*, James Buttery, afflicted by all manner of digital palsies, sounds like a cyborg whose implants and interfaces have come loose, learning to be a man again, and not liking it very much.

North is like Kanye West's 2008 album *808s and Heartbreak* with all the gloss removed. There is the same method melancholia, the same anchoring in early 80s synthpop, explicitly flagged in *808*'s case by the cover design's echo of Peter Saville's sleeves for New Order's *Blue Monday* and *Power, Corruption and Lies*. The opening track 'Say You Will' sounds like it has been worked up out of the crisp synthetic chill of Joy Division's 'Atmosphere' and the funereal drum tattoo of New Order's 'In A Lonely Place'. As with *North*, though, the 80s parallels are disrupted by the digital effects used on the voice. *808s and Heartbreak* pioneered the use of Auto–Tune, which would subsequently come to dominate R&B and hip-hop from the late 00s onwards. In a sense, the conspicuous use of Auto-Tune – that is to say, its use as an effect, as opposed to its official purpose as a device to correct a singer's pitch – was a 90s throwback, since this was popularised by Cher on her 1998 single 'Believe'. Auto-Tune is in many ways the sonic equivalent of digital airbrushing, and the (over) use of the two technologies (alongside the increasing prevalence of cosmetic surgery) result in a look and feel that is hyperbolically enhanced rather than conspicuously artificial. If anything is the signature of 21st century consumer culture, is this feeling of a digitally upgraded normality – a perverse yet ultra-banal normality, from which all flaws have been erased.

On *808s and Heartbreak*, we hear the sobs in the heart of the 21st century pleasuredome. Kanye's lachrymose android shtick reaches its maudlin depths on the astonishing 'Pinocchio Story'. This is the kind of Auto-Tuned lament you might expect neo-Pinocchio and android-Oedipus David from Spielberg's *AI* (2001) to sing; a little like Britney Spears's 'Piece Of Me', you can either hear this as the moment when a commodity achieves self-consciousness, or when a human realises he or she has become a commodity. It's the soured sound at the end of the rainbow, an electro as desolated as Suicide's infernal synth-opera 'Frankie Teardrop'.

A secret sadness lurks behind the 21st century's forced smile. This sadness concerns hedonism itself, and it's no surprise that it is in hip-hop – a genre that has become increasingly aligned with consumerist pleasure over the past 20-odd years – that this melancholy has registered most deeply. Drake and Kanye West are both morbidly fixated on exploring the miserable hollowness at the core of super-affluent hedonism. No longer motivated by hip-hop's drive to conspicuously consume – they long ago acquired anything they could have wanted – Drake and West instead dissolutely cycle through easily available pleasures, feeling a combination of frustration, anger, and self-disgust, aware that something is missing, but unsure exactly what it is. This hedonist's sadness – a sadness as widespread as it is disavowed – was nowhere better captured than in the doleful way that Drake sings, 'we threw a party/ yeah, we threw a party,' on *Take Care*'s 'Marvin's Room'.

It's no surprise to learn that Kanye West is an admirer of James Blake. There's an affective as well as sonic affinity between parts of Kanye's *808s and Heartbreak* and *My Beautiful Dark Twisted Fantasy* and Blake's two albums. You might say that Blake's whole MO is a partial re-naturalisation of the digitally manipulated melancholy Kanye auditioned on *808s*: soul music after the Auto-Tune cyborg. But liberated from the penthouse-prison of West's ego, unsure of itself, caught up in all kinds of impasses, the disaffection languishes listlessly, not always even capable of recognizing itself as sadness.

You might go so far as to say that the introspective turn reached a kind of conclusion with Blake's 2013 album *Overgrown*. In his transformation from dubstep to pop, Blake had gone from digitally manipulating his own voice to becoming a singer; from constructing tracks to writing songs. The initial motivation for Blake's approach to the song no doubt came from Burial, whose combination of jittery 2-step beats and R&B vocal samples pointed the way to a possible vision of 21st century pop. It was as if Burial had produced the dub versions; now the task was to construct the originals, and that entailed replacing the samples with an actual vocalist.

Listening back to Blake's records in chronological sequence is like hearing a ghost gradually assume material form; or it's like hearing the song form (re)coalescing out of digital ether. A track such as 'I Only Know (What I Know Now)' from the *Klavierwerke* EP is gorgeously insubstantial – it's the merest ache, Blake's voice a series of sighs and unintelligible pitch-shifted hooks, the production mottled and waterlogged, the arrangement intricate and fragile, conspicuously inorganic in the way that it makes no attempt to smooth out the elements of the montage. The voice is a smattering of traces and tics, a spectral special effect scattered across the mix. But with Blake's self-titled debut album, something like traditional sonic priorities were restored. The reinvention of pop that his early releases promised was now seemingly given up, as Blake's de-fragmented voice moved to the front of the mix, and implied or partially disassembled songs became 'proper' songs, complete with un-deconstructed piano and organ. Electronics and some vocal manipulation remained, but they were now assigned a decorative function. Blake's blue-eyed soul vocals, and the way that his tracks combined organ (or organ-like sounds) with electronica, made him reminiscent of a half-speed Steve Winwood.

Just as with Darkstar's *North*, Blake's turn to songs met with a mixed response. Many who were enthusiastic about the early EPs were disappointed or mildly dismayed by *James Blake*. Veiling and implying an object is the surest route to producing the impression of sublimity. Removing the veils and bringing that object to the fore risks de-sublimation, and some found Blake's actual songs unequal to the virtual ones his early records had induced them into hallucinating. Blake's voice was as cloyingly overpowering as it was non-specific in its feeling. The result was a quavering, tremulous vagueness, which was by no means clarified by lyrics that were similarly allusive/elusive. The album came over as if it were earnestly entreating us to feel, without really telling us what is was we were supposed to be feeling. Perhaps it's this emotional obliqueness that contributes to what Angus Finlayson, in his review of *Overgrown* for FACT, characterised as the strangeness of the songs on *James Blake*. They seemed, Finlayson said, like 'half-songs, skeletal place-markers for some fuller arrangement yet to come.' The journey into 'proper' songs was not as complete as it first appeared. It was like Blake had tried to reconstruct the song form with only dub versions or dance mixes as his guide. The result was something scrambled, garbled, solipsistic, a bleary version of the song form that was as frustrating as it was fascinating. The delicate insubstantiality of the early EPs had given way to something that felt overfull. It was like drowning in a warm bath (perhaps with your wrists cut).

On Blake's albums, there is a simultaneous feeling that the tracks are both congested and unfinished, and that incompleteness – the sketchy melodies, the half-hooks, the repeated lines that play like clues to some emotional event never disclosed in the songs themselves – may be why they eventually get under your skin. The oddly indeterminate – irresolute and unresolved – character of Blake's music gives it the quality of gospel music for those who have lost their faith so completely that they have forgotten they ever had it. What survives is only a quavering longing, without object or context, Blake coming off like an amnesiac holding on to images from a life and a narrative that he cannot recover. This negative capability means that *Overgrown* is like an inversion of the oversaturated high-gloss emotional stridency of chart and reality TV pop, which is always perfectly certain of what it is feeling.

Yet there's an unconvincing – or perhaps unconvinced – quality to so much of mainstream culture's hedonism now. Oddly, this is most evident in the annexing of R&B by club music. When former R&B producers and performers embraced dance music, you might have expected an increase in euphoria, an influx of ecstasy. But the reverse has happened, and it's as if many of the dancefloor tracks are pulled down by a hidden gravity, a disowned sadness. The digitally–enhanced uplift in the records by producers such as Flo-Rida, Pitbull and will.i.am is like a poorly photoshopped image or a drug that we've hammered so much we've become immune to its effects. It's hard not to hear these records' demands that we enjoy ourselves as thin attempts to distract from a depression that they can only mask, never dissipate.

In a brilliant essay on The Quietus website, Dan Barrow analysed the tendency in a slew of chartpop over the past few years – including Jay-Z and Alicia Keys's 'Empire State of Mind' Kesha's 'Tik Tok', Flo Rida's 'Club Can't Even Handle Me Yet' – 'to give the listener the pay–off, the sonic money-shot, as soon and as obviously as possible'. Pop has always delivered sugar-sweet pleasure, of course, but, Barrow argues, there's a tyrannical desperation about this new steroid-driven pop. It doesn't seduce; it tyrannises. This, Barrow argues, is 'a crude, overdetermined excess, as if pop were forcing itself back to its defining characteristics – chorus hooks, melody, "accessibility" – and blowing them up to cartoonish size.' There's an analogy to be drawn between this artificially inflated pop and Berardi's discussion of internet pornography and drugs such as Viagra, which, similarly, dispense with seduction and aim directly at pleasure. According to Berardi, remember, we are so overwhelmed by the incessant demands of digital communications, we are simply too busy to engage in arts of enjoyment – highs have to come in a no-fuss, hyperbolic form so that we can quickly return to checking email or updates on social networking sites. Berardi's remarks can give us an angle on the pressures that dance music has been subject to over the last decade. Whereas the digital technology of the 80s and 90s fed the collective experience of the dancefloor, the communicative technology of the 21st century has undermined it, with even clubbers obsessively checking their smartphones. (Beyoncé and Lady Gaga's 'Telephone' – which sees the pair begging a caller to stop bugging them so they can dance – now seems like a last failed attempt to keep the dancefloor free of communicational intrusion.)

Even the most apparently uncomplicated calls to enjoyment can't fully suppress a certain sadness. Take Katy Perry's 'Last Friday Night'. On the face of it, the track is a simple celebration of pleasure ('Last Friday night/ Yeah we maxed our credit cards/ And got kicked out of the bar'). Yet it's not hard to hear something Sisyphean, something purgatorial, in the song's evocation of a (not so) merry-go-round of pleasure that Perry and her friends can never get off: 'Always say we're gonna stop/ This Friday night/ Do it all again . . .' Played at half-speed, this would sound as bleak as early Swans. David Guetta's 'Play Hard' calls up a similarly interminable repetition. Pleasure becomes an obligation that will never let up – 'us hustler's work is never through/ We work hard, play hard' – and hedonism is explicitly paralleled with work: 'Keep partyin' like it's your job'. It's the perfect anthem for an era in which the boundaries between work and non-work are eroded – by the requirement that we are always-on (that, for instance, we will answer emails at any hour of the day), and that we never lose an opportunity to marketise our own subjectivity. In a (not at all trivial) sense, partying *is* now a job. Images of hedonistic excess provide much of the content on Facebook, uploaded by users who are effectively unpaid workers, creating value for the site without being remunerated for it. Partying is a job in another sense – in conditions of objective immiseration and economic downturn, making up the affective deficit is outsourced to us.

Sometimes, a free-floating sadness seeps into the grain of the music itself. On their blog No Good Advice, the blogger J describes the use of a sample from Kaoma's 1989 track 'Lambada' on Jennifer Lopez's 2011 hit 'On The Floor': 'The snatch of 'Lambada' functions as a buried-memory trigger, a sort of party hauntology that lends the song a slight edge of wistful, nostalgic sadness.' There is no reference to sadness in the official text of the track, which is a simple exhortation to dance. So it's as if the sorrow comes from outside, like traces of the waking world incorporated into a dream, or like the grief which creeps into all the embedded worlds in *Inception* (2010).

'Party hauntology' might even be the best name for the dominant 21st century form of pop, the transnational club music produced by Guetta, Flo-Rida, Calvin Harris and will.i.am. But the debts to the past, the failure of the future are repressed here, meaning that the hauntology takes a disavowed form. Take a track like the Black Eyed Peas' immensely popular 'I Gotta Feeling'. Although 'I Gotta Feeling' is ostensibly an optimistic record, there's something forlorn about it. Perhaps that's because of will.i.am's use of Auto-Tune – there seems to be Sparky's Magic Piano-like machinic melancholy intrinsic to the technology itself, something which Kanye drew out rather than invented on *808s and Heartbreak*. In spite of the track's declamatory repetitions, there's a fragile, fugitive quality about the pleasures 'I Gotta

Feeling' so confidently expects. That's partly because 'I Gotta Feeling' comes off more like a memory of a past pleasure than an anticipation of a pleasure that is yet to be felt. The album from which the track comes, *The E.N.D. (The Energy Never Dies)* was – like its predecessor, *The Beginning* – so immersed in Rave that it effectively operated as an act of homage to the genre. *The Beginning*'s 'Time (Dirty Bit)' could have actually passed for a Rave track from the early 90s – the crudeness of its cut and paste montage recalls the ruff 'n' ready textures that samplers would construct at that time, and its borrowing from *Dirty Dancing*'s '(I've Had) The Time of my Life' was just the kind of subversion/sublimation of cheesy source material that Rave producers delighted in. Yet, the Black Eyed Peas' Rave-appropriations didn't function so much as revivals of Rave as denials that the genre had ever happened in the first place. If Rave hasn't yet happened, then there is no need to mourn it. We can act as if we're experiencing all this for the first time, that the future is still ahead of us. The sadness ceases to be something we feel, and instead consists in our temporal predicament itself, and we are like Jack in the Gold Room of the Overlook Hotel, dancing to ghost songs, convincing ourselves that the music of yesteryear is really the music of today.

03: THE STAIN OF PLACE

'Always Yearning For The Time That Just Eluded Us' – Introduction to Laura Oldfield Ford's *Savage Messiah* (Verso, 2011)

June 2011

'I regard my work as diaristic; the city can be read as a palimpsest, of layers of erasure and overwriting,' Laura Oldfield Ford has said. 'The need to document the transient and ephemeral nature of the city is becoming increasingly urgent as the process of enclosure and privatisation continues apace.' The city in question is of course London, and Ford's *Savage Messiah* offers a samizdat counter-history of the capital during the period of neoliberal domination. If *Savage Messiah* is 'diaristic', it is also much more than a memoir. The stories of Ford's own life necessarily bleed into the stories of others, and it is impossible to see the joins. 'This decaying fabric, this unknowable terrain has become my biography, the euphoria then the anguish, layers of memories colliding, splintering and reconfiguring.' The perspective Ford adopts, the voices she speaks in – and which speak through her – are those of the officially defeated: the punks, squatters, ravers, football hooligans and militants left behind by a history which has ruthlessly photoshopped them out of its finance-friendly SimCity. *Savage Messiah* uncovers another city, a city in the process of being buried, and takes us on a tour of its landmarks: The Isle of Dogs . . . The Elephant . . . Westway . . . Lea Bridge . . . North Acton . . . Canary Wharf . . . Dalston . . . Kings Cross . . . Hackney Wick . . .

In one of many echoes of punk culture, Ford calls *Savage Messiah* a 'zine'. She began producing it in 2005, eight years into a New Labour government that had consolidated rather than overturned Thatcherism. The context is bleak. London is a conquered city; it belongs to the enemy. 'The translucent edifices

of Starbucks and Costa Coffee line these shimmering prome-
nades, 'young professionals' sit outside gently conversing in
sympathetic tones.' The dominant mood is one of restoration and
reaction, but it calls itself modernisation, and it calls its divisive
and exclusionary work – making London safe for the super-rich
– *regeneration*. The struggle over space is also a struggle over time
and who controls it. Resist neoliberal modernisation and (so we
are told) you consign yourself to the past. *Savage Messiah's*
London is overshadowed by the looming megalith of 'London
2012', which over the course of the last decade has subsumed
more and more of the city into its banal science fiction *telos*, as
the Olympic Delivery Authority transformed whole areas of East
London into a temporary photo opportunity for global
capitalism. Where once there were 'fridge mountains and
abandoned factories' out of Tarkovsky and Ballard, a semi-
wilderness in the heart of the city, now a much blander desert
grows: spaces for wandering are eliminated, making way for
shopping malls and soon-to-be-abandoned Olympic stadia.
'When I was writing the zines,' Ford remembers, 'I was drifting
through a London haunted by traces and remnants of rave,
anarcho-punk scenes and hybrid subcultures at a time when all
these incongruous urban regeneration schemes were happening.
The idea that I was moving through a spectral city was really
strong, it was as if everything prosaic and dull about the New
Labour version of the city was being resisted by these ghosts of
brutalist architecture, of '90s convoy culture, rave scenes, '80s
political movements and a virulent black economy of scavengers,
peddlers and shoplifters. I think the book could be seen in the
context of the aftermath of an era, where residues and traces of
euphoric moments haunt a melancholy landscape.'

All of these traces are to be eliminated from the Restoration
London that will be celebrated at London 2012. With their
lovingly reproduced junk-strata, overgrowing vegetation and
derelict spaces, *Savage Messiah's* images offer a direct riposte to

the slick digital images which the Olympic Delivery Authority has pasted up in the now heavily policed, restricted and surveilled Lee valley. Blair's Cool Britannia provides the template for an anodyne vision of London designed by the 'creative industries'. Everything comes back as an advertising campaign. It isn't just that the alternatives are written over, or out, it is that they return as their own simulacra. A familiar story. Take the Westway, West London's formerly deplored dual carriageway, once a cursed space to be mythologised by Ballard, punks and Chris Petit, now just another edgy film set:

> This liminal territory, cast in a negative light in the 70s was recuperated by MTV and boring media types in the 90s. The Westway became the backdrop for Gorillaz imbecility, bland drum & bass record sleeves and photo shoots in corporate skate parks.

> Cool Britannia. Old joke.
> 'Space' becomes the over arching commodity. Notting Hill. New Age cranks peddling expensive junk. Homeopathy and boutiques, angel cards and crystal healing.

Media and high finance on the one hand, faux-mysticism and superstition on the other: all the strategies of the hopeless and those who exploit them in Restoration London . . . Space is indeed the commodity here. A trend that started 30 years ago, and intensified as council housing was sold off and not replaced, culminated in the insane super-inflation of property prices in the first years of the 21st century. If you want a simple explanation for the growth in cultural conservatism, for London's seizure by the forces of Restoration, you need look no further than this. As Jon Savage points out in *England's Dreaming*, the London of punk was still a bombed-out city, full of chasms, caverns, spaces that could be temporarily occupied and squatted. Once those spaces are enclosed, practically all of the city's energy is put into paying the mortgage or the rent. There's no time to experiment, to journey without already knowing where you will end up. Your aims and objectives have to be stated up front. 'Free time' becomes convalescence. You turn to what reassures you, what will most refresh you for the working day: the old familiar tunes (or what sound like them). London becomes a city of pinched-face drones plugged into iPods.

Savage Messiah rediscovers the city as a site for drift and daydreams, a labyrinth of side streets and spaces resistant to the process of gentrification and 'development' set to culminate in the miserable hyper-spectacle of 2012. The struggle here is not only over the (historical) direction of time but over different uses of time. Capital demands that we always look busy, even if there's no work to do. If neoliberalism's magical voluntarism is to be believed, there are always opportunities to be chased or created; any time not spent hustling and hassling is time wasted. The whole city is forced into a gigantic simulation of activity, a fantacism of productivism in which nothing much is actually produced, an economy made out of hot air and bland delirium. *Savage Messiah* is about another kind of delirium: the releasing of the pressure to be yourself, the slow unravelling of biopolitical identity, a depersonalised journey out to the erotic city that exists alongside the business city. The eroticism here is not primarily to do with sexuality, although it sometimes includes it: it is an art of collective enjoyment, in which a world beyond work can – however briefly – be glimpsed and grasped. Fugitive time, lost afternoons, conversations that dilate and drift like smoke, walks that have no particular direction and go on for hours, free parties in old industrial spaces, still reverberating days later. The movement between anonymity and encounter can be very quick in the city. Suddenly, you are off the street and into someone's life-space. Sometimes, it's easier to talk to people you don't know. There are fleeting intimacies before we melt back into the crowd, but the city has its own systems of recall: a block of flats or a street you haven't focused on for a long time will remind you of people you met only once, years ago. Will you ever see them again?

I got invited up for a cup of tea in one of those Tecton flats on the Harrow road, one of the old men from the day centre I work in. I took him up Kilburn High Road shopping and watered the fuchsias on his balcony. We talked about the Blitz and hospitals mostly. He used to be a scientist and wrote shopping lists on brown envelopes dated and filed in a stack of biscuit tins.

I miss him.

I miss them all.

Savage Messiah deploys anachronism as a weapon. At first sight, at first touch – and tactility is crucial to the experience: the zine doesn't feel the same when it's JPEGed on screen – *Savage Messiah* seems like something familiar. The form itself, the mix of photographs, typeface-text and drawings, the use of scissors and glue rather than digital cut and paste; all of this make Savage Messiah seem out of time, which is not to say out of date. There were deliberate echoes of the para-art found on punk and postpunk record sleeves and fanzines from the 1970s and 1980s. Most insistently, I'm reminded of Gee Vaucher, who produced the paradoxically photorealistically delirious record covers and posters for anarcho-punk collective Crass. 'I think with the look of the zine I was trying to restore radical politics to an aesthetic that had been rendered anodyne by advertising campaigns, Shoreditch club nights etc.,' Ford says. 'That anarcho-punk look was everywhere but totally emptied of its radical critique. It seemed important to go back to that moment of the late '70s and early '80s to a point where there was social upheaval, where there were riots and strikes, exciting cultural scenes and ruptures in the fabric of everyday life.' The 'return' to the postpunk moment is the route to an alternative present. Yet this is a return only to a certain ensemble of styles and methods – nothing quite like *Savage Messiah* actually existed back then.

Savage Messiah is a gigantic, unfinished collage, which – like the city – is constantly reconfiguring itself. Macro- and micro-narratives proliferate tuberously; spidery slogans recur; figures migrate through various versions of London, sometimes trapped inside the drearily glossy spaces imagined by advertising and regeneration propaganda, sometimes free to drift. She deploys collage in much the same way William Burroughs used it: as a weapon in time-war. The cut-up can dislocate established narratives, break habits, allow new associations to coalesce. In *Savage Messiah*, the seamless, already-established capitalist reality of London dissolves into a riot of potentials.

Savage Messiah is written for those who could not be regenerated, even if they wanted to be. They are the unregenerated, a lost generation, 'always yearning for the time that just eluded us': those who were born too late for punk but whose expectations were raised by its incendiary afterglow; those who watched the Miners' Strike with partisan adolescent eyes but who were too young to really participate in the militancy; those who experienced the future-rush euphoria of rave as their birthright, never dreaming that it could burn out like fried synapses; those, in short, who simply did not find the 'reality' imposed by the conquering forces of neoliberalism liveable. It's adapt or die, and there are many different forms of death available to those who can't pick up the business buzz or muster the requisite enthusiasm for the creative industries. Six million ways to die, choose one: drugs, depression, destitution. So many forms of catatonic collapse. In earlier times, 'deviants, psychotics and the mentally collapsed' inspired militant-poets, situationists, Rave-dreamers.

Now they are incarcerated in hospitals, or languishing in the gutter.

No Pedestrian Access To Shopping Centre

Still, the mood of *Savage Messiah* is far from hopeless. It's not about caving in, it's about different strategies for surviving the deep midwinter of Restoration London. People living on next to nothing, no longer living the dream, but not giving up either: 'Five years since the last party but he held his plot, scavenging for food like a Ballardian crash victim.' You can go into suspended animation, knowing that the time is not yet right, but waiting with cold reptile patience until it is. Or you can flee Dystopian London without ever leaving the city, avoiding the central business district, finding friendly passages through the occupied territory, picking your way through the city via cafes, comrade's flats, public parks. *Savage Messiah* is an inventory of such routes, such passages through 'territories of commerce and control'.

The zines are saturated in music culture. First of all, there are the names of groups: Infa Riot and Blitz. Fragments of Abba, Heaven 17 on the radio. Japan, Rudimentary Peni, Einstürzende Neubauten, Throbbing Gristle, Spiral Tribe. Whether the groups are sublime or sub-charity shop undesirable, these litanies have an evocative power that is quietly lacerating. Gig posters from 30 years ago – Mob, Poison Girls, Conflict – call up older versions of you, half-forgotten haircuts, long-lost longings, stirring again. But the role of music culture goes much deeper in *Savage Messiah*. The way the zine is put together owes as much to the rogue dance and drug cultures that mutated from Rave as to punk fanzines; its montage methodology has as much in common with the DJ mix as with any precursor in visual culture. *Savage Messiah* is also about the relationship between music and place: the zine is also a testament to the way in which the sensitive membranes of the city are reshaped by music.

This sombre place is haunted by the sounds of lost acid house parties and the distant reverberations of 1986. Test Department. 303. 808. Traces of industrial noise. The roundhouse was easy to get into, and the depot itself, disused for years is lit up with tags and dubs. You can hear these deserted places, feel the tendrils creeping across the abandoned caverns, the derelict bunkers and broken terraces. Mid summer, blistering heat under the concrete, Armagideon Time(s), a hidden garden, to be found, and lost again.

Superficially, the obvious tag for *Savage Messiah* would be psychogeography, but the label makes Ford chafe. 'I think a lot of what is called psychogeography now is just middle-class men acting like colonial explorers, showing us their discoveries and guarding their plot. I have spent the last twenty years walking around London and living here in a precarious fashion, I've had about fifty addresses. I think my understanding and negotiation of the city is very different to theirs.' Rather than subsuming *Savage Messiah* under the increasingly played-out discourses of psychogeography, I believe it is better understood as an example of a cultural coalescence that started to become visible (and audible) at the moment when Ford began to produce the zine: hauntology. 'The London I conjure up . . . is imbued with a sense of mourning,' Ford says. 'These are the liminal zones where the free party rave scene once illuminated the bleak swathes of marshland and industrial estates.' So many dreams of collectivity have died in neoliberal London. A new kind of human being was supposed to live here, but that all had to be cleared away so that the restoration could begin.

Haunting is about a staining of place with particularly intense moments of time, and, like David Peace, with whom her work shares a number of affinities, Ford is alive to the poetry of dates. 1979, 1981, 2013: these years recur throughout *Savage Messiah*, moments of transition and threshold, moments when a whole alternative time-track opens. 2013 has a post-apocalyptic quality (in addition to being the year of the London Olympics, 2012 is also, according to some, the year that the Mayans predicted for the end of the world). But 2013 could also be Year Zero: the reversal of 1979, the time when all the cheated hopes and missed chances are finally realised. *Savage Messiah* invites us to see the contours of another world in the gaps and cracks of an occupied London:

> Perhaps it is here that the space can be opened up to forge a collective resistance to this neo liberal expansion, to the endless proliferation of banalities and the homogenising effects of globalisation. Here in the burnt out shopping arcades, the boarded up precincts, the lost citadels of consumerism one might find the truth, new territories might be opened, there might be a rupturing of this collective amnesia.

Nomadalgia: The Junior Boys' *So This is Goodbye*

k-punk post, March 4, 2006

Space comes as standard with the Junior Boys. The synthpop that inspired them remained attached, for the most part, to the three-minute format; 'extended' remixes were a concession to the imperatives of dance. Only one of *So This is Goodbye*'s 10 tracks is under four minutes. Space is *integral*, not only to their sound, but to their songs. Space is a compositional component, a presupposition of the songs, not something retrospectively inserted at a producer's whim. The pauses, the imagist-allusiveness of the lyrics, the breathy phrasing would not work, or make much sense, outside a plateau-architecture imported from dance; crushed into three minutes Junior Boys' songs would lose more than length.

House references are everywhere: the title track is gorgeously, oneirically poised on a honeyed Mr Fingers' plateau, and it is not only the arpeggiated synth which drives many of the tracks that is reminiscent of Jamie Principle. Yet the LP does not sound either like House or like most previous attempts to synthesize pop with House. *So This is Goodbye* is like House if it had started in the wilds of Canada rather the clubs of Chicago. Too many House-pop hybrids fill up House's space with business, hectic activity. On *Vocalcity* and, to some extent *The Present Lover*, Luomo did the opposite: dilating the Song into an unfolding driftwork. But the Luomo LPs were more pop House than pop per se. *So This is Goodbye* is, however, very definitely a pop record; if anything, it's even more seductively catchy than *Last Exit*.

The obvious difference between *So This is Goodbye* and its predecessor is the absence of the tricksy stop-start stutter beats on the new record. If Junior Boys' inventiveness is no longer concentrated on beats, that is a reflection as much of a decline of the surrounding pop context as it a sign of the JB's newfound taste for rhythmic classicism. *Last Exit's* reworkings of Timbaland/Dem 2 tic-beats meant that it had a relationship with a rhythmic psychedelia that was, then, still mutating pop into new shapes. In the intervening period, of course, both hip hop and British garage have taken a turn for the brutalist, and pop has consequently been deprived of any modernising force. Timbaland's beat surrealism became water-treading repetition years ago, displaced by the ultra-realist thuggish plod of corporate hip hop and the ugly carnality of crunk; and 2 Step's 'feminine pressure' has long since been crushed by the testosterone-saturated bluntness of Grime and Dubstep. That skunk-fugged heaviness remains the antipodes of the Junior Boys' cyberian, etherealised, plaintive physicality; listening to the Junior Boys after Grime or Dubstep is like walking out of a locker room thick with dope smoke out onto a Caspar David Friedrich mountain. A lung-cleansing experience. (Significant also that those other ultra-heterosexual post-Garage musics should have bred out the influence of House, while the Junior Boys return to it so emphatically.)

But the removal of rhythmic tricksiness perhaps also indicates something of the scale of the Junior Boys' pop ambitions, which are best seen as the pioneering of a New MOR rather than another attempt at New Pop. If there is no cutting edge, then it makes more sense to abandon the former margins and refurbish the middle of the road. The Junior Boys' songs have always had more in common with a certain type of modernist MOR – Hall and Oates, Prefab Sprout, Blue Nile, Lindsay Buckingham – than with any rock. Modernist MOR is the opposite of the discredited strategy of entryism: it doesn't 'conform to deform', it locates the alien right in the heart of the familiar. The problem with current Pop is not the predominance of MOR, but the fact that MOR has been corrupted by the wheedling whine of Indie authenticity. In any just world, the Junior Boys, not the drippy moroseness of James Blunt nor the earthy earnestness of KT Tunstall, would be the globally dominant MOR brand in 2006.

Ultimately, though, *So This is Goodbye* sounds more middle of the tundra than middle of the road. It's as if the Junior Boys' journey into North America Endless has continued beyond the late-night freeways of *Last Exit*. It's like the first LP's city lights and Edward Hopper coffee bars have receded, and we're taken out, beyond even the small towns, into the depopulated wildernesses of Canada's Northern Territories. Or rather, it's as if those wildernesses have crept into the very marrow of the record. In *The Idea of North*, Glenn Gould suggests that the North's icy desolation has a special pull on the Canadian imagination. You hear this on *So This is Goodbye* not in any positive content so much as in the songs' gaps and absences; the gaps and absences that make the song what they are.

Those crevices and grottoes seem to multiply as the album progresses. The second half of the album (what I hear as the 'second side'; one of the most gratifying things about *So This is Goodbye* is that it is structured like a classic pop album, not an extras-clogged CD) diffuses forward motion into trails of electro-cumulae. The title track sets stately synths against the anti-climactic urgency of Acid House's Forever Now: the effect like running up a down escalator, frozen in an aching moment of transition. 'Like a child' and 'Caught in a Wave' immerse the agitated drive of the LP's signature arpeggiated synth in a vapour trail of opiated atmospherics.

The reading of Sinatra's 'When No-one Cares' is the knot which holds together all of *So This is Goodbye*, a clue to its modernist MOR intentions (lines from the song – 'count souvenirs', 'like a child' – provide the titles for other tracks, almost as if the song is a puzzle the whole album is trying to solve). *So This is Goodbye*'s songs bear much the same relation to high-energy as the late Sinatra's bore to big band jazz: what was once a communal, dance-oriented music has been hollowed out into a cavernous, contemplative space for the most solitary of musings. On the Junior Boys' 'When No-one Cares' beats are abandoned altogether, the track's 'endless night' lit only by the dying-star flares and stalactite-by-flashlight pulse of reverbed electronics.

The Junior Boys have transformed the song from the lonely-crowd melancholy of the original – Frank at the bar staring into his whisky sour, happy couples partying obliviously behind him (or in his imagination) – into a lament whispered in the wilderness, icy-breathed into the black mirror indifference of a Great Lake at midnight. It is as cosmically desolated as the Young Gods' version of 'September Song', as arctic-white as Miles Davis' *Aura*. 'When No-one Cares' is one of my favourite Sinatra songs, and I must have first heard it 20 years ago, but with the Junior Boys' version – which makes the catatonic stasis of the original's grief seem positively busy – it is as if I am hearing the words for the first time.

Sinatra's *No-One Cares* (which could have been subtitled: *From Penthouse to Satis House*) was like pop's take on literary modernism, an *affect* (rather than a concept) album, a series of takes on a particular theme – disconnection from a hyper-connected world – with Frank the ageing sophisticate adrift in the McLuhan wasteland of the late 50s, Elvis already here, the Beatles on the way (who is the 'no-one' who doesn't care if not the teen audience who have found new objects of adoration?), the telephone and the television offering only new ways to be lonely. *So This is Goodbye* is like a globalised update of *No-One Cares*, its images of 'hotel lobbies', 'shopping malls we'll never see again' and 'homes for sale' sketching a world in a state of permanent impermance (should we say precarity?). The songs are overwhelmingly preoccupied with leave-taking and change, fixated on doing things for the first or the last time. 'So This is

Goodbye' is not the title track for nothing.

Sinatra's melancholy was the melancholy of mass (old) media technology – the 'extimacy' of the records facilitated by the phonograph and the microphone, and expressing a peculiarly cosmopolitan and urban sadness. 'I've flown around the world in plane/ designed the latest IBM brain/ but lately I'm so downhearted', Sinatra song on *No-One Cares' 'I Can't Get Started'*. Jetsetting is now not the privilege of the elite so much as a veritiginous mundanity for a permanently dispossessed global workforce. Every town has become the 'tourist town' alluded to in *So This is Goodbye*'s final track, 'FM', because now at home everyone is a tourist, both in the sense of permanently on the move but also in the sense of having the world at their fingertips, via the net. If Sinatra's best records, like Hopper's paintings, were about the way in which the urban experience produces new forms of isolation (and also: that such mass mediated private moments are the only mode of affective connection in a fragmented world), then *So this is Goodbye* is a response to the cyberspatial commonplace that, with the net, even the most remote spot can be connected up (and also: that such connection often amounts to a communion of lonely souls). Hence the impression that, if Sinatra's 'When No-one Cars' was an unanswered call from the heartless heart of the Big Apple, then the Junior Boys' version has been phoned-in down a digital line from the edge of Lake Ontario. (Is it accidental that the term 'cyberspace' was invented by a Canadian?)

So this is Goodbye is a very *travel sick* record. It expresses what we might call *nomadalgia*. Nomadalgia, the sickness *of* travel, would be a complement to, not the opposite of, the sickness *for* home, nostalgia. (And what of the relation between nomadalgia and hauntology?) It's entirely fitting that the final track, 'FM', should invoke both 'a return home' and radio (not the only reference to that ghost-medium on the album), since internet radio – with local stations available from any hotel in the world

– is perhaps more than anything else the objective correlative of our current condition. A condition in which, as Žižek so aptly puts it, 'global harmony and solipsism strangely coincide. That is to say, does not our immersion in cyberspace go hand in hand with our reduction to a Leibnizian monad which, although "without windows" that would directly open up to external reality, mirrors in itself the entire universe? Are we not more and more monads, interacting alone with the PC screen, encountering only the virtual simulacra, and yet immersed more than ever in the global network, synchronously communicating with the entire globe?' ('No Sex Please, We Are Post-humans', http://www.egs.edu/faculty/slavoj-zizek/articles/no-sex-please-we-are-post-humans/)

Grey Area: Chris Petit's *Content*

BFI/ Sight & Sound Website, March 2010

At one point in Chris Petit's haunting new film *Content*, we drive through Felixstowe container port. It was an uncanny moment for me, since Felixstowe is only a couple of miles from where I now live – what Petit filmed could have been shot from our car window. What made it all the more uncanny was the fact that Petit never mentions that he is in Felixstowe; the hangars and looming cranes are so generic that I began to wonder if this might not be a doppelgänger container port somewhere else in the world. All of this somehow underlined the way Petit's text describes these 'blind buildings' while his camera tracks along them: 'non-places', 'prosaic sheds', 'the first buildings of a new age' which render 'architecture redundant'.

Content could be classified as an essay film, but it's less essay-istic than aphoristic. This isn't to say that it's disconnected or incoherent: Petit himself has called *Content* a '21st-century road movie, ambient', and its reflections on ageing and parenthood, terrorism and new media are woven into a consistency that's non-linear, but certainly not fragmentary.

Content is about 'correspondence', in different senses of the word. It was in part generated by electronic correspondence between Petit and his two major collaborators: Ian Penman (whose text is voiced by the German actor Hanns Zischler) and the German musician Antye Greie. Penman's text is a series of reflections on the subject of email, that 'anonymous yet intimate' ethereal communication. Some of Penman's disquisitions on email are accompanied by images of postcards – the poignant tactility of this obsolete form of correspondence all the more affecting because the senders and addressees are now forgotten. Greie, meanwhile, produces skeins of electronica that provide

Content with a kind of sonic unconscious in which terms and concepts referred to in the images and the voice track are refracted, extrapolated and supplemented.

One of the first phrases cited in Greie's soundwork – which resembles sketches for unrealised songs – is a quotation from Roy Batty's famous speech in *Blade Runner*: 'If only you could see what I have seen with your eyes.' This is a phrase Penman has made much of in his own writings on recording, technology and haunting – and it brings us to the other meaning of 'correspondence' *Content* plays with: correspondences in the sense of connections and associations. Some of these are underscored by Petit in his dryly-poetic text; others he leaves the viewers to make for themselves.

One of the most gratifying aspects of *Content*, in fact, is that by contrast with so many contemporary television documentaries, which neurotically hector the audience by incessantly reiterating their core thesis, Petit trusts in the intelligence and speculative power of the viewer. Where so much television now involves a mutual redundancy of image and voice – the image is slaved into illustrating the text; the voice merely glosses the image – *Content* is in large part about the spaces between image and text, what is unsaid in (and about) the images.

The use of a German actor and musician and the many references to Europe in *Content* reflect Petit's childhood which, as he describes in the film, was partly spent as a forces child in Germany. But it also reflects Petit's long-standing desire for some kind of reconciliation between British culture and European modernism. Petit has described *Content* as an 'informal coda' to his 1979 film *Radio On* (recently reissued on BFI DVD). With its strong debt to European art cinema, *Radio On* projected a rapprochement between British and European film that never happened – a rapprochement anticipated in the 1970s art pop (Kraftwerk, Bowie) used so prominently in that film. Petit imagined a British cinema that, like that music, could assert its

Europeanness not by rejecting America, but by confidently absorbing American influences. Yet this future never arrived. 'Radio On,' Petit said in a recent interview, 'ended with a car 'stalled on the edge of the future', which we didn't know then would be Thatcherism.' Ahead lay a bizarre yet banal mix of the unprecedented and the archaic. Instead of accelerating down Kraftwerk's autobahn, we found ourselves, as Petit puts it in *Content*, 'reversing into a tomorrow based on a non-existent past', as the popular modernism *Radio On* was part of found itself eclipsed by a toxic-addictive confection of consumer-driven populism, heritage kitsch, xenophobia and US corporate culture. In this light, *Content* stands as a quiet but emphatic reproach to the British cinema of the last 30 years, which in its dominant variants – drab social realism, faux gangster, picture-book costume drama or mid-Atlantic middle-class fantasia – has retreated from modernity. It isn't only the poor and the non-white who are edited out of *Notting Hill*, for example – it's also the Westway, west London's Ballardian flyover, which now stands as a relic of 'the modern city that London never became'.

Yet *Content* isn't just a requiem for the lost possibilities of the last 30 years. In its use of stunning but underused locations – the ready-made post-Fordist science-fiction landscapes of Felixstowe container port, the eerie Cold War terrain of nearby Orford Ness – *Content* demonstrates not only what British cinema overlooks, but what it could still be.

Postmodern Antiques: *Patience (After Sebald)*

Sight & Sound, April 2011

The first time I saw Andrei Tarkovsky's *Stalker* – when it was broadcast by Channel 4 in the early 1980s – I was immediately reminded of the Suffolk landscapes where I had holidayed as a child. The overgrown pill boxes, the squat Martello towers, the rusting groynes which resembled gravestones: this all added up to a readymade science fiction scene. At one point in Grant Gee's *Patience (After Sebald)* (2011) – an essay film inspired by W G Sebald's novel *The Rings of Saturn* – theatre director Katie Williams makes the same connection, drawing a comparison between the demilitarised expanses of the Suffolk coast and Tarkovsky's Zone.

When I read *Rings of Saturn*, I was hoping that it would be an exploration of these eerily numinous spaces. Yet what I found was something rather different: a book that, it seemed to me at least, morosely trudged through the Suffolk spaces without really looking at them; that offered a Mittel–brow miserabilism, a stock disdain, in which the human settlements are routinely dismissed as shabby and the inhuman spaces are oppressive. The landscape in *The Rings of Saturn* functions as a thin conceit, the places operating as triggers for a literary ramble which reads less like a travelogue than a librarian's listless daydream. Instead of engaging with previous literary encounters with the Suffolk – Henry James went on a walking tour of the county; his namesake MR James set two of his most atmospheric ghost stories there – Sebald tends to reach for the likes of Borges. My scepticism was fed by the solemn cult that settled around Sebald suspiciously quickly, and which seemed all-too-ready to admire those well-wrought sentences. Sebald offered a rather *easy difficulty*, an anachronistic, antiqued model of 'good literature' which acted as if many of the developments in 20th century experimental fiction and popular culture had never happened. It is not hard to see why a German writer would want to blank out the middle part of the 20th century; and many of the formal anachronisms of Sebald's writing – its strange sense that this is the 21st century seen through the restrained yet ornate prose of an early 20th century essayist – perhaps arise from this desire, just as the novels themselves are about the various, ultimately failed, ruses – conscious and unconscious – that damaged psyches deploy to erase traumas and construct new identities. The writer Robert Macfarlane has called Sebald a 'postmodern antiquarian', and the indeterminate status of *The Rings of Saturn* – is it autobiography, a novel or a travelogue? – points to a certain playfulness, but this never emerges at the level of the book's content. It was necessary for Sebald to remain po-faced in order for the 'antiquing' to be successful. Some of Gee's images of Suffolk take their cue from the black and white photographs which illustrate *The Rings Of Saturn*. But the photographs were a contrivance: Sebald would photocopy them many times until they achieved the required graininess.

Gee's film was premiered as part of a weekend of events superbly curated by Gareth Evans of Artevents under the rubric *After Sebald: Place and Re-Enchantment* at Snape Maltings, near Aldeburgh, in Suffolk. In the end, however, Sebald's novels fits into any discussion of place and enchantment only very awkwardly: his work is more about displacement and disenchantment than their opposites. In *Patience (After Sebald)*, the artist Tacita Dean observes that only children have a real sense of home. Adults are always aware of the precariousness and transitoriness of their dwelling place: none more so than Sebald, a German writer who spent most of his life in Norfolk.

Patience (After Sebald) follows Gee's documentaries about Radiohead and Joy Division. The shift from rock to literature, Gee told Macfarlane, was one that came naturally to someone whose sensibilities were formed by the UK music culture of the 1970s. If Sebald had been writing in the 1970s, Gee claimed, he would surely have been mentioned in the NME alongside other luminaries of avant-garde literature. Gee started reading Sebald in 2004, after a recommendation from his friend, the novelist Jeff Noon. The film's somewhat gnomic title was a relic of an earlier version of what the film would be. It now suggests the slowing of time that the Suffolk landscape imposes, a release from urban urgencies, but it is actually a reference to a passage in Sebald's novel *Austerlitz*: 'Austerlitz told me that he sometimes sat here for hours, laying out these photographs or others from his collection the wrong way up, as if playing a game of patience, and that then one by one, he turned them over, always with a new sense of surprise at what he saw, pushing the pictures back and forth and over each other, arranging them in an order depending on their family resemblances, or withdrawing them from the game until either there was nothing left but the grey tabletop, or he felt exhausted from the constant effort of thinking and remembering and had to rest on the ottoman.'

Gee had originally intended to make a film about the non-places in Sebald's work: the hotel rooms or railway station waiting rooms in which characters ruminate, converse or break down (Austerlitz himself comes to a shattering revelation about his own identity in the waiting room at Liverpool Street station). In the end, however, Gee was drawn to the book which – ostensibly at least – is most focused on a single landscape.

Gee filmed practically everything himself, using a converted 16 mm Bolex camera. He wanted something that would produce frames that were 'tighter than normal', he said, 'as if a single character is looking'. Gee sees *Patience (After Sebald)* as an essay film, in the tradition of Chris Petit's work and Patrick Keiller's Robinson trilogy. But when I put it to him that *Patience* lacks the single voice that defines Petit or Keiller's essay films, Gee responded self-deprecatingly. He had tried to insert himself into his own films, but he had always been dissatisfied with the results: his voice didn't sound right; his acting didn't convince; his writing wasn't strong enough. In *Patience*, as in the Joy Division documentary, the story is therefore told by others: Macfarlane, Dean, Iain Sinclair, Petit, the literary critic Marina Warner and the artist Jeremy Millar. Millar provided one of the most uncanny images in *Patience*. When he lit a firework in tribute to Sebald, the smoke unexpectedly formed a shape which resembled Sebald's face, something which Gee underlines in the film by animating a transition between Millar's photograph and an image of the novelist.

More than one of the speakers at the Towards Re-Enchantment symposium acknowledged that they misremembered *The Rings of Saturn*. There's something fitting about this, of course, given that the duplicity of memory might have been Sebald's major theme; but my suspicion is that misremembering of a different kind contributes to the *Rings of Saturn* cult; that the book induces its readers to hallucinate a text that is not there, but which meets their desires – for a kind of modernist travelogue, a novel that would do justice to the Suffolk landscape – better than Sebald's actually novel does. *Patience (After Sebald)* is itself a misremembering of *The Rings of Saturn* which could not help but reverse many of the novel's priorities and emphases. In *The Rings of Saturn*, Suffolk frequently (and frustratingly) recedes from attention, as Sebald follows his own lines of association. By contrast, the main substance of the film consists of images of the Suffolk landscape – the heathland over which you can walk for miles without seeing a soul, the crumbling cliffs of the lost city of Dunwich, the enigma of Orford Ness, its inscrutable pagodas silently presiding over Cold War military experiments which remain secret. Sebald's reflections, voiced in *Patience* by Jonathan Pryce, anchor these images far less securely than they do in the novel. At Snape, some of those who had re-created Sebald's walk – including Gee himself – confessed that they had failed to attain the author's lugubrious mood: the landscape turned out to be too energising, its sublime desolation proving to be fallow ground for gloomy psychological interiority. In a conversation with Robert Macfarlane after the screening of the film, Gee said that it was not really necessary that Sebald had taken the walk. He meant that it was not important whether or not Sebald actually did the walk exactly as *The Rings of Saturn*'s narrator described it, in one go: that the novel could have been based on a number of different walks which took place over a longer period of time. But I couldn't help but hear Gee's remark in a different way: that it was not necessary for Sebald to have taken the walk *at all*: that, far from being a close engagement with the Suffolk terrain, *The Rings of Saturn* could have been written had Sebald never set foot in Suffolk.

This was the view of Richard Mabey, cast in the role of doubting Thomas at the Towards Re-Enchantment symposium. Mabey – who has written and broadcast about nature for 40 years, and whose latest book *Weeds* has the glorious subtitle *How Vagabond Plants Gatecrashed Civilisation and Changed the Way We Think About Nature* – argued that Sebald was guilty of the pathetic fallacy. When he read *The Rings Of Saturn*, Mabey said, he felt as if a very close friend had been belittled; although he had walked the Suffolk coastland countless times, he couldn't recognise it from Sebald's descriptions. But perhaps the issue with Sebald is that he wasn't guilty enough of the pathetic fallacy, that instead of staining the landscape with his passions, as Thomas Hardy did with Wessex, or the Brontes did with Yorkshire, or, more recently, as the musician Richard Skelton has done with the Lancashire moorland – Sebald used Suffolk as a kind of Rorschach blot, a trigger for associative processes that take flight from the landscape rather than take root in it. In any case, Mabey wanted a confrontation with nature in all its inhuman exteriority. He sounded like a Deleuzean philosopher when he expostulated about the 'nested heterogeneity' and 'autonomous poetry' of micro-ecosytems to be found in a cow's hoof print; of how it was necessary to 'think like a mountain', and quoted approvingly Virginia Woolf's evocation of a 'philosophising and dreaming land'. I was struck by the parallels between Mabey's account of nature and Patrick Keiller's invocation of lichen as 'a non-human intelligence' in *Robinson in Ruins*. With its examination of the 'undiscovered country of nearby', Robert Macfarlane's film for the BBC, *The Wild Places of Essex,* shown as part of the Towards Re-Enchantment symposium, was also close to Mabey's vision of a nature thriving in the spaces abandoned by, or inhospitable to, humans. (Macfarlane's film now seems like a counterpart to Julien Temple's wonderful *Oil City Confidential,* which rooted Dr Feelgood's febrile rhythm and blues in the lunar landscape of Essex's Canvey Island.) *Patience (After Sebald)* could appeal to a Sebald sceptic like me because – in spite of Sebald – it reaches the wilds of Suffolk. At the same time, Gee's quietly powerful film caused me to doubt my own scepticism, sending me back to Sebald's novels, in search of what others had seen, but which had so far eluded me.

The Lost Unconscious: Christopher Nolan's *Inception*

Film Quarterly, Vol. 64, No. 3, 2011

In Christopher Nolan's breakthrough memory-loss thriller *Memento* from 2000, the traumatised and heavily tattooed protagonist Lenny has a suggestive conversation with a detective:

> TEDDY: Look at your police file. It was complete when I gave it to you. Who took the twelve pages out?
> LEONARD: You, probably.
> TEDDY: No, you took them out.
> LEONARD: Why would I do that?
> TEDDY: To set yourself a puzzle you won't ever solve.

Like Lenny, Christopher Nolan has specialised in setting puzzles that can't be solved. Duplicity – in the sense of both deception and doubling – runs right through his work. It's not only the case that Nolan's work is *about* duplicity; it is itself duplicitous, drawing audiences into labyrinths of indeterminacy.

Nolan's films have a coolly obsessive quality, in which a number of repeating elements – a traumatised hero and his antagonist; a dead woman; a plot involving manipulation and dissimulation – are reshuffled. These film noir tropes are then further scrambled in the manner of a certain kind of neo-noir. Nolan acknowledges *Angel Heart* (1987) and *The Usual Suspects* (1995) as touchstones (he mentions both in an interview which is included on the *Memento* DVD, singling out Parker's film as a particular inspiration), but one can also see parallels with the meta-detective fictions of Robbe-Grillet and Paul Auster. There's a shift from the epistemological problems posed by unreliable narrators to a more general ontological indeterminacy, in which the nature of the whole fictional world is put into doubt. *Memento* remains emblematic in this respect. At first glance, the film's enigma resolves relatively simply. Lenny, who suffers from anterograde amnesiac condition which means that he can't make new memories, is 'setting puzzles for himself that can't be solved' so that he can always be pursuing his wife's murderer, long after Lenny has killed him. But after repeated viewings, the critic Andy Klein – in a piece for Salon.com pointedly entitled 'Everything You Wanted To Know About *Memento*'– conceded that he wasn't 'able to come up with the 'truth' about what transpired prior to the film's action. Every explanation seems to involve some breach of the apparent 'rules' of Leonard's disability – not merely the rules as he explains them, but the rules as we witness them operating throughout most of the film.) The rules are crucial to Nolan's method. If *Memento* is a kind of impossible object, then its impossibility is generated not via an anything-goes ontological anarchy but by the setting up of rules which it violates in particular ways – just as the effect of Escher's paintings depend upon unsettling rather than ignoring the rules of perspective.

Nolan nevertheless maintains that, however intractable his films might appear, they are always based on a definitive truth which he knows but will not reveal. As he said of *Inception* in the interview with *Wired*, 'I've always believed that if you make a film with ambiguity, it needs to be based on a true interpretation. If it's not, then it will contradict itself, or it will be somehow insubstantial and end up making the audience feel cheated. Ambiguity has to come from the inability of the character to know – and the alignment of the audience with that character'. When the interviewer Robert Capps puts it to Nolan that there might be several explanations of the film's ending, that the 'right answer' is impossible to find, the director flatly contradicts him: 'Oh no, I've got an answer.' But Nolan's remarks may only be another act of misdirection; and, if a century of cultural theory has taught us anything, it is that an author's supposed intentions can only ever constitute a supplementary (para)text, never a final word. What are Nolan's films about, after all, but the instability of any master position? They are full of moments in which the manipulator – the one who looks, writes or narrates – becomes the manipulated – the object of the gaze, the character in a story written or told by someone else.

In *Inception*, Cobb is an 'extractor', an expert at a special kind of industrial espionage, which involves entering into people's dreams and stealing their secrets. He and his team have been hired by hyper-wealthy businessman Saito to infiltrate the dreams of Robert Fischer, the heir to a massive energy conglomerate. But this time Cobb's team is not required to extract information, but to do something which the film tells is much more difficult: they are tasked with implanting an idea into Fischer's mind. Cobb's effectiveness as a dream thief is compromised by the projection of his dead wife, Mal, the pathological stain he now brings with him into any dream caper. Mal died after she suffered an apparent psychotic break. She and Cobb set up a lover's retreat in the 'unconstructed dreamspace' that the dream thieves call Limbo. But after she became too attached to this virtual love nest, Cobb 'incepted' in her the idea that the world in which they were living was not real. As Cobb mordantly observes, there is nothing more resilient than an idea. Even when she is restored to what Cobb takes to be reality, Mal remains obsessed with the idea that she the world around her is not real, so she throws herself from a hotel window in order to return to what she believes is the real world. The film turns on how Cobb deals with this traumatic event – in order to incept Fischer, Cobb has first of all to descend into Limbo and defeat Mal. He achieves this by simultaneously accepting his part in Mal's death and by repudiating the Mal projection as an inadequate copy of his dead wife. With the Mal projection vanquished and the dream-heist successfully completed, Cobb is finally able to return to the children from whom he has been separated. Yet this ending has more than a suggestion of wish fulfilment fantasy about it, and the suspicion that Cobb might be marooned somewhere in a multi-layered oneiric labyrinth, a psychotic who has mistaken dreams for reality, makes *Inception* deeply ambiguous. Nolan's own remarks have carefully maintained the ambiguity.' I choose to believe that Cobb gets back to his kids,' Nolan told Robert Capps.

Nolan's films are preoccupied with, to paraphrase *Memento*'s Teddy, 'the lies that we tell ourselves to stay happy'. Yet the situation is worse even than that. It's one thing to lie to oneself; it's another to not even know whether one is lying to oneself or not. This might be the case with Cobb in *Inception*, and it's notable that, in the *Wired* interview, Nolan says that 'The most important emotional thing about the top spinning at the end is that Cobb is not looking at it. He doesn't care.' Not caring whether we are lying to ourselves may be the price for happiness – or at least the price one pays for release from excruciating mental anguish. In this respect, Dormer in *Insomnia* (2002) could be the anti-Cobb. His inability to sleep – which naturally also means an inability to dream – correlates with the breakdown of his capacity to tell himself a comforting story about who he is. After the shooting of his partner, Dormer's identity collapses into a terrifying epistemological void, a black box that cannot be opened. He simply doesn't know whether or not he intended to kill his partner (just as Borden in *The Prestige* cannot remember which knot he tied on the night that Angier's wife died in a bungled escapology act.) But in Nolan's worlds, it is not only that we deceive ourselves; it is also that we are deceived about having a self. There is no separating identity from fiction. In *Memento*, Lenny literally writes (on) himself, but the very fact that he can write a script for future versions of himself is a horrifying demonstration of his lack of any coherent identity – a revelation that his Sisyphian quest both exemplifies and is in flight from.

Inception leaves us with the possibility that Cobb's quest and apparent rediscovery of his children could be a version of the same kind of loop: a Purgatorio to *Memento's* Inferno. 'The urge to rewrite ourselves as real-seeming fictions is present in us all,' writes Christopher Priest in his novel *The Glamour*. It's not at all surprising that Nolan has adapted a novel by Priest, since there are striking parallels between the two men's methods and interests. Priest's novels are also 'puzzles that can't be solved', in which writing, biography and psychosis slide into one another, posing troubling ontological questions about memory, identity and fiction. The idea of minds as datascapes which can be infiltrated inevitably puts one in mind of the 'consensual hallucination' of Gibson's cyberspace, but the dreamsharing concept can be traced back to Priest and his extraordinary 1977 novel, *A Dream of Wessex*. In Priest's novel, a group of researcher-volunteers use a 'dream projector' to enter into a shared dream of a (then) future England. Like the dreamsharing addicts we briefly glimpse in one of *Inception's* most suggestive scenes, some of the characters in *A Dream of Wessex* inevitably prefer the simulated environment to the real world, and, unlike Cobb, they choose to stay there. The differences in the way that the concept of shared dreaming is handled in 1977 and 2010 tell us a great deal about the contrasts between social democracy and neoliberalism. While *Inception's* dreamsharing technology is – like the internet – a military invention turned into a commercial application, Priest's shared dream project is government-run. The Wessex dream world is lyrical and languid, still part of the hazy afterglow of 60s psychedelia. It's all a far cry from *Inception's* noise and fury, the mind as a militarised zone.

Inception (not entirely satisfactorily) synthesizes the intellectual and metaphysical puzzles of *Memento* and *The Prestige* (2006) with the big budget ballistics of *Batman Begins* (2005) and *The Dark Knight* (2008). The problem is the prolonged action sequences, which come off as perfunctory at best. At points, it as

if *Inception*'s achievement is to have provided a baroquely sophisticated motivation for some very dumb action sequences. An
unkind viewer might think that the entirety of *Inception*'s
complex ontological structure had been constructed to justify
clichés of action cinema – such as the ludicrous amount of things
that characters can do in the time that it takes for a van to fall
from a bridge into a river. Blogger Carl Neville complains that
Inception amounts to 'three uninvolving action movies playing
out simultaneously' 'What could have been a fascinatingly
vertiginous trip into successively fantastic, impossible worlds,
not to mention the limbo of the raw unconscious into which a
couple of the central characters plunge,' Neville argues,

> ends up looking wholly like a series of action movies, one
> within the other: "reality" looks and feels like a "globali-
> sation" movie, jumping from Tokyo to Paris to Mombasa to
> Sydney with a team of basically decent technical geniuses
> who are forced to live outside the law, making sure there are
> lots of helicopter shots of cityscapes and exotic local colour.
> Level one dream is basically *The Bourne Identity* . . . rainy, grey,
> urban. Level two is the *Matrix*, zero gravity fistfights in a
> modernist hotel, level three, depressingly, turns out to be a
> 70s Bond film while the raw Id is basically just a collapsing
> cityscape.

The 'level three' snow scenes at least resemble one of the most
visually striking Bond films – 1969's *On Her Majesty's Secret
Service* – but it's hard not to share Neville's sense of anti-climax.
Rather than picking up pace and ramping up the metaphysical
complexity, the film rushes towards its disappointing
denouement. The elaborate set-up involving the 'dream
architect' Ariadne is summarily abandoned, as she is told to
forget the labyrinth and 'find the most direct route through.'
When Ariadne and the film accede to these demands, it as if the

imperatives of the action thriller have crashed through the intricacies of Nolan's puzzle narrative with all the subtlety of the freight train that erupts into the cityscape in an earlier scene.

Neville is right that *Inception* is very far from being a 'fascinatingly vertiginous trip into successively fantastic, impossible worlds', but it is worth thinking about why Nolan showed such restraint. (His parsimony couldn't contrast more starkly with the stylistic extravagances of something like Peter Jackson's *The Lovely Bones* (2009), which aims at the fantastic and the impossible, but ends up CGI-onanistic rather than lyrically oneiric.) One initially strange thing about *Inception* is how *un-dreamlike* the dreams in the film are. It's tempting to see the Nolan of *Inception* as a reverse Hitchcock – where Hitchcock took De Chirico-like dream topographies and remotivated them as thriller spaces, Nolan takes standard action flick sequences and repackages them as dreams. Except in a scene where the walls seem to close in around Cobb when he is being pursued – which, interestingly, takes place in the film's apparent 'reality' – the spatial distortions at work in *Inception* do not resemble the ways in which dreams distend or collapse space. There are none of the bizarre adjacencies or distances that do not diminish that we see in Welles's *The Trial* (1962), a film which, perhaps better than any other, captures the uncanny topographies of the anxiety dream. When, in one of *Inception*'s most remarked upon scenes, Ariadne causes the Paris cityspace to fold up around herself and Cobb, she is behaving more like the CGI engineer who is creating the scene than any dreamer. This is a display of technical prowess, devoid of any charge of the uncanny. The Limbo scenes, meanwhile, are like an inverted version of Fredric Jameson's 'surrealism without the unconscious': this is an unconscious without surrealism. The world that Cobb and Mal 'create' out of their memories is like a Powerpoint presentation of a love affair rendered as some walk-through simulation: faintly haunting in its very lack of allure, quietly horrifying in its solipsistic emptiness. Where the unconscious was, there CGI shall be. In an influential blog post, Devin Faraci argues that the whole film is a metaphor for cinematic production itself: Cobb is the director, Arthur the producer, Ariadne the screenwriter, Saito 'the big corporate suit who fancies himself a part of the game', Fischer the audience. 'Cobb, as a director, takes Fischer through an engaging, stimulating and exciting journey,' Faraci argues, 'one that leads him to an understanding about himself. Cobb is the big time movie director . . . who brings the action, who brings the spectacle, but who also brings the meaning and the humanity and the emotion.' In fact, as a director Cobb is something of a mediocrity (who we must conclude is far less accomplished than Nolan) – as Neville argues, Fischer's 'journey' takes him through a series of standard-issue action set pieces, which are 'engaging, stimulating and exciting' only in some weakly generic way. Significantly and symptomatically, Faraci's hyperbole here sounds as if it might belong in a marketing pitch for Cobb and his team; just as when Cobb and the others eulogise the 'creativity' of the dream architecture process – *you can create worlds that never existed!* – they sound like they are reciting advertising copy or the script from a corporate video. The scenes in which the team prepare for Fischer's inception might have been designed to bring out the depressing vacuousness of the concept of the 'creative industries'. They play like a marketing team's own fantasies about what they themselves are doing: the view from inside an *Apprentice* contestant's head, perhaps. In any case, *Inception* seems to be less a meta-meditation on the power of cinema than a reflection of the way in which cinematic techniques have become imbricated into a banal spectacle which – fusing business machismo, entertainment protocols and breathless hype – enjoys an unprecedented dominion over our working lives and our dreaming minds.

It is no doubt this sense of pervasive mediation, of generalised simulation, that tempts Faraci into claiming that '*Inception* is a dream to the point where even the dream-sharing stuff is a dream. Dom Cobb isn't an extractor. He can't go into other people's dreams. He isn't on the run from the Cobol Corporation. At one point he tells himself this, through the voice of Mal, who is a projection of his own subconscious. She asks him how real he thinks his world is, where he's being chased across the globe by faceless corporate goons.' The moment when Mal confronts Cobb with all this is reminiscent of the scene in Verhoeven's *Total Recall* (1990) when a psychiatrist attempts to persuade Arnold Schwarzenegger's Quaid that he is having a psychotic breakdown. But while *Total Recall* presents us with a strong distinction between Quaid's quotidian identity as a construction worker and his life as a secret agent at the centre of an interplanetary struggle – a distinction that the film very quickly unsettles – *Inception* gives us only Cobb the generic hero: handsome, dapper, yet troubled. If, as Faraci claims, Cobb isn't an extractor and he isn't on the run from faceless corporate goons, then who is he? The 'real' Cobb would then be an unrepresented X, outside the film's reality labyrinth – the empty figure who identifies with (and as) Cobb the commercially-constructed fiction; ourselves, in other words, insofar as we are successfully interpellated by the film.

This leads to another difference between *Inception* and its Philip K Dick-inspired 80s and 90s precursors such as *Total Recall*, *Videodrome* (1983) and *Existenz* (1999). There is very little of the 'reality bleed', the confusion of ontological hierarchy, that defined those films: throughout *Inception*, it is surprisingly easy for both the audience and the characters to remember where they are in the film's ontological architecture. When Ariadne is being trained by Cobb's partner, Arthur, she is taken round a virtual model of the impossible Penrose Steps. On the face of it, however, *Inception* is remarkable for its seeming failure to explore any paradoxical Escheresque topologies. The four different reality levels remain distinct, just as the causality between them remains well-formed. But this apparently stable hierarchy might be violated by the object upon which much of the discussion of the film's ending has centred: the thimble, the 'totem' that Cobb ostensibly uses to determine whether he is in waking reality or not. If it spins without falling, then he is in a dream. If it falls, then he is not. Many have noted the inadequacy of this supposed proof. At best, it can only establish that Cobb is not in his 'own' dream, for what is there to stop his dreaming mind simulating the properties of the real thimble? Besides, in the film's chronology, the thimble – that ostensible token of the empirical actual – first of all appears as a *virtual* object, secreted by Mal inside a doll's house in Limbo. And a totem, it should be remembered, is an object of faith (it's worth noting in passing that there are many references to faith throughout the film).

The association of the thimble with Mal – there are online debates as to whether the thimble was first of all Cobb's or Mal's – is suggestive. Both Mal and the thimble represent competing versions of the Real. For Cobb, the thimble stands in for the Anglo-Saxon empiricist tradition's account of what reality is – something sensible, tangible. Mal, by contrast, represents a psychoanalytic Real – a trauma that disrupts any attempt to maintain a stable sense of reality; that which the subject cannot help bringing with him no matter where he goes. (Mal's malevolent, indestructible persistence recalls the sad resilience of the projections which haunt the occupants of the space station in Tarkovsky's *Solaris* (1972).) No matter what 'reality level' Cobb is on, Mal and the thimble are always there. But where the thimble supposedly 'belongs' to the 'highest' reality level, Mal 'belongs' to the 'lowest' level, the lover's limbo which Cobb repudiated.

Mal conflates two roles that had been kept separate in Nolan's films – the antagonist-double and the grief object. In Nolan's debut, *Following* (1998), the antagonist-double of the unnamed protagonist is the thief who shares his name with *Inception*'s hero. The theme of the antagonist-double is nowhere more apparent than in Nolan's remake of *Insomnia* and *The Dark Knight*, films which are in many ways *about* the proximity between the ostensible hero and his beyond-good-and-evil rival. Nolan's adaptation of Christopher Priest's novel, *The Prestige*, meanwhile, is in effect a film in which there is a defining antagonism but no single protagonist: by the end of the film, the illusionists Angier and Borden are doubled in multiple ways, just as they are defined and destroyed by their struggle with one another. More often than not, grief is the source of these antagonistic doublings. Grief itself is a puzzle that cannot be solved, and there's a certain (psychic) economy in collapsing the antagonist into the grief object, since the work of grief is not only about mourning the lost object, it is also about struggling against the object's implacable refusal to let go. Yet there's something hollow about Cobb's grief; on its own terms, it doesn't convince as anything other than a genre-required character trait. It instead to stand in for something else, another sadness – a loss that the film points to but can't name.

One aspect of this loss concerns the unconscious itself, and here we might take Nolan's script quite literally. For those with a psychoanalytic bent, the script's repeated references to the 'subconscious' – as opposed to the unconscious – no doubt grate, but this might have been a Freudian slip of a particularly revealing kind. The terrain that *Inception* lays out is no longer that of the classical unconscious, that impersonal factory which, Jean-Francois Lyotard says, psychoanalysis described 'with the help of images of foreign towns or countries such as Rome or Egypt, just like Piranesi's *Prisons* or Escher's *Other Worlds*'. (*Libidinal Economy*, Athlone, 1993, 164) *Inception*'s arcades and hotel corridors are indeed those of a globalised capital, whose reach easily extends into the former depths of what was once the unconscious. There is nothing alien, no *other place* here, only a 'subconscious' recirculating deeply familiar images mined from an ersatz psychoanalysis. So in place of the eerie enigmas of the unconscious, we are instead offered an Oedipal-lite scene played out between Robert Fischer and a projection of his dead father. The off-the-shelf pre-masticated quality of this encounter is entirely lacking in any of the weird idiosyncrasies which give Freud's case histories their power to haunt. Cod Freudianism has long been metabolised by an advertising-entertainment culture which is now ubiquitous, as psychoanalysis gives way to a psychotherapeutic self-help that is diffused through mass media. It's possible to read *Inception* as a staging of this superseding of psychoanalysis, with Cobb's apparent victory over the Mal projection, his talking himself around to accepting that she is just a fantasmatic substitute for his dead wife, almost a parody of psychotherapy's blunt pragmatism.

The question of whether Cobb is still dreaming or not at the film's end is ultimately too simple. For there is also the problem of *whose* dream Cobb might be in, if not his 'own'. The old Freudian paradigm made this a problem too, of course – but there the issue was the fact that the ego was not master in its own house because the subject was constitutively split by the unconscious. In *Inception*, the ego is still not a master in its own house, but that is because the forces of predatory business are everywhere. Dreams have ceased to be the spaces where private pyschopathologies are worked through and have become the scenes where competing corporate interests play out their banal struggles. *Inception*'s 'militarised subconscious' converts the infernal urgencies and languid poise of the old unconscious into panicked persecution and a consolatory familialism: pursued at work by videogame gunmen, you later unwind with the kids building sandcastles on a beach. This is another reason that the dreams in *Inception* appear so undream-like. For, after all, these are not 'dreams' in any conventional sense. The designed virtual spaces of *Inception*'s dreams, with their nested 'levels', evidently resemble a videogame more than they recall dreams. In the era of neuromarketing, we are presided over by what J G Ballard called 'fictions of every kind', the embedded literature of branding consultancies, advertising agencies and games manufacturers. All of which makes one of *Inception*'s premises – that it is difficult to implant an idea in someone's mind – strangely quaint. Isn't 'inception' what so much late capitalist cognitive labour is about?

For inception to work, Arthur and Cobb tell Saito early in the film, the subject must believe that the implanted idea is their own. The self-help dictums of psychotherapy – which Cobb affirms at the end of *Inception* – offer invaluable assistance in this ideological operation. As Eva Illouz argues, discussing the very conversion of psychoanalysis into self-help that *Inception* dramatises, 'if we secretly desire our misery, then the self can be made directly responsible for alleviating it . . . The contemporary Freudian legacy is, and ironically so, that we are in the full masters in our own house, even when, or perhaps especially when, it is on fire.' (*Cold Intimacies: The Making of Emotional Capitalism*, Polity, 2007, 47) Yet our misery, like our dreams, our cars and our refrigerators, is in fact the work of many anonymous hands. This impersonal misery may be what *Inception* is ultimately about. The ostensibly upbeat ending and all the distracting boy-toy action cannot dispel the non-specific but pervasive pathos that hangs over the film. It's a sadness that arises from the impasses of a culture in which business has closed down any possibility of an outside – a situation that *Inception* exemplifies, rather than comments on. You yearn for foreign places, but everywhere you go looks like local colour for the film set of a commercial; you want to be lost in Escheresque mazes, but you end up in an interminable car chase.

Handsworth Songs and the English Riots

BFI/ *Sight and Sound Website, September 2011*

'I'm sure that a group of people who brought the British state to its knees can organise themselves.' So argued John Akomfrah, the director of the Black Audio Film Collective's *Handsworth Songs* at a screening of the film at Tate Modern last month. The film was released in 1986, a year after riots in Handsworth, Birmingham and Tottenham. Not surprisingly, given that the Tate had convened the event as a consequence of the recent uprisings in England, the question of the continuities and discontinuities between the 80s and now hung over the whole evening, dominating the discussion that followed the screening.

Watched – and listened to – now, *Handsworth Songs* seems eerily (un)timely. The continuities between the 80s and now impose themselves on the contemporary viewer with a breathtaking force: just as with the recent insurrections, the events in 1985 were triggered by police violence; and the 1985 denunciations of the riots as senseless acts of criminality could have been made by Tory politicians yesterday. This is why it is important to resist the casual story that things have 'progressed' in any simple linear fashion since *Handsworth Songs* was made. Yes, the BAFC can now appear at Tate Modern in the wake of new riots in England, something unthinkable in 1985; but, as Rob White pointed out in the discussion at the Tate event, there is little chance now of *Handsworth Songs* or its like appearing on Channel 4 now, still less being commissioned. The assumption that brutal policing and racism were relics of a bygone era was part of the reactionary narrativisation of the recent riots: *yes, there was politics and racism* back then, *but not now, not any more* . . . The lesson to be remembered – especially now that we are being asked to defend abortion and oppose the death penalty again – is that struggles are never definitively won. As the academic George Shire pointed out in the Tate discussion, many struggles have not been lost so much as diverted into what he called 'the privatisation of politics', as former activists become hired as 'consultants'. Shire's remarks strikingly echoed recent comments made by Paul Gilroy. 'When you look at the layer of political leaders from our communities,' Gilroy observed, 'the generation who came of age during that time 30 years ago, many of those people have accepted the logic of privatization. They've privatised that movement, and they've sold their services as consultants and managers and diversity trainers.' (See http://dreamof-safety.blogspot.com/2011/08/paul-gilroy-speaks-on-riots-august-2011.html) This points to one major discontinuity between now and 25 years ago. In 1985, political collectivities were in the process of being violently decomposed – this was also the year in which the Miners' Strike ended in bitter defeat – as the neoliberal political programme began to impose the 'privatisation of the mind' which is now everywhere taken for granted. Akomfrah's optimistic take on the current riots – that those who rioted will come to constitute themselves as a collective agent – suggests that we might be seeing the reversal of this psychic privatisation.

One of many striking things about *Handsworth Songs* is the serene confidence of its experimental essayism. Instead of easy didacticism, the film offers a complex palimpsest comprising archive material, anempathic sound design and footage shot by the Collective during and after the riots. The Collective's practice coolly assumed, not only that 'black', 'avant garde' and 'politics' could co-exist, but that they must entail one another. Such assumptions, such confidence, were all the more remarkable for the fact that they were so hard won: the Collective's Lina Gopaul remembered that the idea of a black avant-garde was greeted with incomprehension when the BAFC began their work. Even the sight of young black people carrying cameras provoked bemusement: *are they real?* Gopaul recalled police officers asking as the Collective filmed events in Handsworth and Broadwater Farm 25 years ago.

At a time when reactionaries once again feel able to make racist generalisations about 'black culture' in mainstream media, the Collective's undoing of received ideas of what 'black' supposedly means remains an urgent project. In *The Ghost of Songs: The Film Art of the Black Audio Film Collective*, the outstanding survey of the BAFC's work that he co-edited with fellow Otolith Group member Anjalika Sagar, Kodwo Eshun argued that, for the Collective, 'black' 'might be profitably understood . . . as a dimension of potentiality.' At the Tate discussion, which he chaired, Eshun pointed to the use in *Handsworth Songs* of Mark Stewart and the Maffia's dub-refracted cut-up version of 'Jerusalem': the track makes a bid for an account of Englishness from which 'blackness', far from being something that can be excluded, becomes instead the only possible fulfilment of the millenarian promise of Blake's revolutionary poem. The use of Stewart's music also brings home the extent to which *Handsworth Songs* belonged to a postpunk moment which was defined by its unsettling of concepts of 'white' and 'black' culture. Trevor Mathison's astonishing sound design certainly draws upon dub, but its voice loops and seething electronics are equally reminiscent of the work of Test Department and Cabaret Voltaire. So much film and television now deploys sound as a crude bludgeon which closes down the polyvalency of images. Whooshing sound effects subordinate audiences to the audio equivalent of a spectacle, while the redundant use of pop music enforces a terroristic sentimentalism. By strong and refreshing contrast, Mathison's sound – which is simultaneously seductive and estranging – liberates lyricism from personalised emotion, and frees up the potentials of the audio from the strictures of 'music'. Subtract the images entirely, and *Handsworth Songs* can function as a gripping audio-essay.

Mathison's sound recording equipment captured one of the most extraordinary moments in the film, an exchange between the floor manager and the producer of the long-defunct documentary series *TV Eye* in the run-up to a special edition of the programme which was about to be filmed in front of a Tottenham audience. The exchange reveals that it is not possible to securely delimit 'merely technical' issues from political questions. The producer's anxieties about lighting quickly shade into concerns about the proportion of non-whites in the audience. The matter-of-fact tone of the discussions make this sudden peek into the reality studio all the more disturbing – and illuminating.

The screening and the discussion at the Tate were a reminder that 'mainstream media' is not a monolith but a terrain. It wasn't because of the largesse of broadcasters that the BBC and Channel 4 became host to popular experimentalism between the 60s and the 90s. No: this was only possible on the basis of a struggle by forces – which were political at the same time as they were cultural – that were content neither to remain in the margins nor to replicate the existing form of mainstream. *Handsworth Songs* is a glorious artefact of that struggle – and a call for us to resume it.

'Tremors of an imperceptible future': Patrick Keiller's *Robinson in Ruins*

Sight & Sound, November 2010

In Ellis Sharp's short story 'The Hay Wain', a Poll Tax rioter in 1990 takes refuge in the National Gallery and 'notices what he has never noticed before on biscuit tins or calendars, or plastic trays on the walls of his aunt's flat in Bradford, those tiny figures bending in the field beyond.' Constable's supposedly timeless painting of English landscape ceases to be a kind of pastoral screensaver and becomes what it always really was: a snapshot of agricultural labour. Far from being some refuge from political strife, the English landscape is the site of numerous struggles between the forces of power and privilege and those who sought to resist them. Sharp replaces the dominant pastoral image of the English countryside, not with a deflated quotidian realism, but with a different kind of lyricism, one coloured by revolt: fields and ditches become hiding places or battlegrounds; landscapes that on the surface seem tranquil still reverberate with the unavenged spectral rage of murdered working class martyrs. It is not the sunlit English afternoon that is 'timeless', but the ability of the agents of reaction to escape justice. When the Poll tax rioter is clubbed by police and his blood starts to stain Constable's emblem of English nationhood, we're uncomfortably reminded of more recent episodes. *'He was resisting arrest, right? Right mates?* (Right, Sarge.) . . . *We used minimal force, right?* . . . *Don't piss yourself and we'll see this thing through together, right mates?* . . . *Everyone'll be on our side, remember that. The commissioner. The Federation. The papers. And, if it comes to it, the Coroner. Now fucking go and call for an ambulance.'*

Patrick Keiller's latest film, *Robinson in Ruins*, the long-awaited sequel to his two 1990s films, *London* (1994) and *Robinson in Space* (1997), performs a similar politicisation of landscape. Or rather, it exposes the way in which the rural landscape is always-already intensely politicised. 'I had embarked on landscape film-making in 1981, early in the Thatcher era, after encountering a surrealist tradition in the UK and elsewhere, so that cinematography involved the pursuit of a transformation, radical or otherwise, of everyday reality,' Keiller wrote in 2008, as he was preparing *Robinson in Ruins*. 'I had forgotten that landscape photography is often motivated by utopian or ideological imperatives, both as a critique of the world, and to demonstrate the possibility of creating a better one.' *London* was a melancholy, quietly angry study of the city after 13 years of Tory rule. Its unnamed narrator, voiced by Paul Scofield, told of the obsessive researches undertaken by Robinson, a rogue – and fictional – theorist, into the 'problem of London'. London was the capital of the first capitalist country, but Keiller was interested in the way that the city was now at the heart of a new, 'post-Fordist' capitalism, in which manufacturing industry had been super-seded by the spectral weightlessness of the so-called service economy. Robinson and his narrator friend bitterly surveyed this brave new world with the doleful eyes of men formed in a very different era: a world in which public service broadcasters could commission films of this nature.

London was as remarkable for the unique way that it combined fiction with the film-essay form. The film was composed of a series of striking images captured by Keiller's static camera, which unblinkingly caught the city in unguarded epiphanic moments. *Robinson in Space* retained the same methodology, but broadened the focus from London to the rest of England. Rural landscapes featured in *Robinson in Space*, but as something which Keiller's camera looked *over* rather than *at*. In the first two films, Robinson's interest was in the cities where capitalism was first built, and in the non-places where it now silently spreads: the distribution centres and container ports that are unvisited by practically anyone except Robinson and his narrator-companion, but which web Britain into the global market. Keiller saw that, contrary to certain dominant narratives, the British economy was not 'declining'. Rather, this post-industrial economy was thriving, and that was the basis of its oppressive and profoundly inegalitarian power.

London and Robinson in Space were made in the space between two political non-events, the general elections of 1992 and 1997. 1992 was the year when change was supposed to come – the end of Tory rule was widely expected, not least by the Conservative Party itself, yet John Major was re-elected. 1997 saw the long–anticipated change finally arrive, but it turned out to be no kind of change at all. Far from ending the neoliberal culture that Keiller anatomised, Tony Blair's government would consolidate it. Robinson in Space, largely assembled in the dying days of the Major government, was made too early for it to properly register this. Yet its focus on the banal, Ballardian infrastructure of British post–Fordist capitalism made it a deeply prophetic film. The England of Robinson in Space was still the England presided over by Gordon Brown a decade later.

The traumatic event which reverberates through Robinson in Ruins is the financial crisis of 2008. It's still too early to properly assess the implications of this crisis, but Robinson in Ruins shares with Chris Petit's Content – a film with which it has many preoccupations in common – the tentative sense that a historical sequence which began in 1979 ended in 2008. The 'ruins' which Robinson walks through here are partly the new ruins of a neoliberal culture that has not yet accepted its own demise, and which, for the moment, continues with the same old gestures like a zombie that does not know that it is dead. Citing Fredric Jameson's observation in The Seeds of Time that 'it seems to be easier for us today to imagine the thoroughgoing deterioration of the earth and of nature than the breakdown of late capitalism; perhaps that is due to some weakness in our imaginations',

Robinson nevertheless dares to hope, if only for a moment, that the so-called credit crunch is something more than one of the crises by which capitalism periodically renews itself.

Perhaps strangely, it is the 'thoroughgoing deterioration of the earth and nature' that seem to give Robinson some grounds for hope, and the most evident difference between *Robinson in Ruins* and the previous films is the emergence of a radical Green perspective. In part, Keiller's turn towards Green themes reflects changes in mainstream political culture. At the time of the previous two Robinson films, Green politics could still appear to be a fringe concern. In the last decade or so, however, anxieties about global warming in particular have come into the very centre of culture. Now, every corporation, no matter how exploitative, is required to present itself as Green. The emergence of ecological concerns gives Keiller's treatment of landscape a properly dialectical poise. In the opposition between capital and ecology, we confront what are in effect two totalities. Keiller shows that capitalism – in principle at least – saturates every-thing (especially in England, a claustrophobic country that long ago enclosed most of its common land, there is no landscape outside politics); there is nothing intrinsically resistant to capital's drive to commoditisation, certainly not in the 'natural world'. Keiller demonstrates this with a long excursus on how the prices of weight increased in the immediate wake of the 2008 crisis. Yet from the equally inhuman perspective of a radical ecology, capital, for all that it may burn out the human environment and take large swathes of the nonhuman world with it, is still a merely local episode.

Environmental catastrophe provides what a political uncon-scious totally colonised by neoliberalism cannot: an image of life after capitalism. Still, this life may not be a human life, and there is the feeling that, like the narrator's father in Margaret Atwood's coldly visionary novel *Surfacing*, Robinson may have headed off into some kind of dark Deleuzean communion with Nature. As with *Surfacing, Robinson in Ruins* begins with a disappearance: Robinson's own. Paul Scofield having died in 2010, the narration is no longer handled by Robinson's friend, but by Vanessa Redgrave, playing the head of a group seeking to reconstruct Robinson's thinking from notes and films recovered from the caravan where he was last known to live. If the Redgrave narration doesn't quite work, then that is partly because there is a feeling that Keiller has slightly tired of the Robinson fiction, or it has ceased to serve much of a function for him. For what seems like large parts of the film, the Robinson framing narrative disappears from view, to the extent that it can be something of a jolt when Robinson is mentioned again. Lacking Paul Scofield's sardonic insouciance, Redgrave's narrative is often oddly tentative, her emphasis not quite mustering Scofield's assured mastery of Keiller's tone.

In tracking the historical development of capitalism in England, and the sites of struggle against it, *Robinson in Ruins* shows a sensitivity to the way that landscape silently registers (and engenders) politics that echoes the concerns of Danièle Huillet and Jean-Marie Straub. As in Straub-Huillet's films, *Robinson in Ruins* returns to landscapes where antagonism and martyrdom once took place: Greenham Common, the woodland where Professor David Kelly committed suicide.

Keiller's decision to retain film rather than switch to a digital medium carries more charge now than it did when he used a cine camera for *London* and *Robinson in Space*. In many ways, even in 1997, we had yet to really enter the digital realm; now, with cyberspace available on every smartphone handset, we are never outside it. The return to film made him appreciate the materiality of the medium in a new way. 'Compared with videotape,' Keiller has written, 'film stock is expensive to purchase and process, and the camera's magazine holds only 122m of stock, just over 4 minutes at 25fps. Film hence tends to involve a greater commitment to an image before starting to turn the camera, and there is pressure to stop as soon as possible, both to limit expenditure and to avoid running out of loaded film. Results are visible only after processing, which, in this case, was usually several days later, by which time some subjects were no longer available and others had changed, so as to rule out the possibility of a retake. I began to wonder why I had never noticed these difficulties before, or whether I had simply forgotten them. Another problem was that, with computer editing, it is no longer usual to make a print to edit. Instead, camera rolls are transferred to video after processing, so that the footage is never seen at its best until the end of the production process. This hybridity of photographic and digital media so emphasises the value of the material, mineral characteristics of film that one begins to reimagine cinematography as a variety of stone-carving.'

When we hear early on in the film that Robinson has made contact with a series of 'non-human intelligences', we initially suspect that he has finally succumbed to madness. Yet the 'non-human intelligences' turn out not to be the extra-terrestrials of a florid pulp science fiction-inspired psychosis, but the intra-terrestrial lifeforms that an ecological awareness reveals growing with a silent stubbornness that matches the brute tenacity of capitalism. In one of the many slow spirals that typify Keiller's approach in *Robinson in Ruins*, the lichen that his camera lingers on in an early shot, apparently for merely picturesque effect, will eventually come to take centre stage in the film's narrative. Lichen, Robinson comes to realise, is already the dominant lifeform on large areas of the planet. Inspired by the work of American biologist Lynn Margulis, Robinson confesses to a growing feeling of 'biophilia', which Keiller seems to share. While his camera lingers tenderly on wildflowers, the film's verbal narrative is suspended, projecting us for a few long moments into this world without humans. These moments, these unnarrativised surveys of a non-human landscape, are like Keiller's version of the famous 'Straubian shot', the cut-aways to depopulated landscapes in Straub and Huillet's films. Robinson is drawn to Margulis because she rejects the analogies between capitalism and the biological that are so often used to naturalise capitalist economic relations. Instead of the ruthless competition which social Darwinians find in nature, Margulis discovers organisms engaging in co-operative strategies. When Keiller turns his camera on these 'non-human intelligences', these mute heralds of a future without humanity, I'm reminded of the black orchids in Troy Kennedy Martin's *Edge Of Darkness*, those harbingers of an ecology that is readying to take revenge on a humanity that thoughtlessly disdained it. Kennedy Martin's inspiration was the anti-humanist ecology of James Lovelock, and Lovelock's apocalyptic message seems to haunt *Robinson in Ruins* too. Keiller finds extinction looming everywhere – species dying off at a far faster rate than scientists had thought possible only a few years ago. The emphasis on extinction means that the concerns of *Robinson in Ruins* rhyme with the preoccupations that have emerged in speculative realist philosophy, which has focused on the spaces prior to, beyond and after human life. In some respects, the work of philosophers such as Ray Brassier and Tim Morton re-stages the old confrontation between human finitude and the sublime which was the former subject of a certain kind of landscape art. But where the older sublime concentrated on local natural phenomenon such as the ocean or volcanic eruptions which could overwhelm and destroy the individual organism or whole cities, speculative realism contemplates the extinction, not only of the human world, but of life and indeed matter itself. The prospect of ecological catastrophe means that disjunction between the lived time of human experience and longer durations is now not just a question of metaphysical contemplation, but a matter of urgent political concern, as one of Robinson's touchstones, Fredric Jameson, noted. '[A]s organisms of a particular life span,' Jameson writes in his essay 'Actually Existing Marxism', we are poorly placed as biological individuals to witness the more fundamental dynamics of history, glimpsing this or that incomplete moment, which we hasten to translate into the all-too-human terms of success or failure. But neither stoic wisdom nor the reminder of a longer-term view are really satisfactory responses to this peculiar existential and epistemological dilemma, comparable to the science-fictional one of beings inhabiting a cosmos they do not have organs to perceive or identify. Perhaps only the acknowledgement of this radical incommensurability between human existence and the dynamic of collective history and production is capable of generating new kinds of political attitudes; new kinds of political perception, as well as of political patience; and new methods for decoding the age as well, and reading the imperceptible tremors within it of an inconceivable future. (*Valences of the Dialectic*, Verso, 2010, pp369-70)

Amongst its requiem for neoliberal England, *Robinson in Ruins* gives us some intimations of those imperceptible tremors and inconceivable futures.

Contemporary culture has eliminated both the concept of the public and the figure of the intellectual. Former public spaces – both physical and cultural – are now either derelict or colonized by advertising. A cretinous anti-intellectualism presides, cheerled by expensively educated hacks in the pay of multinational corporations who reassure their bored readers that there is no need to rouse themselves from their interpassive stupor. The informal censorship internalized and propagated by the cultural workers of late capitalism generates a banal conformity that the propaganda chiefs of Stalinism could only ever have dreamt of imposing. Zer0 Books knows that another kind of discourse – intellectual without being academic, popular without being populist – is not only possible: it is already flourishing, in the regions beyond the striplit malls of so-called mass media and the neurotically bureaucratic halls of the academy. Zer0 is committed to the idea of publishing as a making public of the intellectual. It is convinced that in the unthinking, blandly consensual culture in which we live, critical and engaged theoretical reflection is more important than ever before.

.